The Security of South Asia

The Security of South Asia

American and Asian Perspectives

Edited by
Stephen Philip Cohen

University of Illinois Press
Urbana and Chicago

© 1987 by the Board of Trustees of the University of Illinois
Manufactured in the United States of America
C 5 4 3 2 1

This book is printed on acid-free paper.

Library of Congress Cataloging-in-Publication Data
The Security of South Asia.

Includes index.
1. India—Military relations—Pakistan. 2. Pakistan—
Military relations—India. 3. United States—Military
relations—South Asia. 4. South Asia—Military
relations—United States. 5. South Asia—National
security. I. Cohen, Stephen P., 1936–
UA840.S36   1987   355′.033054   86–31784
ISBN 0-252-01394-8 (alk. paper)

If there were only two men in the world, how would they get on? They would help one another, harm one another, flatter one another, slander one another, fight one another, make it up; they could neither live together nor do without one another.

Voltaire, *Philosophical Dictionary,* 1764

Contents

Abbreviations and Acronyms

ADB	Asian Development Bank
ASEAN	Association of Southeast Asian Nations
CENTCOM	U.S. Central Command (replaced RDF)
CENTO	Central Treaty Organization (replaced Baghdad Pact)
EEC	European Economic Community
ERDA	Energy Research and Development Agency
GOI	Government of India
ICBM	intercontinental ballistic missile
IRBM	intermediate range ballistic missile
IAEA	International Atomic Energy Agency (Vienna)
IDA	International Development Association
IOZP	Indian Ocean Zone of Peace
LEU	low enriched uranium
MBFR	Mutual and Balanced Force Reduction talks (Vienna)
MRD	Movement for the Restoration of Democracy (Pakistan)
NAM	Non-Aligned Movement
NEFA	North East Frontier Agency (now Arunachal Pradesh, India)
NIEO	New International Economic Order
NNPA	Nuclear Non-Proliferation Act (U.S.)
NRC	Nuclear Regulatory Commission (U.S.)
NSC	National Security Council
NWFP	North-West Frontier Province (Pakistan)
OECD	Organization for Economic Cooperation and Development
OIC	Organization of Islamic Countries
PDPA	People's Democratic Party of Afghanistan
PPP	Pakistan People's Party
PRC	People's Republic of China

RCD	Regional Cooperation for Development (Turkey, Iran, Pakistan)
RDF	Rapid Deployment Force (later CENTCOM)
SAARC	South Asian Association for Regional Cooperation (after 1985)
SARC	South Asian Regional Cooperation (before 1985)
SEATO	South East Asian Treaty Organization
TAPS	Tarapur Atomic Power Station (India)

Preface

This book examines the relationship between the two militarily important states of South Asia—India and Pakistan—and the involvement of one of the superpowers—the United States—in South Asia. It is not an attempt to survey all South Asian security problems. It does try to dig beneath the surface and to examine some of the underlying causes of the India-Pakistan conflict, and it does try to suggest policies that might enhance regional stability and security and still protect the legitimate interests of outsiders, especially those of the United States. As the reader will discover, the analyses in this book are often contradictory, and the policy suggestions offered by various contributors are often mutually exclusive.

This should come as no surprise, because the views of the contributors to this volume (who include many of India's and Pakistan's leading strategic experts and a number of America's leading South Asian specialists) have long been on public record. If this book makes a contribution to our understanding of the issues and to this peaceful resolution, it is that this is the first attempt to *juxtapose* Indian, Pakistani, and American responses. This is done in two ways.

Part One looks at perceptual and issue-related problems from the standpoint of India, Pakistan, and the United States. We have tried to encourage new thinking by having the major chapters on each country written by nationals from another state. Thus, the major chapter on Pakistani security problems was written by Lt. Gen. Eric Vas, formerly of the Indian army; the companion chapter on Indian security policy was written by Brig. Noor Husain, a retired Pakistan army officer and the director of the Institute for Strategic Studies in Islamabad. Similarly, chapters on Indian and Pakistani regional policies were written by two American authors (Leo Rose and W. Howard Wriggins), while two chapters on American policy and policymaking were written by Indian and Pakistani scholars (R. R. Subramaniam and Pervaiz Iqbal Cheema).

The authors of these chapters were asked to place themselves in the position of their counterparts in another country. How would *they* make policy if they were in power? Would geomilitary reality lead to the same policies that are now being pursued, or would they change things? As the reader will see, the authors responded to this challenge in various ways. For most of the major chapters there is a companion chapter written by a national of the country involved (P. R. Chari, India; M. B. Naqvi, Pakistan; William J. Barnds and Selig S. Harrison, United States).

Part Two takes a different approach. Four of the most distinguished strategic analysts familiar with South Asia were asked to speculate on "the" future, or on various "futures" of the region. K. Subrahmanyam and Jagat S. Mehta (India), Lt. Gen. A. I. Akram (Pakistan), and Thomas Perry Thornton (United States) clearly differ in their views of whether the desirable, the feasible, and the likely are the same.

A concluding chapter summarizes some of the arguments presented in this book, discusses the prospects for future regional peace, and suggests some areas for future research and study.

Some supplementary data on regional arms levels and military balances are presented in Appendix 1, and Appendix 2 provides an important glimpse into the future (or, at least some futures) via Rashid Naim's analysis of the possible consequences of nuclear war in South Asia.

This book was completed in mid-1985, which happened to be a period of great tension between India and Pakistan and great internal developments in those two countries. India held national elections in late 1984, and Pakistan held them in early 1985. Mrs. Indira Gandhi was assassinated and succeeded by her son, Rajiv Gandhi. He and Mrs. Gandhi had earlier issued threatening statements about the prospects for war in South Asia; rumors of a planned Indian attack on Pakistani nuclear facilities were widespread, and Pakistan itself was thought to have moved close to the possession of a nuclear weapon.

Despite these tensions, there is a remarkable degree of optimism in some chapters (as well as outright pessimism in others) about the prospect for substantial normalization of relations between India and Pakistan and the evolution of a coherent and effective South Asia policy by the United States. Yet the striking quality of this book as a whole is that there is no clearcut correlation of nationality with optimism or pessimism. Indeed, the differences among Americans, Pakistanis, and Indians themselves seem to be as great as those among the three groups. Perhaps I am describing the glass as half full, but I am rather optimistic about the future evolution of a secure and stable South Asia and America's relationship with it.

Finally, a personal note. Much of what I know about South Asian security problems and American regional policy I have learned from many of the contributors to this volume—Indian, Pakistani, and American alike—over the past twenty years. I am grateful to these individuals for joining in an unusual project at a moment of great regional tension. I disagree with many of the arguments put forward in this book, but recognize that there is no monopoly in truth. Indeed, on vital issues affecting lives of millions and the survival of states, there will be legitimate differences over what is the "truth." Hopefully, this volume will help clear away some perceptual dead wood and allow us to build upon many shared interests. In view of the presence of one superpower in South Asia, the unpredictable consequences of new technologies, and the shifting influence on vital security issues of volatile domestic politics, failing to cooperate is a luxury we can no longer afford.

This volume is a product of the Regional Security project of the Program in Arms Control, Disarmament and International Security (ACDIS) at the University of Illinois. I wish to acknowledge the continuing and substantial support of the Ford Foundation and the timely assistance of the Office of Public Diplomacy of the Department of Defense. The Program in Arms Control has also received important assistance from the National Strategy Information Center and the MacArthur Foundation.

Finally, particular thanks are extended to Director Edward Kolodziej, Mary Anderson, Roy Roper, and Judy Jones of ACDIS. I would also like to thank three ACDIS fellows, Kanti Bajpai, Sumit Ganguly, and Rashid Naim, for their important substantive contributions to this book, and Merle Levy, for a thoughtful editorial touch.

Part One

South Asian and American
Perspectives

1

India's Regional Policy: Nonmilitary Dimensions

Leo E. Rose

During Mrs. Gandhi's second period as prime minister (1980-84) the tendency in New Delhi was to emphasize India's status as a world power and, in particular, on her role as a world leader through her important positions in the nonaligned movement, in the "North-South" negotiations on a New International Economic Order, and her friendly ties to the leaders of both the superpowers.[1] With the succession of Rajiv Gandhi as prime minister in November 1984 there was, inevitably, a change in style and in rhetoric. The world-leader theme has by no means disappeared, but the focus in his first months in office was more on South Asian regional issues, in particular the bilateral disputes with Pakistan and Sri Lanka over allegations of "interference" in their respective domestic politics through the support of dissident terrorist groups: (1) Pakistani support of Sikh extremists in the Indian Punjab, and (2) Indian support of the Al-Zulfikar terrorists in Pakistan and Tamil insurgents in Sri Lanka.

Although all of these disputes could be defined in regional terms involving common regional problems, the Government of India (GOI) usually downplays their multilateral aspects and urges a strictly bilateral approach to their resolution.[2] This approach is combined, however, with a self-identification of India in regional terms as the "dominant," "paramount," "hegemonic," "preeminent," or just plain "major" (kindly select the adjective preferred) power in South Asia and the rights and privileges that accompany such a status.[3] The dominant power in a region usually insists on operating through a regional system, but India has not seen the situation in South Asia as conducive to easy management on a regional basis, at least until quite recently.

New Delhi's delight in its world role and exasperations with its regional role probably make good sense. India's position on broader Asian or global issues can be safely defined under a set of "principles" that are little more than appealing slogans. It is impossible to define nonalignment in any meaningful way today given the extremely diverse composition of the nonaligned movement. The same laxity does not apply to India's relations with the other South Asian states, as these are both too important and too specific to be handled by slogan-mongering. A well-defined and explicit Indian policy toward South Asia as a region cannot be avoided in the mid-1980s, particularly with an institutionalized regional system finally beginning to emerge.

India's policy objectives in the region, both formal and informal, are beginning to be expressed in more explicit terms. There is now a broad consensus among most Indian leaders and commentators that a primary objective is to obtain the acceptance of India's status as *the* major regional power in South Asia from both the other regional states and from the major external powers. But just what this would involve in policy terms is still uncertain. In its actual policies toward the region (although not always in statements by government leaders), the GOI does not appear to be demanding hegemony in the way that term is normally used, that is, the acceptance of a client status by subordinate states in the system. But at least as the minimum, New Delhi does insist that the foreign policies of the other South Asian states must take into consideration India's interests, policies, and status, and must not conflict with these too overtly—at least on those international issues that are important to India. Furthermore, the other regional states must exercise self-restraint in seeking support from or affiliating with outside powers, on what are defined as primarily regional issues by New Delhi.

One other frequently noted policy objective of the GOI is a preference for dealing with its neighbors in the region on a bilateral basis, thus excluding international forums or agencies, external powers, and even other South Asian states from the negotiation process. This would seem to conflict with New Delhi's growing interest in developing a regional system in South Asia to handle *some* subjects and issues. There is an evident interest in India with the development of a regional economic system, though on rather unique terms. As defined by India, the South Asian system would function through the greater coordination of India's *bilateral* economic relations with the other regional states; any substantial integration of the economies of the other states (e.g., Pakistan and Sri Lanka or Nepal and Bangladesh) or any use of a multilateral approach to regional economic issues (e.g., the river systems of Nepal, Bhutan, Bangladesh, and India) should be discouraged. Economically this is reasonable, since there is only a very limited potential as yet for economic interaction between the other states in the region; but politically it is an unacceptable principle in most capitals in the region.

Indian Responses to Regional Systems Proposals

The immediate reaction in New Delhi to Bangladesh's 1980 proposal for the establishment of a South Asian system was something less than enthusiastic.[4] The GOI had reservations about how this would serve India's interests, and the prevailing view was that it might be preferable to continue to deal with neighboring states on a strictly bilateral basis. Moreover, there were some doubts in India that a real regional system would be acceptable to the other South Asian states. The applicability of the often-cited Association of Southeast Asian Nations (ASEAN) model —in which there is an approximate balance of power among the participants—to South Asia is doubtful since India's dominant position is probably unavoidable and a deterrent to participation by the other states. A showpiece regional institution that lacked any substantial powers or responsibilities might be more acceptable to these other states, but what the Indian government wants is a system that encourages cooperation focused around India on cultural, diplomatic, and even some economic issues.

Thus, a properly defined regional system held some attractions for New Delhi: it could provide an institutional channel for the expansion and coordination of some economic and cultural relations among the participants, with India serving as the conduit. But probably more important to New Delhi, a regional system would enhance the sense of identity with South Asia and thus over time might reduce the evident tendency among most of India's neighbors to seek affiliations with alternative regional systems—Pakistan with the Islamic states of Southwest Asia, Sri Lanka and Bangladesh with ASEAN, and Nepal as a neutralized "zone of peace" between South and East Asia.

One unique aspect of South Asia as a region is that all the other states in the region have a common border only with India and not with each other (if Afghanistan is not defined as a South Asian state), and thus must interact with each other through India. As a consequence, a sense of common identity as South Asian states is still poorly developed among these states. New Delhi considers it important to encourage a South Asian identity among its neighbors for good Indian reasons, and any overt opposition to the regional system proposed by Dhaka would have been counterproductive.

To almost everyone's surprise the South Asian Regional Cooperative (SARC) forum has developed much faster and more substantially than anyone would have predicted in 1980 when all the South Asian states responded rather tentatively to the proposal by President Ziaur Rehman of Bangladesh. For very different reasons, the Indian and Pakistani initial reservations about SARC seemed muted by 1984. During the four foreign secretary level meetings held from 1981 to 1984 and the two meetings held at the foreign minister level in 1983 and 1985, the number of subjects with which SARC has been empowered to deal through the establishment of multilateral subcommissions has increased from five to twelve. These subcommissions have begun to function, and we can expect a virtual flood of reports from them over the next few years.[5]

It was also symbolically significant that the SARC foreign ministers conferences in the fall of 1983 and February 1985 coincided with an outburst of extreme Tamil-Sinhala communal clashes in Sri Lanka. Sri Lankan suspicions that, with the knowledge of the GOI, Indian Tamils had provided assistance to the Ceylon Tamil insurgents has led to a mini-crisis in Indian-Sri Lankan relations. It was also at this time that India and Pakistan were exchanging allegations of interference by the other government in their respective domestic politics. But these worsening bilateral relations between India, on one hand, and Sri Lanka and Pakistan on the other, were not allowed to interfere with the SARC meetings, an encouraging sign that the regional organization had already achieved a position somewhat above and beyond the bilateral disputes and outbursts that periodically strain South Asian intraregional relations.

One reason that this is possible, however, is the very limited scope of responsibilities assigned to SARC. The more important and controversial intrastate issues are not even discussed in or through SARC. The subjects assigned to the SARC subcommissions are the more perfunctory cultural, technological, or bureaucratic (e.g., postal) issues in which the states have only minor interests involved and no basic differences in views. The more important economic relationships among the regional states have been excluded from consideration by SARC and are still managed on a bilateral basis. It would probably be unavoidable in any South Asian regional system whatever New Delhi's position might be, given the geopolitical and economic framework within which the regional states must interact. All of the states in the region (except, in some years, Pakistan) have their largest intraregional economic relations with India rather than with the other South Asian states. Thus, the only regional international economic system of any significance is based upon each state's bilateral economic relationship with India. Despite some public relations efforts in some South Asian states to proclaim an interest in developing an economic relationship with states other than India in the region, this has not occurred on any scale as yet, even where there would appear to be some basis for trade—for example, Pakistan and Bangladesh. Until there is something that can be classified as a regional economic system above and beyond each state's bilateral relationships with India, nothing much should be expected of SARC in this sphere.

Nor is there as yet any evident interest on any side in the transformation of SARC into a regional security system, as has gradually happened with ASEAN since 1965.[6] New Delhi's views on this subject would seem to waver, as there are both advantages and disadvantages for India. The major security problems for most of the countries in South Asia concern their relationship with India: for example, India-Pakistan tensions; Sri Lanka's apprehension over the possibility of Indian intervention in support of Tamil dissidents; Nepal and Bangladesh's persistent sense of insecurity in their relationship with India.[7] (Pakistan is the only state that faces a two-front threat, but it is only in the context of an Indo-Soviet cooperative policy that the Soviet threat from Afghanistan constitutes a serious problem at this point in time.) Thus, any security system in South Asia would have to reassure India's neighbors about New Delhi's intentions, and this the GOI has been unable—or at least unwilling—to do.

India's Bilateral Relations with South Asian States

Economic Relations

There is no doubt about the keen interest in India to expand economic relations with other regional states through bilateral arrangements, because New Delhi has usually adopted a quite liberal position in negotiation with its neighbors over the past decade. The Janata government (1977-79) was particularly forthcoming in this respect and seemed on the verge of major breakthroughs in improving relations with neighbors, not only on economic but on most issues.[8] After her return to power in 1980, Prime Minister Indira Gandhi maintained or even expanded the liberal approach to economic relations inherited from the Janata government, but on occasion in the context of strained political and security relations that often frustrated efforts to improve economic ties.

Pakistan. India still has only a very limited and spasmodic economic relationship with Pakistan, the consequence primarily of Pakistan's determined efforts from 1947 to 1971 to eliminate the subcontinent-wide economic system that had developed during the British period. This was not easily accomplished, for East Pakistan had been integrated with and dependent on neighboring areas of what became northeast India after 1947. But the government of Pakistan carried out this policy more thoroughly and effectively in West Pakistan after the 1965 Indo-Pakistani War, which ended the few remaining economic ties between West Pakistan and India. After the 1971 Indo-Pakistani war, a virtual iron curtain was constructed between what remained of Pakistan (i.e., West Pakistan) economically, culturally, and politically, and the prospects of any substantial improvement in this relationship seemed very remote in the early 1970s.

New Delhi had never been happy with this situation and "in the spirit of Tashkent" (that is, the 1966 Tashkent Agreement) after the 1965 war had made overtures to Pakistan on various aspects of their relationship. This was attractive to the Indians for both economic and political reasons. Until the latter half of the 1970s, however, there were invariably negative responses from Pakistan. Perhaps coincidentally, it was only in the post-Bhutto period that some reconsideration of Pakistan's policy on economic relations became evident. It was clear to responsible Pakistanis that their country had paid a high price for its policy of avoiding economic relations and presumably economic dependence on India. Pakistan often found itself importing consumer products or machinery from third countries at considerably higher prices than the prices on the Indian market, and was, moreover, paying for these imports with scarce foreign exchange. Also, the lack of an economic relationship with India had deterred the improvement of political relations with India, an objective of Islamabad's foreign policy by the late 1970s when Pakistan's close relationships with Iran, Turkey, the United States, and even China had diminished in both scope and utility.

There were a number of ad hoc economic agreements between Pakistan and India in the 1970s, but the need for a more systematic and coordinated economic relationship was recognized by both governments. Reaching an agreement on the terms of an "economic treaty" required extensive negotiation and bargaining. Pakistan was still not prepared for a wholesale trade opening with India that might (1) make it overly dependent on India for some vital imports, and (2) expose Pakistan's "infant industries" in several fields to "unfair" competition from the better established and, supposedly, more efficient Indian industries. New Delhi was understanding of the Pakistani view on these matters, and in the bargaining process did incorporate some concessions to Pakistan in an effort to mitigate Islamabad's concern over the domestic impact of an economic relationship with India.

These negotiations collapsed, at least temporarily, because of a series of developments in the 1980s that tended to increase tension and reduce the scope for compromise between the two countries. Pakistan was obviously less interested in an economic opening to India, in part because developments in Afghanistan revived and expanded more attractive alternative sources of economic aid, trade, and capital investments. Pakistan's economy has flourished in recent years, and its foreign exchange holdings now seem adequate for its economic requirements. At the same time, India's liberality on the trade issue has been obfuscated by the enhanced concern in the GOI on regional security and political issues. The discussions continue in a low key, in part through the new Indo-

Pakistani Joint Commission that was established in 1983, but the prospects in the immediate future for expanded economic relations between the two states would appear to be quite dismal. Negotiations through the Joint Commission were suspended throughout 1984 when relations between the two countries were particularly tense, but there would appear to be good prospects for their renewal in 1985.

Bangladesh. It has been particularly galling to the GOI that economic relations with Bangladesh have gone the way of those with Pakistan in recent years. Before 1971, one of the basic complaints of the Awami League Party in East Pakistan against the Pakistan government was that the latter's economic policy had obligated East Pakistan to make major sacrifices that hampered its economic development because of the obstacles to economic exchange with India. The high price that India paid in the liberation of Bangladesh and immediately thereafter in a massive economic aid program to the new state had led most Indians to assume that relations between the two governments on *all* subjects would be close and cooperative. Bangladesh's "gratitude" lasted only a few months. By the last year of the Mujib period (1972-75), the Bangladesh government had quietly initiated some policies that deemphasized economic ties with India. In the eighteen months between Mujib's assassination in August 1975 and Mrs. Gandhi's removal from office by the voters in March 1977, this became government policy in Dhaka in the context of Indian support of and direct involvement in terrorist campaigns directed against the Bangladesh authorities. Formal relations improved during the Janata period and have not deteriorated much since January 1980, but it has remained Dhaka's objective to limit as far as possible Bangladesh's economic relations with India. The Bangladesh consumer pays a steep price for this policy in terms of the high cost of imported commodities. This makes no sense in terms of economic development; but the highest priorities in Bangladesh go to political and security considerations, and on these levels a friendly but distant relationship with New Delhi is what has been desired. As a result, India is a minor factor in Bangladesh's official trade and aid relationship with foreign powers in the 1980s (i.e., when the extensive smuggling of commodities between the two states is not included), and little movement on either side to change this situation to their mutual economic advantage was evident by the end of 1984.

The distribution of the waters of the Gangetic and Brahmaputra river systems between the two countries has absorbed the attention of the Indian and Bangladesh governments for a decade. The dispute over the Farakka barrage in India has yet to be resolved, and the short-term agreement on the distribution of the Ganges waters deals only with the fringe issues involved. The Indian government has proposed a link canal between the Ganges and Brahmaputra as an ultimate solution, but Dhaka's response has been very negative, although the link canal would seem to meet both India's and Bangladesh's water requirements. Here again, political factors may be superseding economic considerations in Dhaka's decision making on this issue, as the control points on both ends of the canal would be in Indian territory and thus subject to Indian control, providing New Delhi with a powerful bargaining weapon in any Indo-Bangladeshi disputes. Bangladesh, in turn, has proposed concentration on building a large reservoir system on the Ganges and subsidiary rivers, most of which would be located in Nepali territory. India has no objections to this, but the Nepal government has not been prepared to sacrifice large segments of its scarce cultivable land for these reservoirs that would benefit India and Bangladesh, but not Nepal. The deficiencies of India's insistence on bilateral rather than multilateral approaches to the resolution of such issues is readily evident in this case.

Sri Lanka. The island state of Sri Lanka had never been integrated very extensively into the mainland economies on the subcontinent even during the British period, and this continues to be the case. Some efforts to expand Indo-Sri Lanka economic relations have been introduced in the past decade, in particular through capital investments by the Indian private sector in the free industrial zones sponsored by the Sri Lankan government as well as a limited expansion in trade. But the improvement in economic relations between the two countries has not yet led to an agreement on the most important subject—cooperation in Indian and Sri Lankan tea exports to the outside world. The suggestion that the two countries would profit from a coordination of tea prices and quantities exported has been met in both Colombo and New Delhi by focusing on the problems rather than the opportunities of devising a cooperative system. For Sri Lanka, the economic gains would be attractive, but the political cost of integrating its main export product into an Indian-dominated trading system is a disincentive.

Sri Lanka has made several overtures for membership in the ASEAN system, first in 1981 and then in 1984. Sri Lankan public statements usually explain this policy in economic terms, in particular Colombo's interests in attracting ASEAN capital into their free industrial zones under preferential ASEAN terms. But it should be noted that intraregional economic relations within the ASEAN system have not developed extensively as yet, and the few agreements between participant countries are mostly bilateral in nature. It is probable that Sri Lanka is more interested in obtaining support from the informal ASEAN security system which has developed in recent years because of Colombo's apprehensions over the major external threat to Sri Lanka—the possibility of Indian military intervention in Sri Lanka in the context of the serious deterioration in communal relations between the minority Tamil and majority Sinhala communities in Sri Lanka.

Nepal. The two Himalayan kingdoms of Nepal and Bhutan differ from the other South Asian states in that their primary international economic relationship is with India. Despite nearly a quarter century of intensive efforts at trade diversification, approximately two-thirds of Nepal's foreign trade is with India under the official figures, and this would rise to 85 to 90 percent if the large scale "unofficial" smuggling between India and Nepal is included. Kathmandu has had more success in diversifying sources of economic assistance, but here also the fundamental programs in economic development, whatever their aid source, are heavily dependent on a cooperative relationship with India. It took some time, but this basic fact of life finally got through to the authorities in Nepal in the 1970s when some efforts were made to expand economic interaction with India—a policy that had been unacceptable from the early 1960s until then. An agreement was reached with India in 1979 on private Indian investment in joint projects in Nepal to hasten the process of industrialization, which had been stagnant for a decade despite a few Chinese and Soviet-aided show projects. The results of the joint projects have been minimal, more because of the incredibly complex bureaucratic maze through which such programs must move than because of any disinclination within the Indian private sector to invest in Nepal. Here again it is Kathmandu's concern over the political impact of expanded economic relations with India that has been crucial.

As with Bangladesh, India's most important economic relationship with Nepal involves the control and development of the myriad water systems that debouch out of the Nepal hills onto the plains of India. On some of the most important of these proposed projects, there have been several agreements "in principle" between New Delhi and Kathmandu but few agreements in fact. There are differences over the kind of projects—for example, one huge hydroelectric complex or numerous smaller water control and power projects—but the major dispute has been over funding of the projects. Nepal prefers multilateral projects that have multilateral funding; India wants bilateral projects in which third parties are excluded, even though it accepts the need for multilateral funding of these projects. The floods, silting, erosion, deforestation, and power shortages go on at an ever-growing pace, but this does not impel the incredibly cautious bureaucracies in both countries that have been assigned responsibility for the negotiation of these agreements to move expeditiously. Substantial progress was made in 1984 toward an agreement of the basic issues in dispute, and there was some optimism in Kathmandu in early 1985 that the new Rajiv Gandhi government in India might be more sensitive to Nepali concerns and needs.

Bhutan. Bhutan's international aid and trade relations are almost exclusively with India. The government in Thimphu has indulged in a symbolic diversification of economic aid policy, with the appropriate United Nations agencies or smaller "noncontroversial" Asian or European countries. The basic effort has been (1) to improve the terms under which aid is provided by the GOI, and (2) to reduce the need for aid by a sensible redefinition of Bhutan's economic development programs that would make them self-supporting. The results to date have been quite encouraging. Indian aid is now given in lump sum form for utilization on projects at the discretion of Thimphu, a contrast with the project-related Indian aid program in Nepal. Bhutan's economic development program has been decentralized in an effort to make it self-supporting and thus less dependent on Indian aid. The hope is that eventually the transfer of funds from India to Bhutan will lose the "aid syndrome" character, but rather will be the result of the sale of hydropower from Indian-aided hydel projects in Bhutan to power-hungry areas in northeastern India. Although there still are some tensions in Indo-Bhutani relations, these would appear to be much reduced over those of ten years ago and minor in comparison to India's economic relations with other South Asian states. A great deal can be accomplished when two South Asian governments decide to behave sensibly and liberally in their economic interactions!

In any case, the news is not all bad on the GOI's determined effort to develop a South Asian regional economic system based on any interlinking of India's bilateral relations with several neighboring states. Pakistan and Bangladesh remain largely outside this system, and it seems unlikely that this will change very rapidly no matter how liberal and farsighted the GOI may be in devising economic policies that are mutually advantageous as well as sensitive to political concerns of the neighboring states. But Nepal, Bhutan, and on certain subjects, Sri Lanka are accommodating themselves to a regional economic system in which India is the fulcrum. None of the South Asian states today has an explicitly anti-Indian policy on economic issues, as was the case in the 1950s, 1960s, and into the 1970s, even though they still have reservations about expanding bilateral relations with New Delhi on aid and trade issues.

There is an agreement among all the SARC states on the basic issue of the proposed "New International Economic Order"—namely extracting greater amounts of capital and related resources from the "developed" world on very soft terms. They all advocate a substantial expansion of contributions from the "North," and all criticized the Reagan administration for "reducing" American contributions to the sources of international largess. But even on this issue, in which their rhetoric tends to be the same, there are some subtle but important differences between India and the other South Asian states on one critical issue—the criteria to be used in setting priorities for the distribution of these funds. India is a strong supporter of the system under which it has long been the recipient of the largest sums from such institutions as the World Bank and the International Development Association. The other countries generally seem to prefer a distribution system under which need rather than sheer size would provide the basis for the distribution of funds. Since the current efforts are concentrated on increasing the total amount available for distribution, the tendency has been to avoid a public debate on the distribution system. But India's recent interest in acquiring access to Asian Development Bank (ADB) funds is looked upon with some apprehension by the other South Asian states because this could eventually reduce the amount available to them from the ADB. When China gains admission as well, the small, poorer states are likely to have reduced access to an important source of assistance. This is another example of a case in which a consensus on broad principles can disintegrate when more specific policies have to be decided.

"Migrant" Communities in South Asia

One of the consequences of the unification of the subcontinent during the colonial period had been the resettlement of large migrant communities outside their traditional cultural and linguistic areas of origin.[9] This process of migration continued and even expanded—not always voluntarily—after the division of British India into successor states with more firmly defined boundary lines and more rigorous controls over entry and residence. In the last decade, the status and rights of several of these migrant communities has become a critical issue in both the domestic and international politics of several South Asian states—in particular India, Sri Lanka, Bangladesh, and Nepal.

Public attention in 1983-85 has focused on two cases in which the migrant community issue was the central theme in violent communal clashes—the Tamil-Sinhala confrontation in Sri Lanka and the Assamese-Bengali riots in northeast India. In Sri Lanka, it is straining the definition of the term to classify the Tamil minority as "migrants" because the most active of the Tamil dissidents come from families that have resided in Sri Lanka for at least several hundred years and are Sri Lankan citizens.[10] But the conflict between this element in the Tamil community and the majority Sinhala community was internationalized when, almost inevitably, the GOI was brought into the dispute because of the response of some political elements in Tamilnadu in India to the treatment of their "brothers" across the straits in Sri Lanka. That the "Ceylon Tamil" community has been totally disinvolved with any Indian political or social system for a millennium or more (the more recent "Indian Tamil" migrant community in Sri Lanka has tried to keep out of these communal clashes, although not always successfully) has not preempted the Tamil insurgent elements from suddenly discovering a sense of identity with the Tamil "homeland" in India that was never noted in the past, nor their proclivity for seeking support from political organizations in Tamilnadu and from the Indian government against the Sinhala-dominated government in Colombo. This raised such basic concerns in Colombo as to persuade the government of the need to seek effective counters to the perceived threat of Indian intervention.

Initially, New Delhi's involvement was restricted to the diplomatic level as a "nonaligned" but interested party to these developments in Sri Lanka. Mrs. Gandhi's personal envoy, G. Parthasarathy, helped to negotiate an agreement between Colombo and the main Tamil political group on what appeared to be mutually acceptable terms. He also reduced somewhat the apprehension over the possibility of Indian military intervention in Sri Lanka among the Sinhala public and political leaders, removing the threat of a serious break in Indo-Sri Lanka relations. The Sri Lanka Foreign Minister attended the SARC meeting in August 1983 —to the surprise of some other participants—thus reasserting Colombo's active support of a South Asian regional system. At the same time, however, Sri Lanka renewed its application for membership in ASEAN, an indication of a desire in Colombo to maintain an option on the regional identity issue.

The communal strife in Sri Lanka continued and, indeed, worsened in 1984-85, eventually leading to serious strains in Sri Lanka-India relations. The GOI continued to advocate a reasonable compromise of the issues in dispute and rejected the proposals for the division of the island and the establishment of an independent state in the Tamil majority areas in the north. Until mid-1985, when Indian policy changed, New Delhi had not taken any action against the training camps established for the Ceylon Tamil insurgents in Tamilnadu that had been clearly identified in the Indian press, nor halted the shipments of men and arms to Sri Lanka from Tamilnadu—also described in detail by Indian reporters who accompanied some of these "fishing boats" in their illegal missions.[11] In New Delhi, meanwhile, there was some dismay over the failure of the Sri Lanka government to make the concessions that were considered necessary if a political solution was to be achieved between the principal Sinhala and Tamil political organizations. But by early fall 1985, Prime Minister Rajiv Gandhi was applying very strong pressure on the Ceylon Tamil insurgent factions to suspend armed resistance and to negotiate with the Sri Lanka authorities. At the same time he placed quiet pressure on Colombo to offer more liberal terms to the Tamils. Negotiations were held, under tacit Indian sponsorship, between the Sri Lanka government and the Tamil insurgents in October 1985 in Thimphu, Bhutan. Although these only set the basis for further negotiations between the two sides, they did reduce the concern that had been felt in Colombo about an Indian intervention in support of the Tamils. And, of course, the other South Asian states have been following all these developments with great interest as possible portents in their own relationship with New Delhi.

Indo-Bangladeshi perceptions of migrant community conflicts differ in some key respects from the Sri Lanka case, but are no less serious. The primary issue in the 1980s concerns the large number—according to dissident Assamese calculations—of recent Bangladeshi migrants into Assam and the neighboring hill states in northeast India, in particular Tripura, Meghalaya, and Mizoram. Dhaka denies that there has been any substantial migration of Bangladeshis into India since 1971 and insists that members of the Bengali community that is the target of "sons of the soil" movements in the northeast are Indian citizens for whom Bangladesh has no responsibility. Dhaka bitterly resents some of the concessions New Delhi has made to the Assamese, in particular the fence that has been ordered constructed along the entire Indo-Bangladesh border. It is assumed in Dhaka that this is a largely symbolic gesture by the GOI to mollify the Assamese, and that this extremely expensive fence will probably never be completed. Nevertheless, it is considered a demeaning act toward Bangladesh and indication of New Delhi's insensitivity to the feeling and concern of its neighbors in the region.

The Indian government faces a welter of conflicting interests and issues in the agreement that was reached with the Assamese movement in July 1985, and decision making on this issue was extremely difficult because it had to be done within the framework of policy principles that would have to be applied to the entire country, not just Assam. The Assamese movement, directed at what are called "Bangladeshi Muslim migrants," was in reality against all Bengalis, whether Muslim or Hindu, who have swarmed into the fertile, comparatively underpopulated Assam valley since 1951. Acceptance of the Assamese demands would also have raised questions about the citizenship of the Bengali *Hindu* refugees from East Pakistan who entered India between 1951 and 1971, and thereafter. Moreover, although the Assam crisis has more the character of an ethnic than a religious communal issue, it is nevertheless certain that the large Muslim minority elsewhere in India has carefully watched how New Delhi responded to what they interpret as a campaign against Muslims.

Another more persistent if less critical issue in Indo-Bangladesh relations concerns the tribal communities that straddle the border in the Chittagong hills and the neighboring states of Meghalaya and Mizoram in India. Tribal separatist movements have been active on both sides of the border for some years, and both Dhaka and New Delhi have accused each other of providing assistance to the tribal dissidents in the other state. This seems most unlikely to have occurred on any scale, as both New Delhi and Dhaka have a major stake in stability and peace in their respective tribal areas and dissidence on one side of the border almost inevitably will have repercussions on the other side. But this is another of these difficult trans-border ethnic issues that are justifiably matters of concern in both countries and, moreover, can be easily exploited by political forces that are prepared to sacrifice good relations between the two neighbors for narrow political advantage.

The disturbances in India's northeast have also had a negative impact on Indo-Nepali relations recently. Although the Assamese and hill tribal movements are usually defined as directed against Bengali migrants, the large Nepali migrant community residents in the fringe areas of Assam valley and the lower hills of the northeast hill states have also been subjected to attack. Some of these Nepalis—most of whom are third or fourth generation residents in India and, hence, Indian citizens—have found the situation so intolerable that they have returned to Nepal as refugees.

Using the issue for narrower interests, several political factions in Nepal have taken up the "cause" of the Nepali returnees, demanding that countermeasures be taken against the large Indian "migrant" community in Nepal, most of whom have also been resident in that country for at least two generations but still have problems with their Nepali citizenship as ascertained by Kathmandu. This reaction has led to demands in Nepal that all "Indians" be required to hold Indian passports and obtain Nepali visas or else be expelled from Nepal, which is not required under present rules. Other Nepalis, including some voices from the Nepalis residing in India, have argued in rebuttal that India would certainly retaliate in kind and that this could be a major problem both for the Nepalis permanently residing in India and for the thousands of hill people in Nepal who go down into India in search of short-term employment for several months each year. The Nepal government will probably resist the pressure being placed upon it to move against the "swarm" of Indians "occupying" the Nepal-Terai and lower hills—the highly exaggerated language used by some of the Nepali political forces—but the issue is sure to be a difficult one for both Kathmandu and New Delhi.

There are no serious migrant community issues in Indo-Pakistani relations unless one wants to interpret the post-1947 dispute over divided Kashmir in these terms. Although both New Delhi and Islamabad have liberalized the terms under which nationals of the other country visit relatives and friends from the families that were "divided" by partition, the large refugee communities that moved into the territory of the other state in the partition period are not considered migrants. Certainly New Delhi asserts no responsibility for the Muslims who moved to Pakisan nor Islamabad responsibility for the Hindus and Sikhs who moved to India in 1947, although, rather incredibly, some Indian extremists accused the Pakistan government of this in the disturbed situation that evolved in Punjab in 1984 which led to the Indian army's seizure of the Sikh's "Golden Temple" in Amritsar in June, and then the assassination of Mrs. Gandhi by two of her Sikh security guards on October 31, 1984.

One internal development in India that is peripherally related to the migrant community issue, however, is the 1983 resettlement act of the government of Jammu and Kashmir, under which Kashmiris, wherever currently resident, can return to Jammu and Kashmir and claim land and property lost when they fled from the state. The GOI is not at all enthusiastic about this Jammu and Kashmir law and has accused the Farooq Abdullah government—deposed by a New Delhi-managed coup in 1984—in Jammu and Kashmir of everything from communalism to pro-Pakistani sentiments. But since India claims all of the pre-1947 state of Kashmir as rightfully Indian, it would be embarrassing to argue that Kashmiris on the other side of the "line of control" in Kashmir, in Pakistan, or in third countries do not have a legitimate claim to Indian citizenship.[12] Islamabad has kept out of the issue because it is not any more enthusiastic about this Jammu and Kashmir law than New Delhi, if for different reasons. But this is another instance of the way in which trans-border ethnic considerations complicate decision making on both domestic and international policy issues in South Asia.

The extremely complex ethnic, religious, linguistic, and tribal factors that strongly influence the sense of identity among social groups along and across national borders in South Asia cannot avoid being a serious problem in both the domestic and international politics in these countries. In most instances, the governments in South Asia had sought to downplay the international aspects of these issues when they arose and to try and resolve them within the domestic political context. This is less evident today, and particularly in India where prominent Indian leaders have made irresponsible off-the-cuff comments on occasion about their duty to assist "Indians"—most of whom are not Indian nationals—in their disputes in their country of residence. This relic of the old "Akhand Bharat" (Greater India) war cries of extremist elements of the Indian nationalist movement in the British period cannot help but increase the concern and trepidation with which the other regional states view their emerging relationships with New Delhi. There is some hope and expectation that the Rajiv Gandhi government in India will exercise more restraint on the rhetoric used on this subject.

Diplomacy

Under this very broad heading I discuss two currently important factors in India's relations with other South Asian states: (1) the differences in views and policies between the Indian and other governments in the region on both regional and extraregional international issues, and (2) some territorial disputes that still affect intrastate relations in South Asia.

Regional and Extraregional International Issues

It is quite evident that there is considerable dissatisfaction in all of the other regional states with New Delhi's policy positions on recent developments in areas within or immediately adjacent to South Asia—more specifically, Afghanistan, Southeast Asia, and the Indian Ocean. India's docile acceptance of Soviet aggression against the Afghan people, at least in some Indian public statements, is widely viewed as an abnegation of Indian responsibilities as the self-proclaimed dominant power in the region as well as a violation of the principles of nonalignment. The apparent failure of New Delhi to offer support or even to make an effort to understand the problem that recent developments in Afghanistan pose for Pakistan and Iran, as well as the self-serving proclivity of New Delhi to concoct security threat scenarios from Pakistan, has appalled and mystified the other SARC states. India is accused of failure to uphold its responsibilities as the key participant in its own regional security system. As one South Asian leader expressed it, India wants all the advantages of being the major power in the region but is reluctant to assume the unpleasant duties that go along with this status.

India's failure to respond forcefully to Soviet intervention in Afghanistan has caused Pakistan to turn again to the outside powers for assistance and support after trying unsuccessfully to establish a working relationship with India on security matters. Although all the other states would have preferred to avoid the reinvolvement of the United States in a South Asian security system, they recognized that it is the inadequacies, deficiencies, and the tendency to toady to Moscow's sensitivities in defining New Delhi's policies that have been primarily responsible for this unfortunate development.

This distress with India's "leadership" on a critical issue in or near the subcontinent is also evident in the policy positions of the other South Asian states on several other important foreign policy issues. All of these governments (even Bhutan!) now take different positions from India's on those broader Asian issues that are seen as most relevant to their interests—Afghanistan, Kampuchea, and, more subtly and indirectly on the Indian Ocean as a Zone of Peace (IOZP) proposal. SARC has not yet demonstrated any signs of maturing in the way that ASEAN has in such situations—that is, by the member-states usually sublimating their different perspectives on such critical issues as Kampuchea, Vietnam, and China in order to maintain a unified front. In other words, the ASEAN regional system has become more important than specific national perspectives and interests in defining their foreign policies; there is no sign as yet of such a process at work in SARC—now SAARC.

Obviously it will take some time and will require basic changes in attitude and behavior by the South Asian states for SAARC to emulate ASEAN in this respect. Moreover, the differences in national power relationships within SAARC, where India claims dominance, when compared to ASEAN, in which no participant claims the status of a dominant power, may make a consensus system implausible in the South Asian system. Fortunately, SAARC is taking a very flexible and creative approach to its regional system and is not trying to emulate ASEAN, the European Economic Community (EEC), or even the OAU. This humble approach is probably most sensible, but it does mean that anything like a coordination of policy on political, economic, or security issues is highly unlikely in South Asia for some time to come.

Another difference in the Indian and the other regional states' perspective on diplomacy is evident in their attitude toward the role of the superpowers, "developed world," and China in South Asia. Indian policy seeks to exclude these external powers from any substantial influence on political and security issues and even advocates keeping economic relations to a level that would avoid the dependency syndrome that is usually interpreted as integral to "neocolonialism." Although the other regional states express their determination to avoid domination by any outside power, they also insist upon their right to establish broad-based relations with the superpowers and other external states and to try and use these relationships effectively in intraregional developments. It should be noted, however, that this difference in perception between India and its regional neighbors exists more in theory than in practice. Whenever New Delhi has found it necessary or convenient to solicit the involvement of external powers in support of India's regional interests, this has been handled quite effectively—for example, United States and British support in the 1962 war with China; Soviet support in the mid-1960s against China and in 1971 against Pakistan. It would appear that India's "exclusion" policy is intended more as a working principle for the other South Asian states than for itself.

Territorial Disputes

Old-fashioned types of boundary disputes are not very evident in South Asia in the 1980s. There are India's periodic disputes with Nepal when a border river changes its course, with the issue usually whether the old or the new river bed should constitute the boundary. A minor dispute with Bhutan in the one area in which the boundary is not determined by the line where the plains end and the foothills begin has been settled "in principle" but not by an actual border demarcation. Sri Lanka and India did settle their dispute over several small islands in the straits area between the mainland and Sri Lanka, with the latter the beneficiary of generous terms. But the water boundary issue has risen again in a threatening form in the context of Sri Lankan efforts to intercept the shipments of men and arms to the Tamil insurgents in Sri Lanka from Tamilnadu, and the GOI's concern with protecting Tamilnadu fishermen, some of whom are involved in these smuggling operations, in Indian territorial waters.

The long-term Indian-Bangladesh dispute over the enclaves held by one state in the territory of the other continues to complicate their relationships, although more on the access to enclaves issue than on the enclaves themselves. A much more difficult territorial dispute concerns the islands at the mouth of the river systems in the Bay of Bengal directly to the south of both Indian and Bangladesh territory. The result of vast deposits of silt from the rivers into the Bay of Bengal, these newly emerging islands are located in areas where the territorial waters of India, Bangladesh, and Burma merge, presenting all three governments with a legal basis for the assertion of their claims. The islands are also in areas where it is projected that there may be large offshore oil and gas resources awaiting exploitation, and ownership of these islands will help determine which country has jurisdiction over their development. The issue is still under negotiation, with both India and Bangladesh preparing their cases on the basis of conflicting interpretations of international law and the law of the seas. A premature Indian landing of a small military unit on the principal island in dispute while the issue was under discussion was strongly resented by Bangladesh and considered improper behavior by the other countries in the region. But if oceanographers are right, it is possible the issue will disappear, along with the islands, when the next major cyclone hits the Bangladesh and West Bengal coast.

The much older and potentially more explosive dispute between India and Pakistan over Kashmir has never been formally resolved and is still a subject of intense and often flamboyant debate in both countries. The new "line of control" that replaced the old 1949 cease-fire line after the 1971 Indo-Pakistani war was accepted as the de facto dividing line in

Kashmir by both India and Pakistan in the 1972 Simla Agreement. Unfortunately, some sections of the line of control in the more remote areas of northwestern Ladakh were never demarcated on the ground, and there are still differences in the Indian and Pakistani versions of the line in this area, leading to occasional clashes between the small border guard units that patrol this area. Some of the more irresponsible sections of the press, particularly in India, have tried to project these small-scale clashes as the opening stage of yet another Indo-Pak war, but it would seem unlikely that either side would select such an inconvenient and difficult area to start a conflict when there are so many better-situated and much more vital areas that could serve this purpose.

Kashmir remains an issue in dispute, one that Pakistan will occasionally raise in a formal, rather unobtrusive fashion in the appropriate international forums. India does not raise the Kashmir issue internationally, but does use—or, on occasion, misuse—the dispute in its domestic politics or in relations with Pakistan. Both were evident in 1984 during the viciously communal Congress (I) campaign directed at the National Conference government in Jammu and Kashmir, which culminated in the toppling of the Farooq Abdullah government, as well as in the ludicrous scenario that Pakistan intended to redo 1965—that is, launch a limited war in Kashmir in order to "internationalize" the dispute and then force India into concessions. Although these allegations made sense in terms of Prime Minister Indira Gandhi's 1984 electoral strategy, they also constitute a potentially serious setback to India's relations with Pakistan and other regional states. The Pakistan government responded carefully and cautiously to the Congress (I) propaganda campaign on the assumption that it was a temporary phenomenon contrived for electoral purposes, as indeed seems to have been the case. But the Pakistani public may not respond with such restraint. President Zia may owe the Indian government a vote of thanks for providing him with something he has had difficulty developing on his own, a solid support base in Pakistan!

Conclusion

Let me conclude with a few comments on the way in which the other South Asian states view India's record in the region since 1947. What is usually mentioned by the politically active public both in and outside of their governments is the readiness of India to intervene militarily, directly or indirectly, in neighboring areas when circumstances permitted or Indian interests required. Usually mentioned are Indian interventions in Junagadh, Hyderabad, and Kashmir in 1948, Nepal in 1950-51, Goa in 1961, East Pakistan in 1971, Sikkim in 1975, and Bangladesh in 1976-77. The concern is that the success India has had in these interventions has made the policy attractive and thus, that there is no sense of assurance that New Delhi will resist temptation to do so again if this is seen as useful or necessary. What is usually *not* noted by the other regional states is the restraint with which India has used its power on other occasions when opportunities for intervention have arisen. But then governments are usually judged by what they do rather than what they do not do. The caution and apprehension with which the other regional states view their relationship with India is understandable, given their perception of India as a neighbor. New Delhi may benefit from this in some ways, at least in the short run. But it does raise the question about how these states would react to a major domestic or international crisis in India.

NOTES

1. For recent surveys of Indian foreign policy under Mrs. Gandhi see Surjit Mansingh, *India's Search for Power* (Beverly Hills, Calif.: Sage Publications, 1984), and Shashi Tharoor, *Reasons of State: Political Development and India's Foreign Policy under Indira Gandhi 1966-1977* (New Delhi: Vikas, 1982).
2. For an early analysis of regionalism in South Asia, see Sisir Gupta, *India and Regional Integration in Asia* (Bombay: Asia Publishing House, 1964).
3. Recent Indian strategic thought is summarized in U. S. Bajpai, ed., *India's Security: The Politico-Strategic Environment* (New Delhi: Lancers, 1983).
4. For a range of views see K. Satya Murty, ed., *South Asian Regional Cooperation* (Hyderabad: Institute of Asian Studies, 1982), and M. S. Agwani et al., eds., *South Asia: Stability and Regional Cooperation* (Chandigarh: Centre for Research in Rural and Industrial Development, 1983).
5. In mid-1985 SARC became SAARC the South Asian Association for Regional Cooperation.
6. For an Indian comparison of SARC and ASEAN see R. V. R. Chandrasekhara Rao, "South Asian Regional Cooperation," *Roundtable* 293 (1985):53-65.
7. A Nepali analysis is in Lok Raj Baral, *Nepal in Regional Cooperation: Quest for a More Equitable Relationship* (Kathmandu: Centre for Economic Development and Administration, 1984).
8. See Shrikant Paranjpe, *India and South Asia since 1971* (New Delhi: Radiant Publishers, 1985).
9. For an overview of the migrant problem, see Myron Weiner, *Sons of the Soil* (Princeton, N.J.: Princeton University Press, 1978). The broader problem of national integration is surveyed in A. Jeyaratnam Wilson and Dennis Dalton, eds., *The States of South Asia: Problems of National Integration* (Honolulu: University Press of Hawaii, 1982).

10. A comprehensive survey of the Sri Lanka situation is in James Manor, ed., *Sri Lanka in Change and Crisis* (New York: St. Martin's Press, 1984).

11. See the reports in *India Today*, especially by Shekhar Gupta, March 31, 1984.

12. For a detailed Indian study of the Kashmir problem, see Sisir Gupta, *Kashmir: A Study in Indo-Pakistan Relations* (Bombay: Asia Publishing House, 1966).

2

India's Regional Policy:
Strategic and Security Dimensions

Noor A. Husain

The foreign policy of a country, especially its strategic and security dimensions, is largely conditioned by its geopolitical and geostrategic environment, by its domestic milieu, and by the dynamics of the international system. Policies, like conflicts, are conceived in the minds of leaders, who are affected by distortions in perceptions caused by historical, cultural, and ethnic factors. This is perhaps more true in developing societies, where think tanks and public policy institutes do not exist, or have very little say in policy formulation or objective analysis, societies that are not free of misplaced chauvinism, whipped up in total disregard of smaller neighbors and their sensitivities.

Indian Foreign Policy Concepts: Pre-1947

This has been equally true with respect to India. "Foreign Policy as such is a low priority area in Indian politics . . . two factors explain the relative indifference of most parties to foreign policy matters. . . . India as an international actor does not play a global role . . . foreign affairs only marginally influence national politics. Indian national life is so problem-ridden as to leave the parties with little time for the luxury of indulging in affairs beyond the frontiers of India. As a result, foreign policy becomes essentially the preoccupation of the party in power or, to be more precise, the government. And as Gabriel Almond theorized years ago, whatever policy the government chooses to follow before long acquires popular approval."[1] Like her father, Jawaharlal Nehru, Indira Gandhi presumed popular support for her foreign policy until there was either a faux pas or an outcry against it. "Many of us in India have a passive view of foreign policy. Such an approach comes naturally to us. So we find whatever excuse comes handy. . . . It does not even occur to us that this show of pusillanimity does not, and cannot, win us anyone's respect and often it is a convenient cover for lack of diplomatic skill."[2] "In India exposure to press opinion on foreign policy matters is confined to a narrow elite class."[3]

India's foreign and security policy and strategy during the last thirty-seven years has been based more in terms of power and interest, with a veneer of both idealism and globalism, than on a systematic approach, and Nehru himself was its main architect. As prime minister, he was at the helm of affairs for seventeen and a half long years, both as the choice of the Congress Party and as elected head of the government of India. He and his party survived three general elections, in 1952, 1957, and 1962. Before 1947, for twenty years Nehru had been the main thinker on foreign affairs in the Indian National Congress and its "Foreign Department" created around 1927. "After the Bolshevik Revolution in Russia in 1917, the abject poverty of the teeming millions of India made some Indian Congress leaders, notably Nehru, enthusiastic converts to the views of Lenin that imperialism was the last stage of capitalism, and increased their fascination for the Soviet Union as a land free from capitalism and thus likely to remain free from imperialism."[4] The participation by Nehru as an accredited representative of the Indian National Congress in the International Congress against Imperialism held at Brussels in February 1927 is a landmark in the evolution of the Indian outlook on world affairs. "He was a member of the Presidium of that Congress and delivered one of the opening addresses on the first day. . . . The Brussels Congress greatly influenced him and through him, the Indian National Congress."[5] "So I turned inevitably with goodwill towards Communism, for whatever its faults, it was, at least not hypocritical and not imperialistic," wrote Nehru.[6] His views were echoed by his mentor, Mahatma Gandhi: "I have never believed in the Bolshevik menace."[7] Ironically, this was the time in Central Asia when the Soviets were completing the conquests of the Khanates. "So far as Nehru was concerned he made it clear that he did not envisage any danger to India from the Soviet Union."[8] Subsequently, in 1936 at the Lucknow Congress session, Fabian socialist Nehru proclaimed his faith in the reconstruction of society on the basis of socialist principles, and in the Working Committee he nominated three leaders of the Congress Socialist Party. By the 1930s both Gandhi and Nehru, and some others, were reflecting and writing on India's defense and security problems. Which country could be a threat to India, they asked each other. After listing the United States, Japan, China, the West European powers, Afghanistan, and the Soviet Union, "by a process of elimination the Soviet Union remained the sole country which might threaten India's freedom, but in Nehru's opinion there was no ground to fear any invasion from her."[9] Gandhi agreed with Nehru. If there was a threat or an invasion, both felt, India would resist by nonviolent means and by economic sanctions alone! Whether this threat perception was based on the Soviet-German Accord of 1940 cannot be established; the accord proclaimed "the area South of Batum and Baku in the general direction of the Persian Gulf is recognized as the center of the aspirations of the Soviet Union."[10] The success of the Soviets in defending Russia during World War II against the Nazi onslaught, and their subsequent offensive capturing Berlin and over-running half of Eastern Europe further built up the Soviet image in the Indian National Congress and the Communist Party of India. After release from prison in 1944, Gandhi, when asked his views on Allied and Axis powers engaged in a global war, remarked, "If I sail in either direction, I suffer shipwreck. Therefore I have to be in the midst of the storm."[11]

The next pre-independence influence on India's foreign policy was the San Francisco Conference of the United Nations in April 1945. While the United States reportedly remained silent on the question of India's independence, the USSR openly supported it together with independence for other Asian and African countries. Even later, when Nehru was convinced that the Soviet Union was following an expansionist policy in Europe and West and East Asia and pressing demands on Turkey, Iran, and Japan, he remained cautious in his comments, and defended Soviet policy as being based upon a fear of encirclement.

The post World War II period was also the birth of another strategic concept in Nehru's mind in New Delhi in March-April 1947, at the Asian Relations Conference sponsored by the Indian Council of World Affairs. Mindful of China's size and position in Asia (particularly South Asia), Nehru was careful enough not to talk of leadership or preeminence, but reiterated what he had said earlier of India being "the center of things in Asia" and "the focal point of the many forces at work in Asia." This concept was to clash later in the 1950s with that of Mao, who considered China the center of the universe, the Middle Kingdom, around which the rest of the world revolved.

The Region

Before analyzing Nehru's strategic and security policy after 1947, a brief historical and geopolitical survey of the region is necessary. The British Raj in the "subcontinent," as distinct from South Asia, was handed over to two dominions, with smaller and militarily weaker Pakistan embodying the strategic and geopolitical crossroads of Central Asia, South Asia, and West Asia as the traditional warden of the marches, and larger India embodying the strategic center of gravity, namely the Indo-

Gangetic plains—the traditional seat of central power in the vast subcontinental peninsula with all its ethnic linguistic disparities and traditional domestic turbulence and instabilities.

To India's north, Tibet and China's Sinkiang region share with India 3,000 kilometers of common border, which has given them, and especially China, from time immemorial, a geographical South Asian connection and a South Asian power status whenever they felt militarily strong. They were at various times able to assert themselves all along and, often across, the Himalayas and the Karakorams, from Gilgit, across Ladakh, Nepal, Sikkim, Bhutan, and Northeastern India, all of which had tributary ties with both Tibet and China. "In 7th century A.D. Tibetan military expansion was rapid which took them to the plains of India. They dominated Nepal for a time and penetrated the whole cis-Himalayan region."[12] In the eighth century, Chinese and Tibetan troops moved into Gilgit to help the Raja of Gilgit against the Turks and stayed for five years. The same ethnic and religious groups inhabit both sides of the Himalayas and Karakorams—Buddhists and Muslims, respectively, with cultural ties cutting well across political boundaries and ranges. "Nepal since the earliest times had served as the entrepot of trade between the Indo-Gangetic valley and Tibet and China."[13] For some time Nepalese coins were legal tender in Tibet. Between the fifth and fifteenth centuries Chinese imperial documents recorded an exchange of about 150 diplomatic missions with cis-Himalayan states.

The British Raj was conscious of China's South Asian connection and status, and of Tibet and Sinkiang as (security) zones of South Asia (no less than the Hindukush and Southern Afghanistan), especially after China's attempt early in this century to form a Himalayan Confederacy with Nepal, Sikkim, Bhutan, and Tibet under Chinese patronage as they were all "subjects of China"; hence, the presence of British consulates, trading marts, listening posts, and soldiers in three Tibetan towns, and in Kashgar in Sinkiang until 1947. In geographic terms, both cartographic map projections (Mercator's showing correct shapes and Arno Peters' showing correct sizes) leave no doubt that Tibet and Sinkiang were geographically contiguous to South Asia. The same is true of the springboard area south of Hindukush; it belongs ethnically and linguistically to South Asia, with another 3,000 kilometers of common border with present-day Pakistan's North-West Frontier Province.

The other popular regional misconception pertains to the so-called Indian Ocean. In ancient times, even in the Indian epic *Mahabharata,* this waterbody is called "Daksina Samudra" (southern sea), a name current in local accounts up to the twelfth century. Until not long ago the Arabs who used this ocean for trade and commerce called it Al Bahar Al Muhit (the enclosed ocean), the Arabian Sea being the Sea of Fars (Persia), and the Bay of Bengal being the Sea of Hind or Sea of Harkand. The subcontinental influence extended only down to the Equator and the Maldive Islands with their ethnic mixture of Arabs, Sinhalese, and some Aryans and Dravidians. It was the British Raj and its global maritime power that conceived it as an imperial Indian lake, although the littoral of Eastern Africa, Southeast Asia, and Western Australia is five times greater than that of peninsular India. It is therefore as obvious a misnomer as "Middle East"—neither middle nor east from the point of view of the subcontinent. This subcontinent contains a quarter of the human race, densely packed, and characterized by the "triple crises of slow economic development, insufficient political integration and a disorderly arms race, [which] interact with and feed upon each other."[14] The region's defense expenditure is approximately 2.9 percent of the GNP, which is lower than that of East Asia and about a third of West Asia's.

These geopolitical and now geostrategic factors have to be seen in their true perspective for a proper realization of the security dilemmas that the region faces; the evolution of India's security policies and strategy often disregards or relegates these obvious factors to a position beneath their proper importance.

Indian Security Policy Evolution: Post 1947

After independence in August 1947, "India's foreign and security policy has tended to operate in three concentric circles, namely the Superpowers, the Third World and the Neighbors. The outer most circle received the most attention, while the closest one received the least. This state of affairs, more than any other, has been responsible for the nation's difficulties and is an indication of misplaced priorities."[15] Although a "soaring idealist" and an agnostic humanist, Nehru attempted to construct free India's foreign policy on the Mandala (circle with a center or nucleus) doctrine of *Kautilya Arthashastra* of 300 B.C., based on the geopolitical assumption that the immediate neighbor state is to be treated as a real or potential enemy, and a state next to the immediate neighbor as one's friend. At the same time he drew upon the ancient Buddhist precept of "Panch Sheela" (or five principles of "peaceful coexistence," a term coined by Lenin, according to Soviet Orientalist E. M. Zhukov) involving neutrality and noninterference, and nonalignment in respect of equal or bigger neighbors. (The term *noninterference* was first used by Viceroy Lawrence of India about policy toward Afghanistan.) Nehru had appreciated before 1947 that the struggle between the West and the Communist world would be decided in the Third World and therefore through nonalignment the best of both camps could be obtained. Yet while ostensibly condemning power politics, within two months of becoming prime minister and foreign minister of India, Nehru manipulated the accession of the state of Jammu and Kashmir and launched the Indian army in a prolonged fifteen-month conflict with India's immediate neighbor, Pakistan, creating the first subcontinental strategic schism, one with far-reaching consequences.

Jammu and Kashmir became the nucleus of the "Mandala" doctrine around which revolved Mr. Nehru's foreign and security policy and India's relations with regional and external powers of all sizes. Mr. Nehru took the Kashmir dispute to the United Nations and internationalized what was essentially a combined domestic, regional, and subcontinental security issue. Military intervention in Jammu and Kashmir was strategically as much an effort to get a stranglehold on Pakistan as it was, geopolitically, to "reach out" to distant neighbors, the Soviet Union, and Afghanistan. The more the western powers in the Security Council backed the principles of self-determination and a plebiscite in Kashmir (based on Nehru's own pledges), the more he attempted to cultivate the Soviet Union for its power of veto. The realization dawned on Nehru that he had committed a strategic schism in a fit of pique and that a plebiscite would go against India!

The Soviet Relationship

The Soviet Union established diplomatic relations with India in June 1947 at the time of the interim government two months before independence. In spite of Nehru's socialist bias, Soviet orientalists considered Indian leaders as "reactionaries" and "pro-imperialists," Gandhi the "apostle of backwardness," and Indian independence as "fictitious," brought about as it was by a British head of the Indian State (Mountbatten), and compromised as it was to become by the Commonwealth and increasing economic connections. Nehru's appointment of his sister Mrs. Pandit as ambassador to Moscow did not effectively thaw Stalin's attitude. The Soviet representative to the United Nations, Andrei Vyshinsky, said: "At best you are dreamers and idealists, at worst you don't understand your own position and camouflage horrible American policy."[16] Significantly, during this period from 1947 to the 1950s, Nehru also most ardently courted the friendship of neighboring China and was aware of China's South Asian power status, which is discussed in detail below.

Stalin's death in 1953 brought a softening in the Communist ideological crusade toward the Third World and India, while the West continued its antipathy to Nehru's neutralism and maintained a Cold War confrontation with the Communist bloc. The new Soviet leaders felt that in India, as in other Third World countries, national liberation movements could be led by the vocal and growing communist parties of India and the bourgeoisie. Soviet condemnation of Nehru's "nonalignment" was suddenly and drastically reversed to one of praise and appreciation. The Soviet Union had finally chosen India. The first step was a trade agreement in December 1953. By 1964 Soviet trade was to increase to 16 percent of India's total foreign trade; by the 1970s India was the Soviet Union's largest trading partner, and also providing more than 50 percent of India's military hardware. This was followed by Soviet pressure on the Communist Party of India to support Nehru's foreign policy in opposing American "imperialism." Nehru needed Soviet aid for India's second Five Year Plan and the Soviet Security Council veto on disputed Jammu and Kashmir. The Soviet Union needed Nehru's help to break out of the Western strategic naval encirclement.

In June 1955 Nehru visited Moscow at the Soviet's invitation, followed by the hasty, unprecedented and historic visit of Bulganin and Khrushchev to India. At the conclusion of the visit, Nehru said, "These last four days that they were here, I think, are historic and a great deal will be written about it in our history."[17] This sentiment was echoed by the Supreme Soviet a few days later. For Nehru's security policy and strategy, the visit was indeed historic. After a seven-year effort he had at last succeeded in changing the Soviet stand on disputed Jammu and Kashmir; he had also secured the Soviet veto should Pakistan raise the Kashmir issue again and be supported by the West. Speaking in Kashmir, Khrushchev had said that the "people themselves had decided that Kashmir is one of the states of the Republic of India,"[18] and he pledged future Soviet support to India, both directly and in various indirect forms. Simultaneously, "India supported, if not instigated the Pakhtoonistan dispute."[19] This action raised a two-front threat to Pakistan. India also stepped up its effort to modernize the Afghan army and air force. In 1957, and later in 1962 and 1964, Nehru used the Soviet veto to block U.N. resolutions proposing a U.N. force for a demilitarized Kashmir and a solution to the dispute. When Sino-Indian border differences became public in 1959 and China firmly asserted its South Asian power-status, Nehru, under the pretext of Pakistan's links with the United States, CENTO, and SEATO, turned more heavily to the Soviet Union to counterbalance China.

Beginning with approximately 196 Indian delegations to the Soviet Union between 1954 to 1957,[20] economic and cultural ties expanded many fold. By the mid-1960s, about seventy public sector projects had been launched with Soviet aid. In 1959, Ayub Khan's offer of "joint defense" to Nehru was rejected, because Nehru had decided on the Soviet Union as the underwriter of India's security and the guarantor of India's hold on Kashmir. This decision perpetuated the strategic schism in the region. Even India's occupation of Portuguese Goa in 1961 received Soviet praise.

If a veto on Kashmir in 1957 was the first security link with the Soviet Union, then the purchase of 24 Ilyushin—14 transports and 26 helicopters in the early 1960s—was the second. This was followed by the third step: the purchase of 100 MiG 21 fighter planes (and a manufacturing agreement), and the subsequent purchase of landing crafts, fast patrol boats, submarines, frigates, and motor torpedo boats on concessionary terms in subsequent years.

By 1962, Nehru (with tacit Soviet support) felt emboldened enough to challenge openly China's status as a South Asian power, and ordered the Indian Army "to eject the Chinese out." The disastrous consequences resulted, in Nehru's words, in an "agonizing reappraisal of India's foreign policy" and in the realization that "the world was cruel." China had militarily established itself as a South Asian power, a fact that Nehru had attempted to wish away for fifteen years. Kautilya's Vijigishu (victory) doctrine, applied by Nehru in the case of Jammu and Kashmir, Goa, and elsewhere, lay shattered. In panic after a cold Soviet response, Nehru turned to the Western powers and asked for military aid, requesting President Kennedy to rush forty squadrons of the United States Air Force (and the Strategic Air Command) to operate from bases in India against China. Some weapon systems for mountain warfare were flown to India, including radar and communications equipment worth $82 million; (United States participation with $500 million in India's First Defense Plan (1964-69) failed to materialize). Eager to have Nehru close the Jammu and Kashmir strategic schism in South Asia, the United States and Great Britain pursued diplomatic initiatives resulting in bilateral Indo-Pakistan talks, which came to nothing. When the Kashmir issue was raised in the United Nations in 1962, Nehru had the Soviet Union block it again.

India now faced an extension of the strategic schism along the 3,000 kilometers of India's northern frontier involving China, a bigger South Asian power than India, which had its own thirty-year treaty with the Soviet Union (dating back to 1950). Faced with a triangular choice, Nehru reinforced his links with the neighboring USSR and went through with the MiG-21 deal. Nehru felt the Soviet Union's long, common, and disputed frontiers with China in Asia made it geostrategically better placed to neutralize China's South Asian power status and guarantee India's security than the distant United States which was allied to Pakistan. The domestic pressures of the vocal and growing Communist Party of India, with its splinter groups, was also a factor influencing Nehru, both

internally and externally. Between 1960 and 1964 the Indian armed
forces increased from 535,000 to 869,000 and defense spending tripled.
In 1964 "Nehru died a saddened man who had not accomplished his mission in life, either domestically or internationally,"[21] while his emissary
Sheikh Abdullah, the Kashmiri leader, was in Pakistan negotiating a settlement of the Kashmir issue on his behalf. The issue remained unresolved, the strategic schism continued; large parts of India's northern
frontiers continued as disputed territory. Such was the security and strategic legacy of Jawaharlal Nehru to his successor, Lal Bahadur Shastri,
whose two-year term of office saw two Indo-Pakistan conflicts over disputed territories in the Rann of Kutch and Jammu and Kashmir, both in
1965. Soviet mediation resulted in the Tashkent declaration of January
1966; Moscow's strategy was to deny China its South Asian status, to
stake a claim for a similar South Asian status, or both.

1966–84: Indira Gandhi as Prime Minister

Mrs. Gandhi's security and strategic perspective could be best
summed up in her oft-quoted remark, "He [her father] was a saint who
strayed into politics; I am a tough politician."[22] Security, military power,
territory, victory (Kautilya's Vijigishu), prestige, all the tangible attributes of power, were to be the pillars of her strategy, but again under a
veneer of peace, cooperation, and nonalignment. Her opponent, Morarji
Desai, commenting on her strategy of political expediency, opined "She
would ally herself with the devil if she thought it served her purpose."[23]
Whatever policy she adopted during her tenure acquired popular support.
Security policymaking institutions were virtually nonexistent in India.
Indira Gandhi picked yes men as foreign and defense ministers and was
"a Prime Minister who permitted—or encouraged—personal allegiance
and medieval intrigue to flourish around her. . . . In international politics as a whole Mrs. Gandhi was less impressed by the sway of moral influence or universalist principles. . . ."[24] Security policy and strategy
decisions were made in her secretariat rather than in the Ministry of External Affairs. Her Kashmiri Principal Secretary, P. N. Haksar, wrote in
later years, "I do not recall a single occasion during the last 31 years
when problems of our country's security were discussed seriously or in
depth."[25] "Indira Gandhi's recognition of power as a crucial determinant in international relations was her main contribution to India's foreign policy."[26]
The most notable security and strategic policy of Mrs. Gandhi during
her first terms as prime minister was increased reliance on the Soviet
Union as the main source of military power. India launched three de-

fense development plans: the first was from 1964 to 1969, the second from 1969 to 1974; "by 1977 India had acquired the world's third largest standing army, fifth largest air force, eighth largest navy. Its indigenous armament industry was the largest in the Third World non-Communist states in value, volume, diversity of manufacture, and R & D facilities."[27] Since 1964 the Soviet Union had become India's major arms supplier; from 1968 onward India manufactured crucial items of Soviet origin under license—a very special privilege. Between 1974 and 1984 there was a 200 percent increase in the defense budget, which tripled in ten years to $6.8 billion. During the same decade, military modernization deals were also concluded with the Soviet Union, United Kingdom, West Germany, and France, to the tune of about $15 billion, those with the Soviet Union being on very concessionary terms.

After the first defense plan was completed, Mrs. Gandhi covertly supported the East Pakistani Awami League Party in the 1970 Pakistan election. Its ethnic Bengali nationalism, built around a core of the Hindu population, was directed against Islamabad, and when the party swept the polls, Mrs. Gandhi infiltrated Indian paramilitary forces and saboteurs into East Pakistan, supporting civil disobedience, arson, and sabotage. She also readied the Indian armed forces for open aggressive intervention in 1971 in support of secessionist elements.

India's "moral" justification for intervening was built upon fiction, exaggeration, and propaganda regarding the mass exodus of ten million Hindus as well as genocide by West Pakistani rulers. Here was "the chance of the century" for her "to cut Pakistan to size," avenge the humiliations of both the 1962 and 1965 wars, tidy up eastern India's backyard of Nagas, Mizos, and Naxalities, challenge China's status in South Asia as an ally of Pakistan, and confront the United States and Chinese presence in the region with the Soviet Union. Kissinger's trip to China via Pakistan in July 1971 gave a ruffled Mrs. Gandhi the excuse to pull out and sign a proposed Treaty of Peace, Friendship, and Cooperation with the Soviet Union, thereby formalizing a security guarantee relationship that had in any case existed since the late 1950s. The stage was again set to implement the Vijigishu doctrine of Kautilya, out of the strategic reach of Pakistan, the United States, and China during the snow-bound Himalayan winter months. Mrs. Gandhi had tacitly acquiesced to the Soviet Union being a South Asian power within a decade of China's military assertion as such.

The fall of Dacca in December 1971, with Soviet political and military support, was acclaimed by Mrs. Gandhi as a victory in a "1000-year struggle" from the ramparts of the Red Fort in Delhi. Premier Chou En-Lai declared that the fall of Dacca would be the beginning of endless explosions when international frontiers are disappearing, old spheres of influence are crumbling, new ones are emerging, and it will be chaos for the next twenty-five years. Gradually and imperceptibly Brezhnev's Asian Collective Security System was coming into being, with India and Afghanistan as its main pillars; the Soviets schemed to link the region by roads to Central Asia, through Afghanistan and Iran; their presence increased in the "Indian Ocean," Communism became a mass movement in West Bengal, and Assam gradually slipped into a state of advanced semi-insurgency. The *Statesman* newspaper of India was to remark, "Gauhati (capital of Assam) has found its place on the terrorist map of the North East (India)." Ethnic issues came to the forefront in eastern and southern India, Punjab, Haryana, and Ladakh; in Nepal, Bhutan, and Sikkim, ethnic nationalism surfaced. Mrs. Gandhi had championed its cause militarily in East Pakistan. In trying to undo the two-nation theory, with Soviet help Mrs. Gandhi had created three nations and sown the seeds of many more in northeast and northwest India. Destabilization of the region had set in. Soviet oriental scholars had earlier written about sixteen nationalities inhabiting the subcontinent! From Tashkent in 1966, to the Friendship Treaty in 1971, and culminating in the invasion of Afghanistan in 1979, the Soviets continued their moves on the South Asian chess board. Apart from other compulsions, the Soviet move in 1979 was a strategy to acquire a South Asian status to match China's. Soviet and Indian security interests have thus converged in more ways than one. Both China and Pakistan have been confronted with a two-front strategy, irrespective of the diplomatic gloss on this policy and statements from Mrs. Gandhi. Moreover, she must have been convinced by Brezhnev's visit in 1980 that the Soviet move into Afghanistan was in their overall regional security interests—to prevent the Islamic revival (that earlier created Pakistan) in Iran and Afghanistan from spilling over to Pakistan, Kashmir, India, and Bangladesh, not to mention the Soviet Central Asian Republics), which would threaten India's fragile secular nationalism. She must also have been convinced that in their continuing support for Indian action in Kashmir and East Pakistan, the Soviet Union expected Indian support on Afghanistan. Mrs. Gandhi's responses on Afghanistan cannot as yet be justified except in the light of this strategy of expediency, which finally sacrifices the long-term security imperatives of the region.

The American Factor

Since World War II the West Asian strategic environment has been the main determinant of United States interests in and relations with

South Asia. Nehru's pro-Soviet leanings before and after independence were known in the United States. He had "scoffed at United States fears of Soviet expansionism and scorned any suggestion that India should play the role of an American surrogate."[28] As compared to neighboring "Asiatic" USSR, Nehru considered the United States a distant power with its "cultural imperialism" and its provocative global military stance; the United States had to be kept away from South Asia. His moralistic, self-righteous, sermonizing pronouncements, often contradicting vital U.S. strategic interests in the Korean War, the Japanese peace treaty, and elsewhere, irked the United States; yet that country voted in the United Nations for a resolution of the Kashmir problem in keeping with Nehru's own pledges. U.S. strategists considered India of marginal interest, whereas Pakistan was situated at the crossroads of Central, South, and West Asia. It is at the "fulcrum" of security in the region, hence its several military pacts and membership in both CENTO and SEATO. There developed a sharp divergence in security and strategic perceptions between the United States and Nehru, often causing tense and acrimonious relations in the 1950s, especially after the Soviet Union had chosen India (around 1955) to further its own interests. That did not prevent Nehru from drawing maximum benefit from the United States in the economic, cultural, and educational fields. India obtained wheat to feed its starving millions, at one time receiving almost half the total U.S. output.

After the Sino-Indian conflict in 1962 and Nehru's offer of bases for the United States Air Force, the United States provided some essential military hardware and discussed participation in India's First Defense Plan, while pressing for correction of the strategic schism in the subcontinent caused by the Kashmir dispute. India was also provided in 1963 with an $80 million loan for India's first nuclear power station at Tarapur after Nehru's private and public assurance that "for myself and my government and for future Indian governments, I will say that India will never make atomic weapons."

Although Nehru drew solace from the United States' anti-China policy, he had failed to wean the United States away from Pakistan. The Soviet Union moved closer to India by reversing its earlier pro-China, neutral stand to a pro-Indian position with regard to both the strategic schisms—Kashmir's and India's northern borders. The United States policy of supplying arms on cash sales both to India and Pakistan on a nondiscriminatory basis continued until the outbreak of the 1965 Indo-Pakistan conflict, when it was reversed.

Mrs. Gandhi continued her father's policies, building on the Soviet connection as the guarantor in India's security, military power, and hegemony. In February 1966, within months after taking over as prime minister, she signed a communique in Moscow referring to the "imperialist in South East Asia." Her perception of the goals and strategies of the two super powers was not very different from that of her father. In an interview in *Forbes* magazine in later years she said, "The global strategy of the United States administration does not find a place for India," whereas "We think that the Soviet Union is not fighting for Communism, it is fighting for nationalism . . . after World War II their system and survival go together."

Through the Treaty of Peace, Friendship, and Cooperation with the Soviet Union in 1971, Mrs. Gandhi carried her father's anti-U.S., pro-Soviet strategy to its fulfillment, exposed the United States as a distant and doubtful ally to its friends in Asia, avenged the humiliation of the 1962 (and 1965) wars, challenged China's South Asian power status, and had India emerge as the major power in the subcontinent with the assistance of neighboring "friends in need" (as she termed the USSR). In terms of the internal security of South Asia, this was the beginning of the "spring thunder over India," with increases in ethnic violence and insurgencies, evident even today. "Revolution is India's manifest destiny," wrote H. V. Hodson, a perception that is apparently shared both by USSR and China.

Some Indian analysts have blamed the United States and the West for failing to cater to India's economic and military needs, thereby forcing India to turn to the Soviet Union, considered by others as a "twentieth century success story'—a model of power, if not of economic growth—to be copied. Others have felt "that it was important to understand that the United States was neither a malevolent nor a benevolent power" and "despite the assertion that the United States was a declining power. . . it was a nation with extraordinary resources."[29] The United States setback in Vietnam, the events in Iran and Afghanistan, the delinking of the dollar from the gold standard, and the collapse of the Bretton Woods economic system may have shaped this perception, although the United States continued to challenge Soviet expansionism globally. The United States-British decision to create the British Indian Ocean Territory, an increased United States naval and air presence on Diego Garcia (to counter a growing Soviet naval presence in the region) was considered by Mrs. Gandhi a challenge to Indian maritime strategy. The creation of the Rapid Development Force (RDF) and the Central Command (CENTCOM) has also been viewed by India as an attempt to trespass on Indian power and influence projection in West Asia. The ruling All-India Congress Committee meeting on April 4, 1983, echoed Mrs. Gandhi's perception that India is "encircled on all sides" and accused the Reagan administration of "heightened tension" in the region around India without safeguarding security. The Soviet defense minister's visits in 1982 and 1984, and his one-to-one, ninety-minute audiences with Mrs. Gandhi must have helped to shape these perceptions.

Thus, President Reagan's decision to provide $3.2 billion aid to Pakistan has come in for greater and sustained attacks by Mrs. Gandhi than the Soviet's military occupation of neighborly nonaligned Afghanistan, largely because Reagan's action retards India's attainment of hegemony in South Asia. The only course for India, it is argued, is to develop nuclear weapons on the pretext that China has them and Pakistan is likely to get them. The acquisition of Jaguar and MiG-27 aircraft and the development of short and long range rockets (begun in 1967) are aimed at increasing India's strategic and nuclear reach. "Between 1970-74 the space research establishment in India had developed and tested inertial guidance systems, telemetry equipment, rate gyroscopes, heat shields, nose cones, electronic payload systems, and a wide variety of high specific impulse solid and liquid propellants."[30] India is well on the way to producing missiles of 1,800-2,000 miles range.

In December 1963, after the Sino-Indian conflict, Nehru welcomed elements of the U.S. Seventh Fleet into the Indian Ocean. In December 1971, during India's aggression against East Pakistan, Mrs. Gandhi condemned the arrival of a carrier group of the Seventh Fleet, although a Soviet naval flotilla was in the region. India's "Indian Ocean" policy seeks regional maritime hegemony under the pretext of declaring it a zone of peace to keep other, bigger powers out. A formidable naval infrastructure buildup at Port Blair in the Andamans, at Cochin, and possibly Laccadive Island—as well as an increase in the surface and subsurface fleet —is well underway. India's fond hope is some day to convert the Afro-Asian Ocean into an Indian Ocean and to gain eventual control of the seventeen choke points, the maritime lanes, and the economic zones that are shared by almost thirty-six littoral states around this ocean and by many more states from other continents.

The China Factor

As an ardent student of history, Nehru was aware of China's South Asian connection and status. The Anglo-Tibetan convention of 1904, the Anglo-Chinese convention of 1906, and finally the Anglo-Russian convention of 1907 had expressively recognized China's suzerainty over Tibet while giving the British Raj facilities for trading marts. In 1910, covert activities of the British forced the Chinese to move forces into

Lhasa, which resulted in the flight of the Dalai Lama to India. On the outbreak of the revolution in China (which led to the fall of the Manchu dynasty), the British Raj concluded the Simla Agreement with China and Tibet in 1913, conceding both Chinese suzerainty over Tibet and demanding autonomy for it. This convention was never ratified by China, but was upheld by both the British and Tibet. After the transfer of power in India in August 1947, "The Tibetan Government . . . sent a message to the Indian Government demanding the return of extensive territories spreading from Assam to Ladakh, including Darjeeling and Sikkim."[31] A similar demand was made by Peking in later years.

From 1947 to 1949 Nehru was preoccupied with military action in Kashmir and Ladakh. In October 1949 the People's Republic of China (PRC) was proclaimed and was duly recognized by India. India's military occupation of Ladakh in 1948 and Sikkim in 1949 was perceived as a threat to Tibet and its vulnerable western link to Chinese Sinkiang. China's reaction was sharp and sudden. Chou En-Lai reiterated his government's determination to "liberate the people of Tibet and stand on guard at the Chinese frontiers."[32] In spite of diplomatic pressure from India, China moved into Tibet in the late 1950s to counter Indian military action in Ladakh and Sikkim. China was also apprehensive of Indian activities in Nepal, Bhutan, and the North East Frontier Agency. Tibet was in China's regional security zone, vital for her South Asian power status.

Moving cautiously, while talking of good relations with China, Nehru consolidated his grip on Nepal, Sikkim, and Bhutan. Finally in 1954 he signed an agreement with China that recognized the Tibet Region of China, removed Indian military personnel from Gyantse and Tatung, abandoned, on payment, rest houses and communication facilities, and conceded the right to China to have trade agencies in Calcutta, Kalimpong, and New Delhi on a reciprocal basis. Nehru had tacitly accepted the PRC as a South Asian power, hoping to make the Himalayas and the Karakorams the great divide of spheres of influence. Militarily, he had no choice; diplomatically, he continued his efforts to woo the Soviet Union as a counterbalance. The famous Panchsheel agreement gave both countries time to consolidate, until 1959, when their differences over the northern boundaries became public. Chou En-Lai accused Nehru of trying to reap the benefits of British imperialism, inciting a revolt in Tibet through Khampa tribes, and infiltrating guerrillas with Western help from the Kalimpong base in India. Under dubious circumstances, the Dalai Lama fled from Lhasa and was granted political asylum in India. When questioned in the Lok Sabha about who incited the revolt against the Chinese, Nehru replied "I cannot say who began it, but it began." As a moralist he could not misstate facts, nor for security reasons confess the truth. The result was the end of Sino-Indian friendship; 50,000 square miles of territory became openly disputed along the 3,000-kilometer frontier stretching from Aksai Chin across Uttar Pradesh, Himachal Pradesh, Punjab, and NEFA, and also along China's boundary with Nepal, Sikkim, and Bhutan, which China regarded as outside the Indian sphere of security interests.

China had signed border-demarcation agreements with Burma and Nepal in 1960-61 (with Afghanistan in 1962 and with Pakistan in 1963) as proof of its nonbelligerent security policies with smaller South Asian neighbors. Nehru confessed in the Rajya Sabha on November 9, 1962 that his government had, from the entry of the Chinese into Tibet in 1950-51, been engaged in developing a war machine for the inevitable "confrontation with China"[33] while preaching peaceful coexistence and disarmament and condemning the arms race.

For almost two decades until 1983, the Indian Ministry of Defense Annual Report had highlighted China (and Pakistan) as posing security threats to India in order to justify the three Defense Development Plans that had run from 1964 to 1979. India today has a regular army of more than one million, an armored force of about 3,000 tanks, a 45-50 squadron air force, missiles, and other sophisticated military hardware and in 1984-85 spent approximately $7 billion on defense. But for the first time in two decades China has been completely omitted from the *Annual Reports* as posing any threat. The latest *Annual Reports* of both the external and defense ministries concentrate on military threats emanating from Pakistan and the Indian Ocean, not China. This is a marked departure from the past; it is perhaps based on Soviet assurances, and serves to isolate Pakistan as India's main perceived "threat."

China's offer of a package deal of the disputed territory granting Arunachal Pradesh to India in spite of the disputed McMahon Line, and keeping the vital strategic link, Aksai Chin, has been rejected by India in four rounds of talks during the last several years. India seeks recognition of its control over Kashmir and Sikkim, which China refuses. Mrs. Gandhi knew that China's track record was not one of expansionism, that the 3,000 kilometers of common northern borders are virtually indefensible even with present army strength, and that China's South Asian identity and power status cannot be denied as long as it has the capability of supporting Indian radicals and insurgents in Assam, Mizoram, Manipur, Nagaland, Tripura, and even in the Indo-Gangetic delta regions of West Bengal and Bangladesh. India justifies its conventional military buildup and quest for nuclear weapons on the grounds of a perceived threat from China, and on the grounds that China and Pakistan had signed pacts with the United States to provide nuclear weapons.

India's Northern and Eastern Borders

The emergence of the People's Republic of China as a power adds a new strategic dimension to India's long and vulnerable borders, which are punctuated by three soft, strategically placed, yet assertive states: Nepal, Sikkim, and Bhutan. Eager to reap the benefits of the British Raj, consolidate India's authority, and get a stranglehold on Pakistan, in 1948 Nehru airlifted the Indian army into Ladakh, which has 480 kilometers of common border with Tibet, and in 1949, India occupied Sikkim, with its direct route to Lhasa. This action posed a threat to Tibet, Nepal, and Bhutan, and led to protests first from the Kuomintang and then from Peking. These two actions, separated in time and space, were to activate the otherwise-dormant northern border of India, to become the defense planners' nightmare, and to change the geostrategic map of South Asia within three decades. Subsequently, by the 1954 Sino-Indian Treaty, Nehru not only recognized Tibet as part of China but tacitly accepted China's South Asian status. He bought time, not security. By 1962, China had impressed its South Asian power status not only on India, but on all kingdoms and territories along the Karakoram and Himalayan ranges.

Nepal, with its 960 kilometers of border and over twenty posts with Tibetan China, was the first to recognize emerging security and strategic realities. There was a frontier demarcation settlement with China in 1961, and Nepal accepted Chinese economic aid in the form of two vital strategic roads—one connecting Kathmandu to Kodari and Tibet, the other from Bhadrapur to Olangchung in eastern Nepal. These routes out-flank Sikkim, which was integrated into the Indian Union in 1975 (but which China still regards as a separate country). The 1950 Treaty imposed by India involves Nepal in the Indian security system, although the Indian military mission and Indian security personnel on Nepal's twenty or so northern border posts were made to withdraw. India could apply military and economic pressure along its 1,300 kilometers of open border with Nepal, which has been watching developments in Tibet very closely. The construction of the Golmo-Lhasa railroad system, an oil pipeline from Lanchow to Lhasa, innumerable all-weather airfields, and improvement of the road network joining areas of Yunnan, Sechuan, Qinghai, and Xinjang (all providing the capability to deploy from twenty to thirty divisions) are changing Nepal's strategic environment. Hence, Nepal's zone-of-peace proposals have been endorsed by thirty countries, including the United States, China, and Pakistan, but were rejected by India, which ironically advocates zones of peace elsewhere. India's rejection is based on denying China an equal status in South Asian affairs; China, in turn, has repeatedly warned India that any intervention in Nepal will be regarded as *casus belli* by China.

Bhutan occupies the pivotal strategic position from where both Sikkim and Arunachal Pradesh could be outflanked. It faces a part of Tibet that is well served with a road network; and with eastern Nepal, Sikkim, and Western Arunachal, it covers the fertile and populated West Bengal, Bangladesh, and Assam. In the 1962 conflict it was isolated and outflanked on its eastern and western borders by Chinese forces, which emphasized its vulnerability. The majority of Bhutan's population is of Tibetan stock, and Lamaism is the prevailing religion. By a 1949 treaty, its foreign relations, economy, and security are controlled by India. A 1981 offer of direct talks with China on demarcation of the 200-mile border with Tibet was vetoed by India, although Bhutan is a member of the United Nations, and has established relations with Nepal, India, Bangladesh, and Kuwait, and, like Nepal, is trying to overcome the handicap of its land-locked status.

Arunachal is the northeastern frontier of India with its vulnerable and disputed McMahon Line. The Chinese broke through Arunachal in the 1962 conflict, threatening the fertile Assam valley to the south. A conglomeration of small, ethnic mountainous tribes of Mongoloid origin populate this region; they look north to the victorious for inspiration and sympathy, not to the plains to the south. The security situation is compounded by the open rebellion, for almost three decades, of the Naga and Mizo tribes on the southeastern fringes of Arunachal adjoining the Burmese border.

Between Ladakh and Nepal is the so-called middle sector of the northern border covering Punjab, Himachal Pradesh, and Uttar Pradesh. Here there also is a common border with Tibet and a dozen major posts, some of which were the scenes of clashes between Indian and Chinese forces. Other than barren, open, inhospitable Ladakh, the rest of the 3,000 kilometers of the heavily vegetated, mountainous northern frontier of India, Nepal, and Bhutan, with historical and cultural ethnic links to Tibetan China, is susceptible to a Vietnam-like subversion and insurgency that could be a perpetual security problem and could even tie down an army of one million. Such an insurgency could spill over into the fertile valleys, urban areas, and industrial hinterland to the south, seething with poverty and discontent.

To note one final strategic fallout from the McMahon Line dispute:

after it, India stopped backing Afghanistan's claims against Pakistan on the Durand Line.

The Pakistan Factor

In Nehru's quest for a doctrine that would make India "the center of things in Asia," Pakistan's two-nation theory, and even its legitimate, agreed creation, provided both an expedient strategic rationale and an unrealistic obsession. When the coercive diplomacy of withholding Pakistan's agreed share of financial assets and military equipment failed to bring the collapse of the new state in 1947, Nehru resorted to direct intervention, using force under false pretenses in strategic Jammu and Kashmir within two months of independence. At the same time, he began courting the USSR and China for diplomatic support of a preeminent Indian hegemonic role in the region. Within a year of the ceasefire, having failed to overrun Jammu and Kashmir, Nehru concentrated the Indian Army against West Pakistan. Wiser counsel prevailed. As Nehru pondered, Communist China emerged as a South Asian power in Tibet and Sinkiang and challenged his coercive strategy in Ladakh and Sikkim—traditionally Tibetan spheres of influence and power. The strategic schism spread from Kashmir to India's northern borders in the 1950s; Pakistan (and China) became the central issue of a nebulous Nehru security doctrine, drawing strength, from 1955 onward from the Soviet Union.

In thirty-seven years, India and Pakistan have fought four wars. In the last conflict India dismembered a part of Pakistan. For Pakistan, as for other South Asian states, "despite regular denials of harboring hegemonic ambitions, New Delhi is at best an imperial capital,"[34] pursuing policies that are a combination of Kautilya, Curzon, and the British Raj.

Pakistan continues to be the central issue for any security policy or doctrine of India; the more Mrs. Gandhi strove for power under a cloak of peace and security, the greater insecurity she bred in Pakistan and the other states of the region. Neither the Tashkent Declaration of 1966 nor the Simla Agreement of 1972 helped to heal the strategic schism of Jammu and Kashmir nor led to a security understanding among the states of South Asia, including China. Concepts such as a no-war pact, joint defense, and a Treaty of Peace, Friendship, and Cooperation have failed to crystallize mainly because Pakistan is not prepared to accept either Indian-style bilateralism or unequal treaties of the type forced on Nepal, Bhutan, and Bangladesh. Nor is Pakistan prepared to accept Indian preferences that would compromise either its sovereignty or renounce Article 51 of the U.N. Charter (relating to right of individual and collective self-defense). Indian hegemony is not a proper price to pay for long-term penetration by the Soviet Union in this region. Pakistan is prepared to discuss legitimate power requirements of both the countries, but India's reluctance is based on the blank check the Soviets give to India in the region with their veto in the United Nations. India also desires veto powers on U.S. arms supply to Pakistan just as it vetoed Soviet arms sales to Pakistan in the 1960s.

Indian strategists and analysts perceive a conventional guerrilla and nuclear threat from Pakistan. In the past few years there have been weekly orchestrated statements to this effect by civilians and soldiers, although the simple arithmetic of the military balance, troops-to-terrain ratios, and the state of weapon systems highlight the fallacy of such statements. Pakistan's offer to discuss force goals and military readiness evoked a negative response, with a demand to publish its defense budget as a first step!

India's strategic and security relationship with Pakistan has fallen into what Sartre called "bad faith" from the time of the original Sino-Kashmir dispute, and with a few exceptions, Indian leadership over the years has seemed both reluctant to correct the strategic schisms of South Asia and incapable of doing so. "Kashmir remains the single most bitter historic memory in the national consciousness of Pakistan that stands in the way of full Indo-Pakistan reconciliation and future cooperation based on mutual trust and friendship. . . . Until a plebiscite is held under international auspices, Islamabad will persist in believing rightly or wrongly that it was cheated out of an integral limb of its body politic at birth."[35]

The Indian aggression against East Pakistan in 1971 displayed a moral relativism in Mrs. Gandhi's strategy; this belief was confirmed by her abortive 1979 effort to take Kashmir off the U.N. list of disputed territories.

Unfortunately, "no Indian government after 1953 was prepared to make the one magnanimous gesture which might have satisfied Pakistan's yearnings—that is, to conduct a plebiscite in Kashmir and relinquish its hold if the vote went against India. . . . few Indians appreciated the depth of feelings in Pakistan on Kashmir. . . . On the contrary, Pakistan's plea for self-determination for the Kashmiris was routinely interpreted in New Delhi as the first of a series of irredentist claims on India."[36] Virtually all the security problems that South Asia faces today are an outcome of the schism created by Jammu and Kashmir, which now geopolitically involves not only India, Pakistan, and Kashmir but also China and the Soviet Union, and affects the other South Asian states.

Nuclear Issues

Mrs. Gandhi reneged on Jawaharlal Nehru's pledge of 1956, sanctioned a "peaceful nuclear explosion" in 1974 in close proximity Pakistan's borders. India has developed or acquired guidance and delivery systems for both tactical and strategic nuclear weapons in the shape of cannon, aircraft, and missiles. According to an Indian defense analyst, "Pokhran was the first deliberate step along the inevitable path of nuclear weapons."[37] Against the background of four conflicts, Pakistan sees a nuclear threat; there has been an outcry for nuclear parity, and there is a strong belief in Pakistan that, like Israel and South Africa, India already has bombs in the basement. Pakistan's modest peaceful nuclear program for energy needs became the target of world media, led by India, although its nuclear facilities are under International Atomic Energy Authority (IAEA) safeguards, and it has offered to open them for inspection to India on a reciprocal basis. When he was prime minister, Morarji Desai, in his address to the U.N. Special Session on Disarmament, had, like Nehru in 1956, "solemnly reiterated his pledge not to manufacture or acquire nuclear weapons even if the rest of the world did." Shortly after, in the Lok Sabha, he modified his stand and declared that while India would not conduct any further nuclear explosions, this did not exclude nuclear blasts for engineering purposes!

Pakistan is prepared to sign the Non-Proliferation Treaty (NPT) if India does. In 1980 Pakistan sponsored a resolution in the General Assembly establishing a nuclear weapon free zone; since 1978 in several international forums it has sponsored resolutions for denuclearization, asking for assurances to non-nuclear states against the threat or use of nuclear weapons. India has opposed both the NPT and Nuclear Weapon Free Zone (NWFZ), because under the cloak of "moral" principles, it wants to keep its options open. After a recent visit to Pakistan, Hans Blix, Director General, IAEA, publicly declared that "Pakistan had a strong case for acquiring nuclear power and its nuclear program was entirely peaceful in nature." The Indian foreign secretary, Mr. Rasgotra, lost no time in announcing that Pakistan had built and detonated its first atomic bomb in June 1983 in the Lop Nor desert of Chinese Sinkiang.[38] In a seminar in New Delhi in March 1984 the Indian scientist Dr. R. R. Subramaniam had argued that "Pakistan has collected enough fissile matter to produce four to five atom bombs." During his 1984 visit to Washington, Premier Zhao Ziyang declared, "We do not engage in nuclear proliferation, nor do we help other countries develop nuclear weapons." It is evident that India is looking for an excuse, however lame, to make nuclear weapons in spite of solemn public pledges by its founding fathers in the recent past.

South Asian Regional Cooperation

India's attitude to South Asian regional cooperation is character-ized by deliberate soft pedaling. India sees the other regional states as un-stable, suffering from a crisis of identity, weakened by fragile political and social systems that cannot handle domestic upheavals without Indian support, and requiring therefore to be cut "down to size" and "put in their proper place." Security issues are not included in the discussions that have taken place since 1980. India would like to confine SAARC to a bilateralism that has not so far produced tangible peace or security in the case of either Bangladesh, Nepal, or Sri Lanka, and is still being tested out in relations with China and Pakistan. "No Indian version of the Monroe Doctrine has functioned in Southern Asia, nor can it func-tion." As one official in the Ministry of External Affairs put it, "No im-perial solution is workable now in our part of the world."[39]

During the last thirty-eight years Indian leadership has neither devel-oped a sound security policy and understanding, nor even narrowed the credibility gap among the states of South Asia which is evident from the record of conflicts and unresolved regional and boundary disputes in-volving more than 3,000 kilometers of vulnerable northern border areas. As a result, Pakistan has turned to West Asia, Nepal, and Bangladesh, and now Bhutan to China, and Sri Lanka to ASEAN and Southeast Asia for identification and links. For Pakistan (as for one billion people of the Islamic world), West Asia has been and will continue to be the ideological and spiritual center of gravity, irrespective of the future shape of South Asian regional cooperation. India's efforts to extend its strategic reach and security concerns to West Asia, South East Asia, and the "Indian Ocean," without first closing the strategic schism and ac-cepting China as a South Asian power are not likely to improve the re-gional security environment. Perhaps this realization is at last dawning on the intellectuals (although not necessarily on astrologers and policy-makers) in India. At a select gathering of about sixty intellectuals, par-ticipants in a seminar on India's security in New Delhi in March 1982, this feeling was voiced: "It will be wrong to ignore the pressure a great power like China can bring to bear upon its southern periphery. China is the most powerful nation whose pressure is felt throughout South and Southeast Asia."[40]

Conclusion

Indian regional foreign policy, especially its security and strategic dimensions, evolved from distorted perceptions, both with regard to the region and to the historical past. Nehru was its main thinker and architect, influenced by Fabian socialism and the Soviet model and colored by the doctrines of Kautiliya and the Raj. His legacy to his successors was the strategic schisms created by confrontation with Pakistan over the Jammu and Kashmir issue, and with China by challenging its South Asian power status. Pakistan and China thus became the central issue of India's security policy and interventionist strategy, with five conflicts in thirty-eight years, and still many unresolved issues.

Indian leaders over the years have reneged on their international pledges on two major security issues: Jammu and Kashmir, and nuclear explosions. They played the game of nonalignment under blurred rules, preached noninterference and peaceful coexistence while following the policies of coercive diplomacy, and used force against their neighbors. Nonaligned India has aligned with the nearby Soviet Union, which has become the main guarantor of her military strength and hegemonic ambitions. Gradually and imperceptibly over the years, Brezhnev's Asian Collective Security System has come into being, first with India and then Afghanistan as its main pillars. Now the Soviet Union consolidates in the Hindukush—another security frontier zone of South Asia.

India's relations with Pakistan (and China) involve more than 6,000 kilometers of vulnerable borders and continue to be soured by "bad faith" and distorted perceptions. In spite of many U.N. resolutions, the Tashkent Declaration, the Simla Agreement, proposals for Joint Defense, a No-War Pact, Treaties of Friendship, and efforts at South Asian Regional Cooperation, the same "bad faith" also sours India's relations with its other neighbors.

In her quest for power Mrs. Gandhi built a formidable military machine which cannot possibly be used in the Himalayas and which is now aspiring for nuclear weapons. Yet Pakistan's peaceful nuclear energy program causes strategic hiccups among defense analysts and intellectuals. Pakistan is now being singled out by some Indian thinkers and intellectuals as posing a guerrilla, conventional, and nuclear threat to India in spite of the former's offer to discuss force goals, allow inspection of its military and nuclear establishments, and sign the NPT and a no-war pact on a mutual basis.

During a discussion of India's security at a recent meeting of Indian defense intellectuals, it was stated that "while it is perfectly true that security is chimerical if a country suffers from grievous political, economic and social ills, it would be equally dangerous to minimize the impact of external factors on these and our security in general."[41] The external factors in the region have been in fact the creation of India's leaders and their quest for power, based on the imperial concept, in a geopolitical environment that has changed rapidly in Asia since the middle of this century and continues to change. The emergence of Pakistan, then China, and then the Soviet move into the security zone of South Asia, all within three decades, resulted in "small men being moved by great events," to use the words Jawaharlal Nehru uttered at midnight at the transfer of power in 1947. Did the gathering of India's intellectual elite in New Delhi see the whole perspective, or were they influenced by what the Indian writer Y. B. Dhawan has noted: "The Indian intellectual, to say the least, is a self-divided human being. Self-deception on the part of the Indian intellectual consists in seeing clearly what he is, and then denying it. Most of the time he is preaching what he is afraid to practice himself . . . in adopting the cover of bad faith . . . in seeing what one is and then denying it . . . in asserting that one is what one is not. . . . His own blind striving for power takes place at the cost of whatever moral sense he has come to achieve as a human being."[42]

Perhaps this is a sweeping generalization, not quite supported by the facts nor applicable to some security decision makers. Jagat Singh Mehta has a different perspective: "If we discard our intellectual obsessions of the past, the world situation, serious as it is, is not specially hostile to the subcontinent. . . . Our primary foreign policy challenge is in the neighborhood. . . . The resolution of Indo-Pak relations will release the kinetic energy of our diplomatic potential."[43] Or again, could Girilal Jain be right when he says, "We Indians are specialists in building myths. . . . The list of myths that we have invented in our innocence and desperation is a long one. Sometimes it looks as if we have lost control over our political future."[44] Indeed, control over the security zone of South Asia was lost five years ago, and control over the vulnerable northern borders cannot be regained without the goodwill and cooperation of China as a South Asian power.

NOTES

1. P. S. Ghosh and R. Pande, *Asian Survey 23*, No. 3 (March 1983): 273-74.
2. *Times of India* (Editorial), New Delhi, September 1, 1983.
3. Ghosh and Pande, *Asian Survey*, p. 272.
4. Bimla Prasad, *The Origins of Indian Foreign Policy* (Calcutta: Bookland, 1960), p. 6.
5. Ibid., pp. 79-80.
6. Jawaharlal Nehru, *Towards Freedom*, pp. 125-26.
7. *Young India*, May 4, 1921.
8. Prasad, *Origins*, p. 91.
9. Ibid., p. 116.
10. R. J. Sontag and J. S. Beddie, eds., *Nazi-Soviet Documents: 1939-41* (New York: Didier, 1948), pp. 251-57.

11. Gandhi to P. C. Joshi, Secretary General of the Communist Party of India,
     July 30, 1944, in Pyarelal, *Mahatma Gandhi: The Last Phase (1956),*
     vol. I, p. 49.
12. Ravuri Dhanalaxmi, *British Attitude to Nepal's Relations with Tibet and
     China 1814-1914* (Chandigarh: Bahri, 1981), p. 8.
13. Ibid.
14. Stephen Philip Cohen, *A Special Report of the Rockefeller Foundation on
     International Relations Research in South Asia* (New York, 1982), p. 1.
15. Baljit Singh, *Indian Foreign Policy: An Analysis* (New York: Asia Publish-
     ing House, 1976), p. 82.
16. *Times of India,* New Delhi, December 3, 1952.
17. Ibid.
18. *New Times* (Supplement) No. 52 (1955), p. 19.
19. Jawaharlal Nehru, *India's Foreign Policy* (New Delhi: Ministry of Infor-
     mation and Broadcasting, 1961), p. 47.
20. F. C. Barghoorn, *The Soviet Cultural Offensive: The Role of Cultural Ex-
     change in Soviet Foreign Policy* (Princeton, N.J.: Princeton University
     Press, 1960), p. 77.
21. Arthur Lall, *The Emergence of Modern India* (New York: Columbia
     University Press, 1981), p. 167.
22. Indira Gandhi: *The Years of Endeavor* (New Delhi: Government of India,
     1975), p. 590.
23. "Mrs. Gandhi's Opposition: Morarji Desai," *The New Republic* 163,
     Nos. 5, 6 (August 1975).
24. Surjit Mansingh, *India's Search for Power* (Beverly Hills, Calif.: Sage,
     1984), p. 34.
25. P. N. Haskar, "Appearance and Reality," Seminar on India's search for
     power (New Delhi, May 1978), cited in Mansingh, *India's Search,* p. 60.
26. Mansingh, *India's Search,* p. 32.
27. Onkar Marwah and Lawrence Ziring, eds., *The Subcontinent in World
     Politics* (New York: Praeger, 1978), p. 35.
28. Mansingh, *India's Search,* p. 74.
29. U. S. Bajpai, ed., *India's Security* (New Delhi: Lancers, 1983), pp. 21-22.
30. Onkar Marwah, "India's Nuclear and Space Programs: Intent and
     Policy," *International Security* 2, No. 2 (Fall 1977).
31. Nancy Jetley, *India-China Relations: 1947-1977* (New Delhi: Radiant,
     1979), p. 144.
32. Bhabani Sen Gupta, *The Fulcrum of Asia* (New York: Pegasus, 1970)
     p. 104.
33. Lorne J. Kavic, *India's Quest for Security* (Berkeley and Los Angeles: Uni-
     versity of California Press, 1967), p. 5.
34. Mansingh, *India's Search,* p. 238.
35. William J. Barnds, *India, Pakistan, and the Great Powers* (New York:
     Praeger, 1972), p. 197.
36. Mansingh, *India's Search,* pp. 292-93.
37. Ibid., p. 59.

38. *Financial Times* (London), March 27, 1984.
39. Mansingh, *India's Search,* p. 240.
40. Bajpai, *India's Security,* p. 108.
41. Ibid., p. 3.
42. Y. B. Dhawan, *Times of India,* New Delhi, October 24, 1982.
43. Jagat S. Mehta, "The Regional Priorities," *Seminar* No. 281 (January 1981).
44. Girilal Jain, *Times of India,* February 2, 1984.

3

Security Aspects of Indian Foreign Policy

P. R. Chari

The many bonds linking South Asian countries include a shared civilization, ethnic ties, linguistic, religious, and social commonalities, trade, and, not sufficiently appreciated, similarities in their administrative, legal, and military systems emanating from their British colonial heritage. The differences between these countries stem primarily from political rather than economic or cultural factors: linkages between them, consequently, are easy to establish but difficult to sustain, which may explain why South Asia rivals the Middle East and Southeast Asia as the theater of the most persistent tensions and instabilities since the World War II.

A General Perspective

It is fashionable to suggest that South Asia's security problems derive basically from India's expansionist and hegemonic spectre looming over the region, since the main component of Pakistani, Bangladeshi, Nepali, and Sri Lankan threat perceptions focus upon India. Such misperceptions have been strengthened by theories describing India as one of the new influential countries in the international system, although analyses are not wanting either, that India lacks the will to power. There is the further question of whether or not the history of the subcontinent can be rewritten, at this juncture, in any dramatic way. But there are two major difficulties in sustaining the Indian hegemonism thesis.

First, the superpower role in exacerbating subcontinental tensions, evident from the inclusion of some regional countries in military security arrangements, would have to be ignored. Second, subregional conflicts, arising from sociocultural differences and political dissidence within South Asian countries, would also have to be ignored.

The sum of the subcontinent's regional security problems, however, comprises interactions between extraregional, intraregional, and subregional assymmetries. Viewed from this perspective, India's Manichaean image in South Asia might be somewhat improved.

It is also fashionable to urge that regional concerns truly animated India's foreign policy only during the Janata interregnum (1977-80). Undoubtedly the Janata Party's election manifesto bore a commitment to give relations with neighbors top priority in its foreign relations. The belief that geography dictated the need for good neighborliness, regional cooperation and a community of equal and sovereign nations in South Asia illumined the Janata government's external policies, and the concept of "beneficial bilateralism" entered India's official lexicon.[1] Particularly, relations with Pakistan and China were sought to be consolidated through the foreign minister's visits to these countries. But it would be overstating the case to suggest that similar concerns did not animate Congress governments, and it should be recognized that relations with Pakistan and China had been reestablished earlier, in 1976. In the early, difficult years after Partition, it was Nehru's personal influence which dictated India's moderate approaches toward Pakistan, beginning with the release of cash balances in 1948 despite the Kashmir invasion, the restraining of Indian extremists from exacerbated communal disturbances within East Bengal in February 1950, or his offer of a no-war declaration to Pakistan at that time.[2] Instances of such restraint are numerous. More recently, India has forcefully supported Bangladesh's regional cooperation initiative: its benefits would, quite plainly, accrue equally to India's neighbors as well as to itself.

In essence, a higher or lower priority could have been accorded to South Asia by successive Indian governments within a general foreign policy framework that stresses the need for a balance between good neighborliness and national interests. But Asia and wider global issues have demanded equal attention from India's foreign-policy establishment in consideration of its commitments to the nonaligned movement and the North-South dialogue. It might be added that this dual identification of India's basic foreign-policy interests enjoys broad consensus within the country. This perspective might clarify three dilemmas underlying any regional security policy that India might devise.

First, India's size, natural resources, population, gross domestic product, and other traditional attributes of power cause understandable uneasiness in its South Asian neighbors. It is no comfort to India that other large countries such as the United States, the Soviet Union, and China are similarly viewed by their anxious neighbors.

Second, the belief that unless India displays largeheartedness and magnanimity toward its neighbors it is unlikely to gain their acceptance of its regional preponderance,[3] is clearly a counsel of perfection. Such advice fails to appreciate India's not unreasonable concern with activities prejudicial to its security interests within its geostrategic environment. Arms acquisitions by Pakistan, or the extension of superpower rivalries into the Indian Ocean, or the killing of Tamils in Sri Lanka impinge too vividly on India's external and internal security consciousness for these developments to be ignored. It would be idle, but nevertheless worthwhile to speculate how Indo-Pak relations might have progressed if the Soviet Union had not moved into Afghanistan.

Third, the fluctuating, and often estranged, nature of Indo-Pak relations indubitably prejudices any efforts India could make to develop a regional security policy or to strive for regional harmony within South Asia.

India's Security Concerns

The external threats to India's security can be discussed against this general backdrop. These security concerns have centered around Pakistan and China and the strategic linkages between them. The dimensions of the threats to India's security have been extended to include the Sino-Vietnamese dispute (which could destabilize Southeast Asia), Chinese support to irredentist elements in North Burma, the growing military linkages between Pakistan and the Gulf countries, and the instabilities possible within Southwest Asia owing to the Soviet presence in Afghanistan. Similarly, an exacerbation of superpower rivalries in the western Indian Ocean could prejudice India's security in unpredictable, but dangerous, ways. Indubitably these developments cause a deterioration in India's regional ambience. But the basic external threat to India continues, in our view, to emanate from Pakistan and China, despite the efflorescence in perceptions of threats from other directions.

Of greater significance in this regard is the fully explicable urge of India's neighbors to counterbalance its regional preponderance by obtaining external support and to develop intraregional linkages explicitly designed to contain their giant neighbor. The obvious examples of the former phenomenon are Pakistan's politico-military linkages with the United States, China, and Gulf countries, or Sri Lanka's efforts to seek military reassurance from the United States and China: Sri Lanka's attempts to forge closer ties with Pakistan and Bangladesh's developing entente with Pakistan illustrate the latter phenomenon. It was primarily an effort to counter a perceived Pak-Sino-American entente, incidentally, which forced India to enter the Indo-Soviet Treaty in 1971 and to consolidate the obtaining identity of interests between them. This development has inspired speculation that a Pak-Sino-American axis would confront an Afghan-Indo-Soviet axis in the foreseeable future. All related developments would need India's active consideration.

Two recent developments are of significance here.

First, nuclear developments within Pakistan have clear military overtones, which have been carefully nurtured by ambivalent statements and undeviating actions. The analogy with Israel is perhaps unavoidable in this regard, but a pertinent comparison with the case of India is also possible. The Chinese invasion across the Himalayas in 1962, and China's first nuclear explosion in 1964 seminally influenced India's nuclear policies. Similarly, the emergence of Bangladesh in 1971, accentuated by the Pokharan explosion in 1974, have conditioned Pakistan's nuclear policies. This analogy, however, has its limitations. India has not pursued its PNE to manufacture nuclear weapons in the manner of the five nuclear weapon powers and has divorced, thereby, its technological capabilities from military intent. Given the present state of bilateral relations between Pakistan and India (Pakistan's explosion of its nuclear device could trigger a nuclear arms race in South Asia), it is also possible that India would not be able to restrict itself to constructing a bilateral nuclear relationship with Pakistan, since the need to configure China into its nuclear force structure would also arise. Whether or not the no-weapons-but-no-foreclosing-of-option phase can be stretched out and the Indo-Pakistan adversary relationship kept below the nuclear level raises one set of questions. Whether or not a nuclearized South Asia would be stable, and how it could influence the Sino-Soviet-American triangular relationship raises another set of questions.

Second, another significant development relates to internal discord within India. The Naga and Mizo insurgencies in Northeast India, which have been assisted by external powers, are recognizable in this regard. In recent years the Assam and Punjab issues have gained ascendancy, and their obtuseness needs greater appreciation. Indeed, Indira Gandhi's tragic demise could be ascribed to the recalcitrance of the Punjab problem to yield facile solutions. The origins and contours of these issues are too complex to permit summary description. But the significance of these questions can be exaggerated, despite the situation of the two states on the Indo-Bangladesh and Indo-Pakistan borders, if the size and diversity of India are borne in mind.

India's constitution consciously promotes a pluralistic society. The religious and cultural rights of minorities are preserved therein, and they are provided the opportunity to preserve their own cultural identity, manage their religious affairs, and maintain their own institutions. Given the religious, social, and cultural diversities obtaining within India, it must be expected that periodic eruptions of violence will occur. These conflicts reflect the tensions between India's constitution-provided federal structure and subregional aspirations, which have yet to work themselves out, to harmonize these conflicting interests. Some value might also be attached to the reality of the "din and noise" of democracy, and the latitude given to dissent therein which has permitted India to retain its unity since Independence. But it is indisputable that these disturbances possess considerable potential for exacerbating internal security and provide unique opportunities for the ubiquitous "foreign hand" in subcontinental politics. The veracity of these allegations, of course, is as difficult to establish as the suspected role of foreign money in South Asian elections.

Pakistan's Significance in India's Regional Security Policies

The foregoing discussion indicates that Pakistan looms large in India's security perceptions and explains its importance in India's foreign policy. Unkind critics have, in fact, suggested that India has no foreign policy, but only a Pakistan policy. An element of truth is evident here, because despite the fluctuations in their quality, India's relations with its other neighbors have never remained consistently adversarial. The single exception might be Bangladesh at some date in the future, and one of the ironies of history that might emerge is that Bangladesh would prefer its former subjugators to its former liberators.

The Indo-Pakistan adversary relationship could nullify any efforts to construct an amicable South Asian regime. Moreover, the rapidly escalating conventional arms race between the two countries would further exacerbate the regional security situation. Even a cursory examination of the accelerating weapons-procurement programs of India and Pakistan since 1978 would make this apparent. Significantly these programs include not only high performance aircraft that can reach vital economic, military, and population targets within minutes, but also dual-capable aircraft that can be used as nuclear-weapon delivery systems. Another result of this arms race has been the enormous increase in military expenditures, which have risen between 1978 and 1984 from $819 million to $1.873 billion in Pakistan, and $3.45 billion to $6.326 billion in India.[4] Beside heightening fears and suspicions and worsening bilateral relations, this ongoing arms race, which is sustained by importing technologically advanced weapon systems, will raise the costs of any future Indo-Pak conflict. The arms race also has significant opportunity costs, since increases in defense outlays are invariably made by diverting available resources from the development and social services sectors of national plans; all this is occurring while demographic pressures and rising expectations in the population remain patently unmatched by the capacity of the governments to satisfy these aspirations.

Argued in Indo-centric terms, the options available to guide India's Pakistan policy are:

—seek a negotiated settlement of all outstanding Indo-Pak differences, including Kashmir;

—seek a settlement of these differences on a piecemeal basis, temporarily excluding Kashmir from these negotiations;

—develop a pattern of cooperative linkages, whereby the advantages of continued cooperation would be perceived to outweigh the ephemeral advantages of contrived hostility in both countries.

Undoubtedly, Kashmir is no longer the live issue in Indo-Pakistan relations it was in the past, but it is difficult for the leadership in India and Pakistan to concede this and to exclude Kashmir from consideration in negotiations. Given the contentious nature of the Kashmir question, proceeding along the first option mentioned above would assuredly end in failure. Whether one might proceed with the second option, and the timing of that option is a matter for political judgment which must be left to the leadership of the two countries. For this reason, the last option available to India offers a long-term, perhaps visionary, but lasting solution to Indo-Pak differences. For this third option to proceed, however, a shared belief would be needed in both countries regarding the mutual benefits of cooperative endeavor. Shortly after partition, Nehru had visualized that "It is inevitable that India and Pakistan would draw closer to one another, or else they will come into conflict. There is no middle way, for we have known each other too long to be indifferent neighbors. . . . Any closer association must come out of a normal process, and in a friendly way."[5]

Bilateralism versus Regionalism

The centrality of Pakistan in India's threat perceptions explains the latter's emphasis on bilateralism in their relations, leading to familiar charges that India has emphasized this approach for hegemonistic reasons. A more plausible rationale for India's bilateral approach derives from the present structure of the international system. It remains bipolar essentially in the nuclear sphere. But the incapacity of the United States or the Soviet Union to control events or to influence their allies, visible in the Middle East and Europe, reveals the limits of their power. Simultaneously, the capacity of militarily and economically weak countries to assert their independence from traditional centers of power has resulted in a diffusion of power through the international system, with nationalism serving as the motive force. Third World conflicts, moreover, arise from a medley of historical, ethnic, linguistic, political, and similar factors which are not amenable to outside resolution, although they could be accelerated by external manipulation.

These aspects of the international system require greater appreciation; the Iran-Iraq war dramatically illustrates its complexities. Presently, Iran has abjured the support of the superpowers without any disastrous result; Iraq has the support of both superpowers without any beneficial result. Moreover, the past history of American and Soviet efforts to achieve subcontinental peace and stability, either by drawing India and Pakistan into alliance systems, or the Tashkent process, indicates these efforts have not proved successful. A bilateral approach to divisive regional issues needs to be commended, therefore, on pragmatic considerations rather than by reference to abstract political or moral principles.

Apropos, Indo-Sri Lankan efforts to resolve the Tamil problem have some possibility of succeeding within the bilateral consultative process, however feeble this likelihood may presently appear. The particularities of this question need greater recognition. Anti-Tamil riots have taken place in 1956, 1958, 1962, 1972, 1977, 1981, and 1983. The Tamils in Sri Lanka, numbering some 3 million, form around 20 percent of its population, and 50 million Tamils inhabit the Tamilnadu state in India, which is ruled by an opposition party making center-state relations delicate in the federal context. The Tamil question is too deeply intertwined, therefore, in Indian and Sri Lankan domestic politics to permit any meaningful intercession by third parties. Consequently, India's attempts to insulate this issue from outside intervention have been construed unfairly as imposing a Pax India upon the South Asian region, despite being intended only to resolve a delicate bilateral problem with considerable inflammatory dangers for both countries.

It is possible to overemphasize bilateralism and disregard the potential worth of regional initiatives to operationalize an overall security policy. These initiatives could soften the edges of suspicion to allow an upgradation of mutual relations in various directions which a strictly bilateral approach might not achieve. This assertion can be illustrated by evaluating the significance of the SAARC process for India's regional security policy, and the increasing newer awareness of regional ethno-political problems.

The declaration adopted in August 1983 by the South Asian foreign ministers' conference visualized increased regional cooperation, contacts, and exchanges among the countries of the region to promote friendship, amity, and understanding among their peoples.[6] The principles laid down specifically provide that regional cooperation would not substitute bilateral and multilateral cooperation or be inconsistent with obligations previously undertaken. Geography and economic realities have dictated these caveats, since only India has a common border with the other South Asian states and the natural direction of their trade has also been with India. These realities have generated fears that India will dominate the SAARC system, without appreciating the potential of India's comparative technological progress being utilized (or complementary economic relationships being developed) within the regional cooperation arrangements that might be devised.

In the past, politics rather than economics has guided reservations in Pakistan and Bangladesh, leading to the attenuation of trade links with India at inevitable cost to their economies; this has led critics to argue that regional cooperation must follow, rather than precede, a political accommodation between these countries. In our view, regional cooperative endeavours in extrapolitical directions offer the best hope that such interactions would create the conditions for eroding suspicions and improving the regional ambience. To date, priorities areas for cooperation in various areas have been identified, a South Asian history conference and archeological congress are to be convened, and the EEC has offered help in the transportation, science, and technology.[7] A summit meeting in Dhaka in late 1985 discussed important questions like extension of the SAARC charter and the institutionalization of this movement. Incidentally, the sphere of cultural exchanges between writers, artists, musicians, and academics could, assuredly, foster greater friendships within the region.

The persistance of ethnopolitical problems bedevils the entire South Asian region. They have led to dissident movements in northeast India, Chittagong hill tracts, Jaffna peninsula, North-West Frontier Province, and Baluchistan. The value of a regional approach to such problems is, perhaps, limited. But bilateral consultations on such questions, sharing intelligence reports, and cooperation between armed forces in counterinsurgency operations could become important steps to ease intraregional tensions. Certain ethnopolitical issues relating to external communities like Indians in Nepal, Bangladeshis and Nepalis in northeast India, Sikhs in Pakistan, and Tamils in Sri Lanka spill over national boundaries. Despite their individual particularities, these issues have the common potential to ignite communal passions and escalate into wider intraregional conflicts. The exacerbation of such conflicts by regional adversaries through overt, or covert measures, is easy, given the latent hostile images and perceptions of rival communities in South Asia.[8] (Pakistan's delay of the hijackers' trials and its encouragement of Sikh extremism illustrate such policies.) Recognizably, such efforts are designed to achieve short-term political gains, but a shared conviction of their mutual vulnerability to exacerbation of ethnopolitical problems could, perhaps, reduce such temptations.

Current Indo-Pakistan Differences

Having discussed the value of bilateralism in South Asian relations and the value of regional approaches to stabilize them, I offer a brief overview of the current frictions in Indo-Pakistan relations. A sense of déjà vu pervades the scene.

Discussions between the two foreign ministers—interrupted, but likely to resume—on Pakistan's proposal for a nonaggression pact and India's proposal for a treaty of peace, friendship, and cooperation have their genesis in India's no-war declaration offer in February 1950 and Pakistan's joint defense offer originally made by Mohammed Ali Bogra in 1953. Similarly, Pakistan's proposal for "reciprocal inspection" of each other's nuclear facilities can be traced back to its South Asia nuclear-free-zone proposal. Furthermore, Pakistan's suggestions regarding the establishment of mutual force ratios is complicated by India's oft-reiterated objections that it must deploy sizeable forces along the Sino-Indian border. Both countries must also account for troops required to perform internal security duties. The highly publicized discord in Indo-Pak relations after India's expression of sympathy for democratic aspirations in Pakistan during the MRD agitation in mid-1983, which Pakistan construed as a further interference in its domestic affairs, resembles innumerable past instances of extraneous considerations, like the Kashmir issue which dissipated a developing entente between the two countries.

Some differences, however, are more apparent than real. Kashmir for instance, is no longer the live issue it once was. Nor is there any ambiguity about India's essential position that Soviet troops must be withdrawn from Afghanistan, although differences obtain with Pakistan concerning the mechanics for achieving this objective. India believes the withdrawal should form part of a political settlement that includes the return of refugees to Afghanistan, and an agreement on noninterference in Afghanistan's internal affairs by external powers. Pakistan leans toward the view that a partial solution to this problem might exist. However, beliefs that Pakistan would tilt toward West Asia by Islamizing its polity and emphasizing its Middle Eastern ties fail to appreciate that its basic security concerns derive from its adversary relationship with India and the encroaching Soviet presence in Afghanistan, apart from the militant, but fragile, nature of the Iranian power structure. Consequently, Pakistan's relations with the South Asian region will continue to require considerable investment and interest.

Conclusion

It must be accepted that the three extraregional powers most concerned with the normalization process between India and Pakistan—the United States, the Soviet Union, and China—will have entirely different perceptions and interests in this process. U.S. interest in Pakistan has heightened since Iran left the American strategic system for the Gulf region and relates primarily to the Soviet presence in Afghanistan. Despite India's recent efforts to diversify its arms sources, the Soviet Union remains India's main arms supplier, emphasizing the identity of interests that links the two countries. China has regarded arms transfers to Pakistan as consolidating a special relationship while simultaneously weakening India's geopolitical situation in the subcontinent. Indo-Pakistan relations are influenced concomitantly then by the state of American-Soviet-Chinese relationships. Future developments within these interactions will undoubtedly influence India's security perceptions.

But there is little reason to apprehend that these external powers have a vested interest in the continuance of Indo-Pak asymmetries. For, the progression of these asymmetries, inexorably, to the nuclearization of South Asia would lead to a nuclear arms race between India and Pakistan, with the further likelihood that India would then seek to establish deterrent patterns against China: a triangular Sino-Indo-Pak nuclear interaction would impinge upon superpower political and strategic relations. Consequently, it would serve the self-interests of China and the superpowers to support and not impede the normalization of Indo-Pak relations and regional peace initiatives.

The primary impetus, however, for seeking regional peace and security must come from within South Asia. The fact remains that geography constrains India and its regional neighbors to find their security essentially within the region by, ideally, establishing cooperative linkages and eroding the suspicions prevailing among themselves. The past history of their estrangements, moreover, highlights the need for regional leaders to reduce their public rhetoric and ascribe a greater role to quiet diplomacy. The search for cooperative linkages would have greater prospects of success through little steps over many fields of activity, rather than by the pursuit of any grand design. With its massive popular mandate the Rajiv Gandhi government is well equipped to undertake this difficult endeavor, taking advantage of the coincidence that stable regimes have also established themselves in the other South Asian countries.

NOTES

1. For an authoritative statement of the Janata Government's foreign policy, see Atal Behari Vajpayee "India and the Changing International Order," in K. P. Misra, ed., *Janata's Foreign Policy* (New Delhi: Vikas, 1979), pp. 1-10.

2. Sisir Gupta, "India's Policy towards Pakistan," in M. S. Rajan and Shivaji Ganguly, eds., *Sisir Gupta: India and the International System* (New Delhi: Vikas, 1981), pp. 274-75.

3. Selig Harrison, "Fanning the Flames in South Asia," *Foreign Policy,* 45 (Winter 1981-82): 99.

4. See *The Military Balance 1977-78 and 1984-85* (London: The International Institute for Strategic Studies, 1984).

5. Cited in K. R. Narayanan, *India and America: Essays in Understanding* (Washington: Embassy of India, 1984), p. 66.

6. For the full text of the declaration, see *The Hindu* (International Edition), week ending August 13, 1983.

7. *India Abroad* (New York), March 9, 1984.

8. For an analysis of such beliefs see Stephen P. Cohen, "Image and Perception in India-Pakistan Relations," in M. S. Rajan and Shivaji Ganguly, eds. *Great Power Relations, World Order, and the Third World* (New Delhi: Vikas, 1981), pp. 281-90.

4

Pakistan's Foreign Policy after Afghanistan

W. Howard Wriggins

In December 1979, Soviet troops crossed into Afghanistan and installed a leader of Moscow's choice in place of Hafizullah Amin. It was the first time Soviet troops had been committed outside the Warsaw Pact area, and it involved them in a country that for more than a century had been recognized as a buffer state between the Russian realm and the powers of South Asia. The geostrategic situation in the region had already been dramatically disrupted by the revolution in Iran, which ejected the Shah and brought in a band of religious zealots who quickly dismantled the Shah's proud army and state structure. Now, the superpower nearest the subcontinent had leapt the Hindukush, the natural barrier historically considered the dividing line between the steppes to the north and the subcontinent to the south.

While the United States reacted promptly to these events, the nations most directly affected—India and Pakistan—moved more cautiously. In Washington's eyes, Pakistan overnight became a "front-line" state, sharing a 1300-mile frontier with a country the Soviet Union now sought to control.[1] As the United States president saw it, Soviet success in Afghanistan would pose a great danger to "the region as a whole." Some years earlier, Washington had quietly acquiesced in the British withdrawal from the Gulf. With the collapse of the Shah and the Soviet move into Afghanistan, however, President Carter deemed the Persian Gulf to be of "vital interest" to the United States, and he committed the country to employing military force to defend it, if necessary.[2]

What impact did the Soviet invasion have on Pakistan's situation? In one sense, the changes seemed slight indeed. Perception counts for much in South Asian international politics—as it does everywhere—and a notable aspect of the post-invasion period was the persistence of perceptions which had been commonplace twenty years before.[3] Initial Indian reactions, for instance, suggested a return to the 1950s; to New Delhi's foreign-policy establishment, it appeared to make little difference whether Russian troops were stationed on the Amu Darya or the Khyber.[4] Both Pakistani and Indian troop dispositions changed but little; and well into 1982, private conversations in both Islamabad and New Delhi sounded all too familiar, echoing sentiments expressed over the past twenty-five years.[5]

In another sense, however, the Soviet presence in Afghanistan dramatically transformed Pakistan's geostrategic situation. Instead of being buffered by the mountains, deserts, and ravines of Afghanistan—which for so long had separated Russia from the subcontinent—Pakistan now faced the spectre of Soviet troops virtually everywhere along the 1,300-mile frontier. The shadow of Soviet power hung over the entire subcontinent as never before. Within months of the invasion, Pakistan was inundated by refugees. And Soviet aircraft periodically violated Pakistani airspace, occasionally buzzing refugee camps well within its borders.

What considerations lay behind Islamabad's approach to this new situation? What were its options, however limited? To whom could it turn for support? How could it best deal with the Afghan freedom movement, the refugees, and the Soviet Union? This chapter seeks to reconstruct the Pakistan government's perceptions of its foreign-policy situation after the Soviet invasion. Necessarily speculative, it considers the constraints under which the Pakistanis have operated—as well as their limited options—in their search for an effective response to the Soviet invasion. To American observers, Islamabad's actions have often seemed halfhearted. But one can argue that its policy of "limited liability" has made the most of a much worsened security situation which at the outset its neighbors did little to improve.

The Bhutto Foreign-Policy Legacy

After the dismemberment of Pakistan in 1971, then-President Zulfikar Ali Bhutto actively sought intimate ties with the states of the Gulf and Middle East and associated his country with the nonaligned nations and the Group of 77 at the United Nations. By hosting the Islamic Conference in Lahore in 1972, by providing specialized assistance to various Gulf states, and by adopting pro-Arab positions on Arab-Israeli issues, Bhutto demonstrated Pakistan's utility to the Arab states. At the same time, Bhutto maintained close relations with the Shah. In fact, his problems in Baluchistan were in part the result of having followed the Shah's advice to bear down hard on the NAP government in Baluchistan and the North-West Frontier Province. He obtained from Tehran an explicit commitment of security assistance in the case of need, as well as price concessions on Iranian oil.[6] He also welcomed Iranian help in trying to resolve Pakistani differences with Afghanistan over the status of Pakhtunistan. For such gains, Bhutto had to suppress his earlier enthusiasm for Colonel Qaddafi; but he clearly considered it worthwhile. Finally, although his zeal for developing Pakistan's nuclear capability alienated Washington, the downgrading of his connection with the United States enhanced his stature among the nonaligned countries.

With China, Pakistan had enjoyed profitable relations since the mid-1960s. Not only had the Pakistanis benefited from China's diplomatic support at the United Nations and elsewhere, but Islamabad believed that its ties to Beijing served to deter possible pressures from India. China withheld its recognition of Bangladesh until India released the Pakistanis being held as POWs. And a modest flow of Chinese military assistance helped slow Pakistan's gradual decline in comparison to India's growing capability. During Bhutto's years, the "China connection" was carefully nursed.[7]

Under Bhutto, Pakistan's relations with India also improved to some extent. After the Simla Agreement of 1972, Indo-Pakistan relations became generally less acerbic than before. Once the parameters of the new relationship were staked out, inconspicuous efforts were undertaken to reduce friction: India reassured Pakistan that it was not encouraging disruptive activities in Baluchistan and the North-West Frontier Province; and Pakistan appeared almost ready to abandon its hopes regarding Kashmir. A flurry of fresh diplomatic efforts accompanied the accession of the Janata government in 1977, and serious economic exchanges were negotiated for the first time.[8]

By the time of Bhutto's overthrow by the military in 1977, Pakistan's foreign policy had become more diversified and far less confrontational against India, and its relations with Afghanistan were improving as well.[9] With the Shah's encouragement, Daoud had been persuaded to drop his agitation on behalf of Pakhtunistan, and he and Bhutto had exchanged visits. In March 1978, a month before the bloody coup that overthrew Daoud, Bhutto's successor, Zia ul-Haq, welcomed Daoud to Rawalpindi to dramatize Pakistan's intent to continue to reduce friction between the two countries.

With the overthrow of Daoud in April 1978, however, the new leadership of Afghanistan quickly took up the old Pakhtunistan cry once more —a sure sign of trouble ahead.[10] In addition, the collapse of the Shah less than a year later, in January 1979, dramatically worsened Pakistan's security situation. Instead of having a stable, well-armed conservative power to the west, playing a moderating role in Indo-Pakistan relations and providing presumptive support in the event of trouble, Islamabad could only watch helplessly as authority disintegrated in Tehran. Now, even conceivable United States backing through the Teheran connection was no longer available. Iran was rapidly falling under the domination of puritanical religious enthusiasts. The Khomeini revolution not only destroyed the Shah's regime as an asset to Pakistan's security, it threatened to provoke religious disorders within Pakistan itself.

The Soviet Invasion

In December 1979, Soviet troops moved into Afghanistan. Closer than many other governments to developments in that part of the world, Pakistan was well aware of the growing resistance against the Taraki and Amin regimes. They were, therefore, less surprised than most at the Soviet move. But Pakistani opinions were divided on the implications. The optimists considered the Soviet move to be a response to the deteriorating condition of the Amin government and an essentially defensive effort to retain Afghanistan within the Soviet "scientific socialist" sphere. Others saw it in a more ominous light, as a major step in the "known" long-run Soviet "plan" to penetrate Baluchistan and advance to the Arabian sea.[11] Those concerned about ethnic tensions in Pakistan were wary of Soviet and Afghan efforts to organize Baluch dissidents and resentful that Baluchistan was not being given its due recognition as a full-fledged province of Pakistan. The external threat was thus compounded by internal ethnic politics to complicate Pakistan's security problem.[12]

As thousands of refugees sought sanctuary in Pakistan from Soviet air raids and from sporadic but devastating retaliation against guerrilla attacks on Soviet forces, Islamabad was able to evoke strong protest through the United Nations from virtually all nonaligned members and all the major powers. More significantly, in Pakistani eyes, the Islamic Conference, meeting in Islamabad in January 1980, protested with almost one voice; only Syria, Libya, and South Yemen dissented.[13] Given Pakistan's geopolitical situation and inherent constraints, however, Islamabad could shape no prudent policy without extensive consultations with neighboring and more distant states. Accordingly, President Zia's principal foreign-policy advisor, Agha Shahi, undertook prompt consultation in many capitals. How was Pakistan to respond to the situation?

Major Alternatives

Mending Fences with India: Initial Efforts

One logical option available to Pakistan was to try to mend its fences with India. Indo-Pakistani relations had worsened since Zia had seized power. The Indian government had long expressed its preference for representative government in Islamabad and had appealed to the generals to spare Bhutto's life. Some Pakistani strategists felt that now was the time to seek closer association with India. It was folly, they believed, to try to defend the subcontinent from Soviet encroachment without India's cooperation. It was necessary now to restrain the chauvinists in Pakistan's Punjab—who allegedly persisted in seeing India as the major enemy—and more actively to seek an acceptable accommodation with the Indians.[14]

On the other hand, fear of Indo-Soviet collusion had long prevailed among Islamabad's military planners and many public figures. India's 1971 venture against East Pakistan, launched within months after the conclusion of the Indo-Soviet Treaty of Friendship, lent substance to that fear. Moreover, India had never been able to propose a long-run relationship which both assumed an Indian preeminence in the region and was acceptable to Pakistan.[15]

Although a serious public debate was beginning in India when he visited New Delhi in January 1980, Agha Shahi reportedly found little evidence that India's rulers shared Pakistan's apprehensions regarding either the Shah's collapse or the Soviet invasion of Afghanistan. Indeed, during the January debate at the U.N., the new Indira Gandhi government went so far as to justify Russia's move as a defensive response to the activities of "certain foreign powers," implying American and Pakistani responsibility for the Soviet venture. This surprising position shocked many of India's nonaligned friends. India's initial position may have been more a quasi-automatic response of a regime whose leaders were exhausted from an electoral campaign, and less the result of reasoned analysis. Indeed, by the end of February, New Delhi was publicly criticizing the Soviet government for its presence in Afghanistan.

Nevertheless, the Gandhi government did little to reassure Islamabad in its worsened security situation. To some extent, experienced Pakistani officials understood India's reluctance. After all, more than 70 percent of India's armaments still came from Russia; for years, Moscow had regularly supported New Delhi's positions in various international forums; and Indo-Soviet trade relations were important as well. For India to acknowledge a markedly changed geostrategic situation would raise serious questions about its own future security policy. India was not likely to jeopardize its relationship with the Soviet Union for the sake of standing shoulder to shoulder with its traditional regional opponent. Moreover, India rather likely preferred a "secular" Afghanistan under Soviet control to a religiously zealous Afghanistan which might excite Muslims throughout South Asia.

In New Delhi, President Carter's abrupt about-face of offering military assistance to Pakistan looked, at first, like an attempt to revive the close Pakistani-American relations of the mid-1950s. This obviously called for strong public protests in New Delhi designed to make both Washington and Islamabad think twice. Indeed, it seemed that the hypothetical return of the Americans to South Asia was of greater urgency to New Delhi than the very real presence of the Soviet Union in Afghanistan. Some even argued that a renewed American connection with Pakistan would justify India in welcoming the Russian move: a Soviet presence on Pakistan's eastern frontier might be the best guarantee against Pakistani revanchism.[16] In the light of such reactions, it is not surprising that a number of Pakistanis began to fear the worst—an Indo-Soviet collusion to take all of Azad Kashmir at the propitious moment.

Nevertheless, while India complained vigorously and publicly about the American offer to help Pakistan, it did protest diplomatically to the Soviet Union about its invasion. In the meantime, Indian and Pakistani officials maintained an inconspicuous dialogue, the one hoping New Delhi might come to be more helpful, the other hoping to dissuade Pakistan from repeating its earlier strategy of going too far with the Americans.

Seeking American Assistance: Initial Efforts

Another obvious alternative for Pakistan was to seek the help of the United States. Pakistan's sense of weakness vis-à-vis India had always led it to seek balancing assistance from the outside. The United States had greatly improved Pakistan's military capability in the mid-1950s, and perhaps it might be helpful again.[17] The day after the invasion, President Carter telephoned President Zia and offered his help.[18] Elements of the Pakistan military were enthusiastic about the possibility of renewing the American connection. For those with long memories, Carter's subsequent sweeping commitment in his State of the Union Message to defend the Gulf seemed to presage an end to America's apparent disinterest in the affairs of South Asia. It also suggested that the United States might be prepared to lift its virtual quarantine, first implemented because of Bhutto's nuclear program, and subsequently intensified because of the Zia government's dubious human-rights record.[19]

The professionals in Pakistan's foreign ministry, however, were less enthusiastic than the military. They were aware of the profound doubts in Washington about once again getting involved in South Asia. Pakistan was unlikely to become the Carter administration's favorite overseas partner, and opinion in Washington was divided about the wisdom of becoming too dependent on that country.[20] There were those in Pakistan with different long memories, who saw the United States as fundamentally unreliable. They felt that the United States had "let Pakistan down" in both its 1965 and 1971 wars with India, despite the agreement of 1959 (which the United States had always said was directed only against the Soviet threat, whereas Pakistan often understood it to apply to the Indian contingency as well). Political figures such as Asghar Khan and spokesmen for the Pakistan People's party warned against forging unreliable ties.[21]

When the Americans made their offer of $400 million in February, it confirmed the view of specialists in Islamabad that the United States should not be taken seriously. Even though Washington said the $400 million was only a first installment, who could be sure? Why should Pakistan run the risk of associating with the United States, thereby inviting criticism from the radical left, religious criticism from those inspired by the Iranian revolution, and perhaps diplomatic or even direct cross-border pressure from Moscow, when the United States was simply offering peanuts? Understandably, then, Zia rejected the American offer, and for the next nine months he pursued a policy of engaging in verbal boldness at the U.N. and among his Islamic brethren while exercising caution on the frontier.

In retrospect, one wonders whether a real opportunity was not missed during those nine months. A very different conjuncture might have developed on the subcontinent. Zia's rejection of the American offer might have been seen in New Delhi as proof that Islamabad was not about to drag the United States back into South Asia, as Ayub was accused of having done in the mid-1950s. Quiet but firm reassurance by the Gandhi government—such as some visible troop redeployments away from the Pakistan frontier—and some expression of sympathy for Islamabad's new situation could have given public confirmation that New Delhi understood Pakistan's worsened security position, and also underlined Indian goodwill. Such moves need not have disturbed India's relations with Moscow, but they might have made a substantial impact on Islamabad. To be sure, such policy flexibility is difficult when domestic opponents are ready to pounce on any sign of concern for the worries of an old antagonist. Bureaucracies often miss opportunities; military men dislike the inconveniences brought about by diplomatic considerations. Moreover, the signals from Islamabad were somewhat mixed as well. Nevertheless, there was enough time to reconsider old policies but the opportunity passed.

In view of India's unwillingness to be helpful and the vulnerability resulting from the Shah's demise and the Soviet invasion, the Pakistanis could not help but wonder aloud—especially within earshot of Americans—just how long they would be able to stand firm against Soviet blandishments without substantial support from other powers. In Washington, the Pakistanis argued that only a formal mutual security treaty (requiring Senate concurrence) could induce Pakistan to become an active partner in the new United States containment effort. Knowledgeable Pakistanis must have realized that such an American commitment was highly unlikely at that time—the "Vietnam syndrome" was still very much in evidence; Pakistan's nuclear ambitions and dubious human-rights record simply made the Carter administration's tasks all that more difficult.[22] Moreover, there was some concern that such intimacy with the United States might require a radical increase in Pakistani assistance to the Afghan *mujahiddin*, a step that Soviet Foreign Minister Gromyko warned against during his visit to New Delhi in February 1980. It would also risk alienating nonaligned nations and the important moderate Arabs who had spoken so forthrightly and voted so overwhelmingly with Pakistan at the Islamic Conference and in the U.N.

Obtaining Support from the Middle East

But Pakistan had other alternatives. In the Islamic world of the Gulf, Zia had sources of support that had not been available to his predecessors Ayub and Yahya. After 1973, the states of the Gulf—particularly Saudi Arabia, Kuwait, and the United Arab Emirates—were able to provide a level of financial assistance hitherto unimaginable. And the dependence of western European states as well as the United States on Gulf-state energy resources provided the oil producers with diplomatic influence they had previously lacked. As pointed out above, the Zia government has some major assets in the Middle East. A number of senior Pakistani financial officials and administrators have served in the Gulf region, as have Pakistani military officers, pilots, aircraft-maintenance teams, and logistical specialists. (Zia himself was stationed in Jordan at the time of the expulsion of the PLO in 1970 and was a staunch supporter of King Hussein.) Pakistanis bolster the police force in Bahrain and Oman.[23] As non-Arabs, they are trusted for their detachment from Arab politics, unlike the Egyptians, Palestinians, or even the Lebanese—who, it is said, can never leave politics alone. More than one million Pakistan citizens have labored in the Gulf region and sent home over $2 billion in remittances annually—which has for several years constituted Pakistan's largest single source of foreign exchange.

From the point of view of many Gulf states, a stable Pakistan is in itself a valuable asset. Compared to the seven million citizens in Saudi Arabia and the miniscule Emirates, Pakistan looms as a major regional power. So long as it copes with its own domestic and security problems, Pakistan can be a reliable and predictable force on the eastern marches

of the Gulf. On the other hand, disintegration in Pakistan would pro-
foundly worsen the politicostrategic environment in the Gulf, an area already destabilized by the Iranian revolution and the Soviet intrusion into
Afghanistan.

The Saudi connection has its problems, however.[24] For one thing, decisions can take an excruciatingly long time to emerge from Riyadh—as
can the steps to implement them. The Saudi system moves by consensus
involving a number of senior family leaders and top administrators. The
decision-making process is highly secretive and reportedly hard to influence from the outside.[25] Moreover, Saudi subsidies and assistance transfers, though large when they come, reportedly do not follow a regular
pattern but arrive sporadically in a way that cannot be counted on, and
sometimes only when specific budgetary items are at their most acute
stage. On the other hand, the entire process has the virtue of being highly
discreet and inconspicuous; there is no public embarrassment such as is
nearly inevitable when dealing with the United States over major arms
purchases.[26]

For Pakistan, of course, the Islamic Middle East comprises more than
Saudi Arabia and the Emirates; Iran is also important. In the wake of the
Iranian revolution, it has been hard to maintain constructive relations
with both Riyadh and Tehran. Nevertheless, Zia has attempted to retain
his connections with the Tehran leadership, difficult and unpredictable
as they are. Reportedly, there have been contacts regarding problems in
Baluchistan; there may also have been exchanges of information on security matters, on developments in Afghanistan, and on the indirect
Pakistani-Soviet negotiations.

At the same time, Zia's popular support at home has remained limited,
and religious agitation inspired by events in Iran could very well erupt in
Pakistan. The Shia Muslims constitute between 10 and 20 percent of the
total population (more have appeared since the Iranian revolution than
were evident before), and some key figures in the Pakistan establishment
have Shia affiliations, but the bulk of the establishment—the bureaucracy, the army, and the business community—are Sunni religious moderates. The mosques have been centers of agitation on behalf of "Islamic
values" and the pious life. In Pakistan, as elsewhere, the religiously zealous often have closer relationships with the rural and urban poor than
have the bureaucrats, the businessmen, and the officers. To criticize the
secular tendencies of Bhutto's regime was easy enough. More difficult
has been the shaping of a consensus on what constitutes a truly Islamic
polity for the 1980s. Satisfying the foreign critics in Iran might alienate
Riyadh, and vice versa; responding to the urgings of either could alienate
—or mobilize—important groups at home. Moreover, diverse shades of

Islamic opinion, if activated, could provoke serious disorders as they contend for public support. Shia demonstrations against Zakat obligations in 1981 were a vivid object lesson.[27]

The intricacies of Gulf-state politics presented President Zia with both opportunities and risks. When the Iran-Iraq war broke out, Zia happened to be president of the Islamic Conference; in this capacity, he immediately sought to mediate an end to the conflict that was splitting the oil producers, threatening peace in the Gulf region, distracting attention from the Arab-Israeli conflict, and potentially opening Iran to Soviet penetration. So long as negotiations are underway, the process of mediation usually enhances the stature of the mediator, as the United States discovered after the 1973 Arab-Israeli war. But the process can also backfire on the mediator: both sides may grow angry should the effort fail; or one party may become embittered should the mediator's weight be seen to bear more heavily in favor of the other.

Mediation itself is a difficult enough task; it becomes even more difficult when a number of heads of state are engaged together, as was the case at the start of the Islamic Conference's effort.[28] To go along with Iran's territorial claims against Iraq's unilateral efforts to change them by force would seem to acquiesce in the Iranian religious agitation within Iraq and to imply approval of Shia religious agitation in neighboring countries. Yet, in any way to question Iranian religious agitation in Iraq risked alienating Iran and could even touch off religious turmoil within Pakistan itself. Zia managed to emerge from the mediation process relatively unscathed, having enhanced his standing among the Gulf states, even though the results of mediation were meager.

Seeking Help from China

From the time of Ayub's overtures to China, as we have seen, Beijing had provided a great deal of diplomatic assistance to Islamabad. In effect, China's presence balanced India's and obliged New Delhi to devote substantial efforts to developing its border road system and maintaining substantial forces along the northern and eastern frontiers. China had supplemented Pakistan's American equipment in the late 1960s and, as the American arms embargo persisted, it became an increasingly important arms supplier. By the late 1970s, Pakistan had received more than 1,000 Chinese T-59 tanks (constituting 75 percent of its tank force), and some 300 Chinese aircraft (perhaps 65 percent of its air force). Of the Chinese-supplied aircraft, 144 were MiG-19/F-6s which, together with French Mirage IIIs and Mirage Vs, formed the backbone of Pakistan's air force.[29] The Chinese constructed a tank-rebuild factory and improved a light-arms plant and a repair facility for the MiG-19/F-6s at Kamra near Taxila. They also undertook substantial roadbuilding efforts in the Sinkiang Karakoram area, opening up the remarkable Karakoram Highway over the Khunjerab Pass.

But, if Pakistan were to come into conflict with Soviet forces on the Afghan border, could it really depend on China? Would the latter risk engaging the Soviet Union in Sinkiang in order to divert Soviet resources from Afghanistan and the Pakistan frontier? Very likely not. In any such confrontation, China, being the weaker power, could probably play a cautious hand. Some observers have noted that both the Chinese and Russians usually make threatening noises on behalf of their respective South Asian clients only when the danger of involvement is manifestly behind. Moreover, Chinese policy has had the worrisome quality of veering sharply from one extreme to another; the breathtaking switch from Mao's cultural revolution to Deng Xiaoping's opening to the West could one day be reversed.

From China, therefore, Pakistan could expect quiet support, with a continuing flow of military resources commensurate with China's technological and productive capabilities. Since China's leadership did not need to win public support from an elected congress, they might be steadier than the United States in a crisis and would no doubt continue to stand by Pakistan at the U.N. and in other diplomatic arenas. By itself, however, China would not be likely to initiate the use of force against the Soviet Union, even in the face of possible Soviet intrusions into the North-West Frontier Province, Gilgit, or Hunza.

Seeking U.S. Assistance: Later Efforts

The results of the U.S. presidential election of November 1980 eased Zia's problems considerably. The newly elected Reagan administration was clearly less concerned than its predecessor about the character of Pakistan's domestic politics, and nuclear nonproliferation was considerably lower on the new administration's priorities than was the bolstering of Pakistan's military capability.

The F-16 deal and $3 billion aid package would make an excellent case study of how to negotiate with the United States from a position of weakness. Having played hard to get during the Carter administration, the Zia government was in a strong position vis-à-vis its successor. Moreover, the Reagan administration felt it was urgent to signal Moscow and others that, unlike its predecessor, it could make tough security decisions and get on with the business of supporting its friends. Early on, Pakistan announced its requirement for the most up-to-date aircraft with a usable life of twenty years. The cheaper, less versatile, and less advanced F-5G simply would not do: even though it might be more useful in the Afghan arena, it was not versatile enough to cover all possible contingencies.[30] Meanwhile, United States senatorial legislation regarding nonproliferation focused much of the congressional debate on the question of how to deal with Pakistan's efforts to develop a reprocessing facility rather than on the merits of the sale of the F-16s or on the substance of the aid package itself. In the end, the administration was authorized to sell the F-16s to Pakistan for cash; commercial credits were to be guaranteed for the $1.5 billion worth of other military equipment; and a $1.5 billion balance in economic assistance was also approved.

The implications of these arrangements for United States relations with India were part of the congressional debate, although hardly central to it. At the same time, it was clear that any serious attempt to defend Pakistan must involve the cooperation of India. Early in the course of discussions between the United States and Pakistan it became apparent to both parties that a return to the old and intimate alliance of the 1950s was out of the question. Neither the Americans nor the Pakistanis were willing to go that far. Pakistan's foreign minister, Agha Shahi, neatly epitomized the new relationship as "a handshake not an embrace."[31] It implied a readiness to cooperate on specific issues and to face together certain understood contingencies. It permitted the large, distant power to provide some support without disturbing the recipient's own balance of interests and alternative options. It carried few of the implications of unquestioning support over a range of unspecified contingencies that had so misled both participants in the 1950s.

Once these limits were understood, the worst fears of the Indian government were somewhat allayed. Previously, as we have seen, New Delhi had recoiled from the prospect of a renewed United States-Pakistani alliance reminiscent of the 1950s. When it became clear that such a scenario was most unlikely, the Indian government made no attempt to stand in the way of Pakistan receiving the aid package. Indeed, both the Reagan administration and the Gandhi government now recognized the wisdom of improving relations. In August 1982, Mrs. Gandhi visited Washington and gave a clear impression of wishing to diversify her options. The contentious issue of nuclear fuels was passed to the French. Moscow's sensitivity to this new flexibility was quickly demonstrated when Defense Minister Ustinov and thirty (!) generals rushed to New Delhi with fresh offers of defense collaboration and enhanced trade arrangements.[32] New Delhi picked up some of the Soviet offers, but Mrs. Gandhi appeared determined to maintain a more diversified policy.

Mending Fences with India: Later Efforts

It has proved no easier since 1980 than before to assess the trend in relations between India and Pakistan. As pointed out above, one view of geostrategic logic holds that both countries' positions on the subcontinent would be well served through closer collaboration in the face of the Soviet presence in Afghanistan. Yet, one observer notes, even after the invasion, "Pakistan remained aggravatingly preoccupied with the historic threat from the east to the detriment of common effort vis-à-vis the more real Soviet danger."[33] The same could be said about India's persistent worry about Pakistan's real intentions. To be sure, as the Soviet occupation continued, Pakistan and India appeared to move haltingly toward at least more regularized consultation. But the movement looked like an all-too-familiar minuet.

In the autumn of 1981, for example, Zia took the initiative and offered a "no war" pact to India, a virtual replica of an Indian proposal first offered in 1949, repeated numerous times thereafter, and regularly rejected by Pakistan as meaningless. Zia's offer could have been intended as an attempt to meet India more than halfway by initiating what had been an Indian proposal in the first place. But under the circumstances it was considered in New Delhi as a clever ploy to put Pakistan in a good light with the United States Congress, which was then gearing up to debate the Pakistan aid package. India countered with a proposal for a treaty of peace, friendship, and cooperation—a phrasing more in keeping with India's agreements with other states.

The two states then swapped texts in a search for language that would reflect the different emphases each desired—conveying expressions of reassurance and goodwill without implying specific commitments that might inhibit each party's freedom of action. When New Delhi expressed understandable anxiety about Pakistan's nuclear program, Zia countered with an offer to establish a nuclear free zone. It was a proposal once espoused by India in an effort to inhibit China, but it was certain to be rejected now, for it would require that India open its facilities to international inspection.

Periodically, impatient Pakistanis publicly brought up the unfinished business of Kashmir. The Indians have protested that the Simla Agreement redefined that issue as one to be dealt with bilaterally, and that any public airing of the issue runs counter to such solemn undertakings. Yet at a time when the Zia government was facing severe disorders in Sind, it could hardly have been seen as helpful in Islamabad for Mrs. Gandhi to be commenting publicly on India's preference for democratic governments in Pakistan.

Indeed it is as if the principals on both sides simply cannot refrain from touching each other's raw nerves, rather like siblings who have lived too long in cramped quarters. Whether the difficulties derive from the bitterness of years of intercommunal suspicion, from thirty-five years of conflict-ridden interstate relations, or from the imperative need of hard-pressed leaders to evoke public support by calling up reliable xenophobic emotions, it is hard to say.

Regardless of the substantive limitations of these various proposals, however, each required a quiet, inconspicuous follow-up. And out of it all has emerged at least a joint Indo-Pakistan Commission, designed to institutionalize regular consultations to facilitate trade, cultural, and press exchanges and pilgrimage travel. Thus, from rather grandiloquent proposals may come some concrete measures to ease the frustrations of individuals and groups whose politically innocent activities have been blocked for years.

Policy toward the Soviets in Afghanistan

Bearing in mind Pakistan's assessment of its international assets and constraints, and its dealings with the United States, the Gulf states, China, and India, let us now turn to the debate within Pakistan on how to deal with the Soviet presence. Regional and distant friends are important, and it is well to minimize antagonism of a large neighbor if possible. But the really difficult question has been what policy to follow toward the conflict in Afghanistan.

Views have differed.[34] Some have argued that to act like a front-line state can be risky. According to this view, the Russians are clearly there to stay; Pakistan should, therefore, return to the policies of the late 1960s and seek some kind of accommodation with Moscow. Not only would this course of action be likely to reduce the threat to Pakistan of the Soviet presence in Afghanistan, it might also strengthen Islamabad in its dealings with New Delhi, since Moscow might well downgrade its relationship with India in order to lure Pakistan. In other words, instead of seeking to balance the power of India and Russia with uncertain support from outsiders, perhaps it would be better to climb on the regional bandwagon. The Russians have offered to recognize the Durand Line and promised that the government in Kabul will do the same—a move that could exorcize the Pakhtunistan issue from Pakistan's internal politics. In addition the Russians suggest that such an accommodation could open the way to linking Pakistan into a larger South Asian economic network.

Critics reply that such a move would lock Pakistan irretrievably into a Soviet-dominated trade and security area, and, with Moscow's ally in

Delhi immediately to the east, Pakistan would truly be cornered. An alternative course of action called for more vigorous assistance to the Afghan freedom fighters. This school argued that only if the Russians were truly hard-pressed in Afghanistan would the costs of remaining ultimately outweigh the advantages. The Russians could put up indefinitely with the level of resistance they encountered during their first three years of occupation. Although it was true that Soviet forces controlled only the cities and the arteries between them while the rest of the country remained in the hands of the freedom fighters, their periodic raids into *mujahiddin* strongholds could bring heavy casualties to the population. Over a five-year period, young Afghans would either leave or die; the Russians could stay the course quite long enough in effect to win. Only if the resistance received outside material assistance, this line argued, would the cost to Moscow become steep enough to drive them out.

The latter alternative, of course, carried the risk of bringing Pakistan into direct confrontation with the Soviet Union, and past experience suggested that, should its own activities precipitate such a conflict, Pakistan might well have to bear the brunt alone. The United States would be very unlikely to take on the Russians so far from its own borders in order to rescue the Pakistanis from a crisis of their own making.

Having considered its various options, the government of Zia ul-Haq chose to pursue a course of limited liability. Pakistan's policy regarding the Soviet presence in Afghanistan has four major elements:

1. *Strong Public Condemnation.* As we have seen, Pakistan has managed to rally the overwhelming support of nonaligned as well as OECD members of the U.N. in its public condemnation of Soviet actions. Even more important, however, has been the virtually unanimous protest lodged by members of the Islamic Conference. Heretofore, the Soviet Union has been able to make much of American ties with Israel in its own bid for support among countries of the Muslim Middle East. Now almost the whole Muslim world—even including most of Moscow's more radical Arab friends—has spoken out against Moscow's invasion of a fellow Muslim country. Surely it must be disconcerting to the Soviet leadership to be publicly and universally reminded that its forces are on the wrong side of freedom fighters. More than incidentally, the condemnations have given heart to the *mujahiddin*. (Although successive meetings of the Islamic Conference have continued to condemn Soviet actions, there has been an increasing stress on the desirability of finding a "political solution.")

2. *Formal Refusal to be a Conduit.* Pakistan's openly antagonistic posture, however, has been moderated by its formal and explicit refusal to act as a conduit for military supplies to the *mujahiddin*.[35] No convoys

are to be seen transporting ammunition and military equipment to the frontier. The *mujahiddin,* say the Pakistanis, receive the bulk of their equipment from the Russian occupiers themselves, either by capture or thanks to the defection of Afghan troops. Pakistani tribesmen have always been known for their skill in manufacturing from scrap highly sophisticated copies of the more simple advanced weapons. No doubt some equipment filters in via the China-Karakoram Highway, and there are unconfirmed press reports that Egypt is supplying Soviet weapons, and the Saudis are paying the bill.[36] But the Pakistan government denies any responsibility for such activity, pointing out that it would be impossible to control its permeable border with Afghanistan. Pakistan's policy has been to deny that it is acting as a conduit for arms.

3. *Allowance for Afghan Political Activity in Pakistan.* A third element relates to the Afghans now in Pakistan. The government continues to receive refugees and care for them as best it can. It also welcomes representatives of the mujahiddin and has even allowed them to set up political offices in Peshawar. While it has tried to induce the various refugee groups (six, eight, twenty, or however many there may be) to collaborate, nevertheless the government confronts a genuine dilemma in this regard. For decades, the Pakhtun majority in Afghanistan has agitated among the 7 to 10 million Pushtu speakers in the North-West Frontier Province, calling for greater autonomy and even secession. The 2.8 million refugees now in Pakistan are mainly Pakhtuns; if they were to become consolidated into a strong political movement with an eye to effective concerted resistance to the Russian occupation, an unwanted byproduct could be renewed agitation within Pakistan itself. Since the refugee "leaders" safely lodged in Peshawar are not likely to carry much weight back home should the Russians be driven out, they might eventually want to become a real force within Pakistan. At the same time, should the movement become solidified and go all out against the Russian occupation, that might be the surest recipe for a direct Soviet attack against Pakistan; and some observers fear that India might seize that moment to incorporate Azad Kashmir. To refugee leaders, Pakistan's support seems half-hearted and at times even divisive. Yet they recognize that their political activities, however ineffectual, could not continue without Pakistan's consent, so they remain acquiescent.

4. *Willingness to Talk within Limits.* A fourth element of Pakistan policy became more prominent in 1982 and the spring of 1983—exploring through arm's-length negotiations a political settlement that might lead to the departure of Soviet troops from Afghanistan. In August 1981, Secretary Firyubin first visited Pakistan and proposed three-cornered talks among Teheran, Kabul, and Islamabad. The Pakistanis

rejected that idea, perhaps with encouragement from both Riyadh and Teheran. Later in 1981, Pakistan encouraged the U.N. to appoint a representative to explore the problem of the Soviet occupation of Afghanistan.[37] Moscow initially opposed the idea, but eventually acquiesced in February 1982 in view of the nearly universal support the initiative received.

Perez de Cuellar, the U.N. secretary general's special representative, took preliminary soundings and proposed talks among Afghanistan, Pakistan, and Iran, in order to stress the shared regional interest in a settlement of the Afghan struggle. Islamabad agreed to indirect talks, making clear that communication through the secretary general's good offices in no way implied recognition of the Soviet-implanted Karmal regime. Perez de Cuellar's successor, Diego Cordovez, made a number of visits to Kabul, Islamabad, and Teheran, usually stopping in Moscow at the end of each round on his way back to New York.

In June 1982, and again in April and June 1983, there were "third party" discussions in Geneva. Four principles were eventually agreed upon among the parties: (a) a withdrawal of Soviet troops; (b) an end to "outside interference" in Afghanistan's affairs; (c) a safe return of the refugees; and (d) international supervision and guarantees of the final settlement. Although it is considered "progress" to define such a formula as a basis for negotiations,[38] by the autumn of 1985 there was still a long way to go. Soviet positions had hardened, it seemed.

The government of Pakistan must maneuver within narrow margins. On the one hand, the Russians are in occupation of Kabul and most other cities and are not likely to leave unless a regime acceptable to them is to remain in place. Yet both Muslim fundamentalists and refugees in Pakistan are likely to turn against the Zia regime if it shows insufficient zeal in defending their interests, which involve both a Soviet withdrawal and a change of regime in Kabul. Furthermore, if there is no Soviet withdrawal, the refugees will probably remain in Pakistan as a source of political unrest. Although the bulk of refugees are in the North-West Frontier Province, in Baluchistan the refugee influx is fundamentally altering the ethnic balance.

On the other hand, a sharp increase in support for the freedom fighters, with an eye to speeding the departure of the Soviet troops by raising the cost of its occupation, would risk involving Pakistan in direct conflict with the Soviet Union, which could destroy the very integrity of Pakistan itself. Even if the results were not so dire, it could cause Pakistan once again to become unduly dependent upon the United States, a development that would carry its own serious liabilities.

Meanwhile, periodic talks go on, and as long as they continue, they

minimize the chances of military confrontation, holding out promise to
the different groups concerned that some acceptable solution may eventually be found. Even if the Russians do not withdraw, Pakistan will
have been seen to have done its best to induce them to go. The burden of
having refused to compromise will be on Moscow, not Islamabad.

Conclusions

In summary, the Zia government has thus far followed an adroit
and multifaceted policy. As a state on the Afghan frontier, Pakistan has
faced unavoidable risks, but it has minimized these risks by broadening
its international support and dealing with both India and the Soviet
Union with subtlety and minimum provocation. It has not lost its creden-
tials among the nonaligned, even as it has received substantial commitments of economic assistance and military equipment from the United
States. By calling on its Saudi and Gulf-state Islamic connections, it has
been able to obtain these armaments on terms that minimize both the
reality and the appearance of American leverage on its freedom of action.

At the same time, it has taken steps to allay Indian fears. By maintaining a certain distance from Washington, Pakistan has made clear that it
is not seeking to involve the United States in regional affairs—as it did in
the 1950s. By the autumn of 1983, the quiet dialogue established by India
and Pakistan continued, and both parties were exploring ways of dealing
with specific areas of difference and distrust. To be sure, there were moments of familiar back-sliding. Delhi's difficulties in the Punjab and the
1984 election campaign were both occasions to implicate Pakistan in
New Delhi's difficulties, for example. On balance, however, it appeared
that in the face of the Soviet presence at the door of the subcontinent,
leaders in both Pakistan and India are themselves beginning to change
their sense of priorities. Age-old ethnic hostilities and thirty-five years of
independent existence and mutual conflict cannot be overcome so easily.
Yet for the first time in many years, India and Pakistan are dealing somewhat more constructively with their ancient fears and suspicions.

All in all, Pakistan's foreign policy achievements have been quite impressive. It has vigorously and effectively marshaled world opinion
against the Soviet presence; it has avoided responsibility for the military
supplies that slip undetected across its permeable frontier to the *mujahiddin;* it has both encouraged and restrained political activities on the part
of refugee "representatives" in Peshawar; and it has participated in
third-party consultations under U.N. auspices, to see if some way can be
found to induce the Russians to leave. In short, Pakistan's leaders have
made the best of a very complicated—and unenviable—situation.

NOTES

This chapter is a revision of a paper prepared for a Southern Asian Institute seminar on "South Asia after Afghanistan." Thanks go to the Ford Foundation for its past support of the Institute and the Pakistan Center, and its more recent grant for work on security policies of South Asia. Zalamay Khalilzad, Ainslie Embree, and Philip Oldenburg have read and criticized an early draft, and J. C. Hurewitz and Richard Bulliett have assisted in other ways. They are in no way responsible for the end result. A slightly different version has appeared in *Pacific Affairs* 57, no. 2 (Summer, 1984): 284-303.

1. Thomas P. Thornton, "Between the Stools?: U.S. Policy towards Pakistan during the Carter Administration," *Asian Survey* 22, no. 10 (October 1982): 969.
2. Jimmy Carter, *Keeping the Faith* (New York: Bantam, 1982), pp. 471-72, 483.
3. Robert Jervis, *Perception and Misperception in International Politics* (Princeton, N. J.: Princeton University Press, 1976), chap. 1.
4. Reported by Girailal Jain at a seminar at Columbia University, November 1982.
5. The writer interviewed policymakers and publicists in Islamabad and New Delhi during the summer of 1982.
6. Zubeida Mustafa, "Pakistan and the Middle East," *Pacific Community* 7, no. 4 (July 1976): 608-20; Khalida Qureshi, "Pakistan and the Middle East," *Pakistan Horizon* 19, no. 2 (1966); M. G. Weinbaum and Gautam Sen, "Pakistan Enters the Middle East," *Orbis,* 22, no. 3 (Fall 1978): 595-612; Shirin Tahir-Kheli, "Iran and Pakistan: Cooperation in an Area of Conflict," *Asian Survey* 17, no. 5 (May 1977): 474-90; Zalmay Khalilzad, "The Superpowers and the Northern Tier," *International Security* 4, no. 3 (Winter 1979-80): 6-30.
7. For details of the China connection, see Y. Vertzberger, *The Enduring Entente: Sino-Pakistan Relations, 1960-1980 The Washington Papers, no. 95* (New York: Praeger, 1983).
8. Lawrence Ziring, ed., *The Subcontinent in World Politics* (New York: Praeger, 1982), p. 43.
9. A.T. Chaudhri, "Handshake across the Durand Line," *Pakistan Times,* October 14, 1977; see also Pervaiz Iqbal Cheema, "The Afghanistan Crisis and Pakistan's Security Dilemma," *Asian Survey,* 23, no. 3 (March 1983): 227-43, esp. p. 227.
10. Ibid.
11. Interviews in Washington (Spring 1980), and in New York, Islamabad, and Lahore (Summer 1982).
12. For an analysis emphasizing ethnic divisions within Pakistan, see Selig Harrison, *In Afghanistan's Shadow: Baluch Nationalism and Soviet Temptations* (New York: Carnegie Endowment for International Peace, 1981).

13. For meetings, see *Keesing's Contemporary Archive,* May 9, 1980, p. 30241; August 1, 1980, p. 30385.

14. See G. M. Khar's argument to this effect in *The Economist,* October 31, 1981. Although he was no longer part of the ruling group, his views may well have found sympathy among some thoughtful members of the Pakistan establishment.

15. Interviews in Islamabad, Lahore, and New York, 1980 and 1982.

16. Interviews in New Delhi.

17. W. Howard Wriggins, "The Balancing Process in Pakistan's Foreign Policy," in Lawrence Ziring et al., eds., *Pakistan: The Long View* (Durham, N. C.: Duke University Press, 1977), pp. 301-40.

18. Thornton, "Between the Stools," p. 969.

19. Ibid., passim.

20. Ibid., p. 969.

21. Interviews in New York and Lahore, 1982.

22. Thornton, "Between the Stools," pp. 970-71; author's interviews in Washington (Spring 1980) and Islamabad (1982).

23. See n. 6.

24. See, for instance, Shirin Tahir-Kheli and W. O. Staudenmaier. "The Saudi-Pakistan Military Relationship: Implications for U.S. Policy," *Orbis* 26, no. 1 (Spring 1982): 115-71.

25. Interviews in Riyadh, Islamabad, and Washington (1982).

26. For background, see William Quandt, *Saudi Arabia in the 1980s: Foreign Policy, Security, and Oil* (Washington, D.C.: Brookings, 1981); and Adeed Dawisha, "Internal Values and External Threats: The Making of Saudi Foreign Policy," *Orbis* 23, no. 1 (Spring 1979): 129-43.

27. For background, see Anwar Hussain Syed, *Pakistan: Islam, Politics and National Solidarity* (New York: Praeger, 1982).

28. Interviews in Riyadh and Jeddah (1982).

29. For details, see Vertzberger, *Enduring Entente.*

30. For an analysis, see Rodney Jones, "Mending Relations with Pakistan," in *Washington Quarterly* 4, no. 2 (spring 1981): 17-29.

31. At a Lahore seminar, June 30, 1981.

32. Thomas Perry Thornton, "The U.S.S.R. and Asia in 1982: The End of the Brezhnev Era," *Asian Survey* 23, no. 1 (January 1983): 11-25, esp. p. 20.

33. Thornton, "Between the Stools," p. 971.

34. G. M. Khar considers these options; see n. 14.

35. Pervaiz Iqbal Cheema, "Afghanistan Crisis," p. 236.

36. For a rare published reference, see Leslie Gelb, *The New York Times,* May 4, 1983.

37. [Ed.: For a careful survey of the U.N.-sponsored talks, see Richard P. Cronin, "United Nations Sponsored Negotiations on Afghanistan: An Annotated Chronology and Analysis," mimeo, Library of Congress Foreign Affairs and National Defense Division, 1985.]

38. W. I. Zartman and M. R. Berman, *The Practical Negotiator* (New Haven, Conn.: Yale University Press, 1982), especially chap. 4.

5

Pakistan's Security Futures

Lt. General Eric A. Vas (retd)

History is the raw material of strategy, and human beings act in the light of the collective memory of communities and societies. Any remembered event may influence current action. If the historical background of the present is not kept in view, the latter is likely to become an insoluble puzzle. We therefore begin our examination of Pakistan's security futures with a survey of the past.

The Past

The subcontinent has always absorbed invaders, new religions, ideas, and races. Islamic, Jewish, and Christian communities were well established in India even before the first European set foot in South Asia.[1] When we look back on the history of the Indian subcontinent, we are struck by the fact that the country was so easily overrun by small groups of foreigners. What was the cause? A civilization is not overwhelmed from without until it has destroyed itself within. For 400 years (A.D. 600-1000) India invited conquest.[2] Those centuries saw the triumphant eastward progress of Islam and the eventual establishment of Muslim states in various parts of India. Muslims created a challenge for Buddhists and Hindus no less in their language, eating habits, and clothing than in regard to caste and religion. They created an open society to which everyone could gain admittance simply by accepting the faith; having done that, a person was accepted as an equal. Islam's simple, uncompromising monotheism freed it from theological complications. An insistence upon brotherhood and equality before God, whatever their race, color, or status, made Islam a power in human affairs.

Hindu regimes, which base their polity on orthodoxy and the caste system, contain within themselves the seeds of their own destruction. Loyalty cannot grow where large sections of the public resent the injustice and tyranny of society and suffer the bitterness of public humiliation. Many sought revenge by going over to the enemies of their king and faith. The new power that was Islam was in many ways a historical pruning knife, and it cut off the weeds of Indo-Aryan apathy.

But all was not well with Muslim polity. The power of the military caste had made the mere recital of the Muslim faith a social and political mantra as potent as any Hindu mantra. Nominally based upon the principle of universal brotherhood, the social program of Islam in some respects became more tyrannical than the caste system. In seeking to gain converts by compulsion and by material incentive rather than by appealing to the conscience or intellect, Islam exalted the rights of the individual above the rights of the community. Early Islam produced many Indian Muslims of commanding ability and fine character but never a great dynasty. Thus, in due course of time, Muslim India became as divided against itself as Hindu India had been. For the next 200 years, India again "invited conquest," until the arrival of the Moghuls who ruled from the sixteenth century up to the nineteenth century.

Akbar, the greatest of all the Moghuls, was a profound student of history. He not only understood why the Buddhist and Hindu regimes had failed but also saw the significance of Indo-Aryan secularism. Yet, he was no blind traditionalist. He was a true son of the Renaissance who claimed the right of interpreting the past and Islamic scripture in the light of the knowledge of the time. His religious values reflected not only ancient Indo-Aryan secular concepts but also the principles of the most enlightened Indian Muslims of the sixteenth century, and made a deep and lasting impression upon the masses. Because of the support of the people, so wisely won by Akbar, India enjoyed a long unbroken peace of almost 200 years. It was not until his iconoclastic, intolerant successors crushed the free Indo-Aryan institutions that the splendid fabric of Akbar's statesmanship began to fall in ruins.

The decay of the Moghul Empire fostered a non-Muslim political revival. These new forces attempted to remove the decaying branches of the Moghul tree which had been planted in India. Many look upon the political struggle between the Moghuls, Marathas, Rajputs, and Sikhs as purely a religious confrontation, which it was not.[3] The falsification and distortion of history is an ancient art which has poisoned the minds of many generations of Indians and Pakistanis. The writing of history is a matter of conscience. All orthodoxy, whether Muslim, Hindu, Christian, Buddhist, or Sikh is intolerant and contrary to the true principles of secular Indo-Aryan polity which are universal toleration, freedom, equal justice, and protection—the only successful polity for any state with a composite population. But just as the latter Moghuls pandered to the intolerant political principles of Muslim orthodoxy and crushed Akbar's institutions, so also Shivaji's Brahmin successors, and Ranjit Singh's

successors of the Khalsa, revived the narrow political principles of orthodoxy and were incapable of preserving their heritage.

The seventeenth century saw Maratha, Jat, Rajput, Sikh, and Muslim
powers struggling for domination in South Asia while the Moghul king
was monarch in name only. For the next one hundred years India once
again invited conquest. Present at that time were the Portuguese, Dutch,
British, and French, who sold arms and the services of their trained mili-
tia to the highest warring bidder. Eventually, the British emerged as the
winning European power and began to cut away the weeds of Indian political and administrative inefficiency. The Marathas and the Sikhs were
the last two Indian peoples to go down fighting before British arms.

The British presence had frozen any further symbiosis of Hindu and
Muslim culture, which had been so ably attempted by Akbar; it stopped
the natural evolution of political power in South Asia and fostered religious communalism. But British rule had a number of credits in its imperial ledger, not the least being the introduction of the English language.
The period between the two world wars saw the rise of many national
leaders and the mounting of communal tensions. At the time of Partition, Britain made it clear to the Indian princes that it was up to them to
work out their relationship with free India and Pakistan. The princes began signing instruments of accession. A systematic drive to integrate all
the states was undertaken in India. The state of Jammu and Kashmir ad-
joined both India and Pakistan. Because Kashmir was predominantly
Muslim and India had no direct road link to it, Pakistan was tempted to
organize a tribal force to overrun the state, hoping that there would be a
popular uprising and the Maharaja would be forced to opt for Pakistan.
In fact the reverse took place; Sheikh Abdullah (a staunch secular leader)
became Chief Minister, and the Maharaja opted for India. Direct conflict between the armed forces of India and Pakistan was averted by a
U.N.-supervised ceasefire which saw the partition of the state along the
cease-fire line. These events left residual resentments in Pakistan.

The debacle of the Sino-Indian Conflict of 1962 and Nehru's death in
1964 sobered India, but may have tempted Pakistan to test its strength
once more against what appeared to be an effete society. In 1965 there
were two attacks by Pakistan on India: the first in the Rann of Kutch and
the second in Jammu and Kashmir. These attacks were followed by a major war and another cease-fire.

In 1968, Pakistan held its first conspiracy trial against the East Pakistani leader Sheikh Mujibur Rehman. From then onward, events in East
Pakistan festered. In 1971 they escalated to a full-fledged people's war
fought between Bengali freedom fighters and the Pakistan army, which
culminated in the Indo-Pakistan War of 1971, the surrender and repatri-
ation of 92,000 Pakistanis, and the creation of Bangladesh. Although

Mrs. Gandhi achieved a sweeping electoral victory after the conclusion
of the Indo-Pakistan War of 1971, this gave no stability to India. Ironically, Mrs. Gandhi declared a state of emergency on June 26, 1975,
while Pakistan saw the rise of Z. A. Bhutto, a new phenomenon in the
politics of that country where, for the first time, a leader made the visible
support of the people a source of legitimate power.

All politics is a struggle for power. The creation of Pakistan in 1947
was a reminder of the inability of Hindu and Muslim to accommodate to
each other; the creation of Bangladesh in 1971 was an epitaph on the inability of East and West Pakistanis to share power equally and freely.
Thus we ought not to be surprised that separative tendencies continue in
the diverse constituent nations of South Asia.

The Present

A national security policy implies foreign and internal policies that
embrace diplomatic, economic, social, psychological, and military plans.
A study of the factors that contribute to a national security policy will indicate the range of Pakistan's problems.

Psychological Factors

At the time of its creation there were many within Pakistan itself
who believed that provincial autonomy was one thing, but partition was
absurd. In fact, the number of doubters might have increased after the
creation of Bangladesh. Millions of Muslims are happy to live in India,
where they attain positions of responsibility in every walk of life.[4] This
fact raises questions about the very basic concept of Pakistan as a homeland for the "persecuted" Indian Muslim and also raises secret moments
of self-doubt: was Pakistan a political error? Would the Muslims have
been better off within an undivided independent India, where they would
have formed a powerful voting block?

Ethnic and Linguistic Factors

Pakistani society is complex and diverse, with four major ethno-
linguistic regions. Pakistan's national language, Urdu, is not indigenous
to any of these regions: its cultural soul is in the Delhi-Lucknow region
of India. Its population contains the world's largest tribal society, and
Pakistan's international boundaries were drawn by colonial powers without consideration of geography or race, so that all of its population belongs to linguistic or ethnic groups that have cultural affiliations with
neighbors. This situation results in unstable borders, demands for re-

alignments, safe sanctuaries for dissidents, and difficulties of administration.

The Geopolitical Factor

Although geographically located in South Asia, Pakistan belongs
to West Asia by religion and to South Asia by culture and tradition. To
the west lie Afghanistan and Iran, both Muslim countries with large
ethnic groups allied to Pakistan. Afghanistan has always been the northwestern gateway to the plains of India. The British had twice tried unsuccessfully to occupy Afghanistan to counter Russian advances into Central Asia. Some Pakistanis believe that they have inherited the British
responsibility of protecting the Indian subcontinent from Soviet advances.

Many reasons have been put forward for the Soviet Union's decision
to intervene in Afghanistan in 1980. The Russians knew that Iran would
be hostile irrespective of whether it was under the Shah or an Ayatollah
and were unhappy to have Iran's U.S.-trained forces or resurgent Islam
on their southern flank. Perhaps some Soviet hawks still have an expansionist urge to by-pass Iran and drive southward to the Indian Ocean.
Once an invader is through the Bolan Pass, there are no natural barriers
until one reaches the sea. Thus, one must ensure that Baluchistan is
under control. But after World War II, the Soviet Union was fully committed to building up its ICBM and IRBM nuclear forces to counter the
United States, NATO, and the Chinese and to creating a deep-water
navy, all of which had to be done from scratch. Because of those strategic requirements, the Kremlin could not even afford to occupy Afghanistan, let alone undertake a southern drive through Baluchistan to the
sea. The Soviets, therefore, planned to establish a Marxist puppet state
and to rule Afghanistan by proxy.

Two decades of steady diplomatic effort brought success and saw the
establishment of a pro-Soviet regime. By 1978, the Kremlin controlled
Kabul from Moscow. Then the Soviet scheme began to fall apart. The
April 1978 coup which brought the People's Democratic Party (PDP) to
power came as a surprise to the USSR, which accepted the news with
mixed feelings. A pro-Communist revolutionary regime had little mass
support. Moscow anticipated instability within Afghanistan itself. At
that time, Iran was being swept by a revolutionary fervor and Pakistan
was controlled by a new military dictatorship, which added to the instability of the region and Soviet fears. The situation was aggravated by the
inefficiency of the PDP regime, which introduced radical reforms without adequate preparation and with little regard to the psychological and

social consequences. Opposition turned into a major anti-regime insurgency. Added to this was instability caused by in-house fighting among rival factions of the isolated and unpopular PDP.

Soviet Intervention in Afghanistan

By the middle of 1979 the Russians were looking for ways to retrieve the situation by political means. Their initial plan was to eliminate Hafizullah Amin, blame the excesses on him, abandon some unpopular socioeconomic measures, and establish a broad-based PDP-led government under Nur Mohamed Taraki. Amin got wind of the plan, assassinated Taraki, and began to take steps to protect himself even if it meant switching alliance and expelling the Russians.

The Soviet decision to intervene must also be viewed in the context of its international position, with particular reference to détente. The Afghanistan crisis arose at a time when the Soviet Union believed that the United States was using détente for mounting multiple pressures on Moscow to make concessions at home and abroad. A large and influential body of opinion in the Soviet Union felt humiliated that their leaders had been forced to yield in purely internal matters, such as Jewish emigration and the treatment of dissidents. These concessions were seen as an unnecessary display of weakness in pursuit of détente.[5] Another connected factor is the intensive Sinification of Sinkiang,[6] which had upset the local Kazakh, Uighur, and Kirghiz, some 60,000 of whom had crossed the border into the USSR to join their compatriots on the other side. Further, elements hostile to the new regime in Afghanistan found sympathetic support in Pakistan, where tribal relationships have flourished on either side of the Durand Line from its very inception. Moscow had to take into consideration the nature of the support being given to the guerrillas operating against Kabul from areas of Pakistan.

Thus the Russian decision to intervene was a deliberate defensive measure which, under different circumstances, may have been avoided. The Soviet dilemma was that it could not disown the coup without abandoning Afghanistan, while to continue to support Amin inevitably led to being accused of taking up a partisan attitude not only against the opposition but also against the moderates within the regime. The decision to intervene was probably clinched when the Soviets came to the conclusion that President Carter was about to launch a U.S.-inspired military coup in Iran, and the Kremlin cold-bloodedly argued that American intervention in Iran would provide a perfect cover for Soviet intervention in Afghanistan because international reactions would be directed against the Americans as much as the Russians. Whatever the reason, the entry of the Soviet army into Afghanistan enabled Pakistan to gain membership in western strategic plans and served as the justification for massive arms transfers from the United States

Religious and Cultural Factors

The Marxist assault on Islam is new, but the the mullah's exploitation of the Muslim world started soon after the first century of Islam. The list of Imams, scholars, sufis, and others who met the challenges of their time, suffered for their courage, and have been imprisoned, whipped, poisoned, tortured, and executed by the mullah, is long and comprehensive. But such persecution was only possible as long as it could be supported by the establishment. From the nineteenth century until today attempts have been made to reconcile Islamic tradition with modernism, but Islam continues to be controlled by a theocracy that has never been challenged successfully by any break-away reformism. In Islam, theocratic control has been more comprehensive than in Christianity because of historical factors.[7] Nevertheless, with the growth of secular ideologies in the twentieth century, the mullah began to lose his predominant position. The change was most apparent in West Asia, where three main responses to the challenge of modernization can be discerned. Kemal Ataturk's secularism was confined to Turkey, but Nasser's Arabism was intensely national and at one time seemed destined to unite the Arabs. The stunning defeat of Egypt by Israel in its Six Day War (1967) saw the decline of Arabism and the rise of two other streams: one secular and leftist, the other a revived rightist commitment of Islam.

The Islamic path leads Pakistan to look to its Muslim neighbors. But attempts to seek Islamic solidarity with the west (Iran and Afghanistan, the Gulf, and Turkey) have been disappointing. To the east, Pakistan avoids looking too closely at Indian Muslims because of mixed feelings: it raises dangerous doubts of the need for creating Pakistan itself; moreover, Pakistanis would like to believe that the Muslims of India are oppressed and in search of liberation. Further east lie Bangladesh, Malaysia, and Indonesia—all with their own brands of nationalism and individual cultures that do not suit an orthodox Islamic outlook.

Economic and Social Factors

Pakistan's economic history can be divided into four phases. From 1948 to 1958, the economic record was miserable. Pakistan became a foodgrain importer in 1958. In the Ayub decade of 1958-68, economic management improved. The main achievement of the Ayub regime was also a massive restructuring of society; he reduced the power of the landed aristocracy, diluted the influence of the Karachi merchant-industrialist, and curtailed the power of the civil bureaucracy. He encouraged the rise of the middle-class landowner, the urban middle class, and the intelligentsia in the Punjab and the NWFP, and he downgraded the importance of industrial labor and trade unions.[8] By 1968, however, disenchantment had set in. The same planners who were responsible for formulating and implementing President Ayub's policies of growth without controls now began to bemoan the concentration of power that had resulted from these policies. Twenty-two families controlled 66 percent of the industrial assets, 80 percent of the banks, and 70 percent of the insurance companies.[9]

The Yahya period (1969-71) was an interregnum of no economic consequence. Between 1970 and 1974, Bhutto's government nationalized all basic industries, public utilities, and financial institutions; it also executed a comprehensive labor reform package that entailed large increases in monetary and nonmonetary benefits for industrial labor. These populist measures were a disaster, as business and capital fled from Pakistan to Africa and West Asia.

In 1974, Bhutto made overtures to the large landlords who had hitherto not been part of the Pakistan People's Party (PPP) base. He also launched a series of grandiose schemes which included a dozen nuclear reactors and a reprocessing plant.

The first five years of President Zia's rule have seen sustained economic growth and consolidation. In this, the president has been aided by unusually favorable weather and higher remittances from West Asia.[10] In industry, President Zia denationalized small- and medium-sized agroindustries and small engineering enterprises. In February 1980, Zia appointed Karl Schiller, an uncompromising market-economy adherent and Bonn's former economic affairs minister, as his economic adviser. President Zia's Islamization program may run into problems. Interest-free lending, instituted for small farmers in 1979, could develop into an extensive system of subsidized credit, something that Schiller (and the IMF) have inveighed against. Zakat[11] hurts the middle class with fixed incomes and appears to have adversely affected bank deposits. Ushr[12] has a side effect that could hamper expansion in agriculture. In 1983, there was a 40 percent decrease in cotton production. Winter rains were poor, and the production of rice and wheat also fell. Larger imports of vegetable oil and pulses were necessary, and Pakistan's foreign exchange situation was gravely weakened by mid-1985.

The Role of the Military

During the last thirty-five years, Pakistan has faced two military coups d'état, two quasi-military coups, and three attempted military coups. The military has been deeply involved in Pakistan politics almost since the creation of the state. Indeed, some soldiers argue that the army

preceded the state of Pakistan and hence has the right to engage in ortho-
political surgery.[13]   General Yahya Khan was president when East Pakistan broke away in 1971. His military associates withdrew their support,
and he was forced to invite Bhutto to take over the reins of government.
A new constitution was framed in 1973, and Bhutto seemed well set until
his political opponents agitated against his overwhelming electoral victory. He was then forced to call out the army to deal with a difficult law-
and-order situation. Since the Pakistan army had been humbled in Bangladesh, it was assumed that the officer corps would not be able to exploit
the situation. But General Zia ul-Haq dismissed the government, proclaimed martial law, appointed himself as Chief Martial Law Administrator, and promised early elections. Bhutto was arraigned on a murder
charge and then executed, through the due process of law.

The military is perceived as politically incompetent by a wide cross-
section of the public, including elements of the officer corps which oppose prolonged military involvement in civil administration and internal
security duties; this undermines the armed forces' professional compe-
tence and lays them open to temptations that sap morale. But General
Zia ul-Haq has found it difficult to return his army to its barracks because of his concern about his and his associates' future. The 1973 Constitution, which stands suspended but not abrogated, provides severe
penalties for usurping power, which is what Zia and his supporters did
when they staged a coup against Bhutto in 1977. Second, Bhutto's fate
made politicians reluctant to come forward to share power with a dis-
credited junta. The military did contemplate institutionalizing its role in
politics by creating an entirely new Islamic system of political life, which
implied drastic constitutional changes and the uprooting or intimidation
of all independent centers of power, including the press, the judiciary,
student unions, and Pakistan's already enfeebled intellectual class.

In November 1980, there was an attempted coup designed to overthrow the President, but it failed. Meanwhile, a majority of the banned
political parties joined together to form the Movement for the Restoration of Democracy (MRD), which proclaimed as its aim the restoration
of the 1973 Constitution, a revival of politics, and free elections. In January 1982, General Zia nominated a Majlis-e-Shoora (Federal Advisory
Council), claiming that this "had already started the democratic
process." He added that his cabinet was considering the question of
channelizing political activity that had been banned since 1979.

Over the years, the MRD gradually gained in popularity. To offset
this, in early 1983 General Zia promised some form of free elections in
1985. [Editorial note: President Zia conducted a referendum on his own
position and on the Islamization process in January 1985, and Pakistan
successfully held national elections in February 1985. Although there was

a partial boycott of these elections by Zia's opponents, there was a substantial turnout, some cabinet members were defeated, and Pakistan has moved closer to full democracy. Zia has announced that he will retire from the army while remaining president, and the necessary legislation for the withdrawal of the military from politics by the end of 1985 was unanimously passed by the Majlis on October 16, 1985. Pakistan's troubles are not over, however, as Zia and his prime minister, Mohammed Khan Junejo, will test the limits of their power under the new constitutional arrangement, as will the press, intellectuals, and opposition politicians.]

A Threat Analysis

From its very creation, Pakistan has faced dangers and stress. To the east it faces India: vastly superior in industrial resources with a much larger human base. To the west lies Afghanistan, which has never been friendly and is now occupied by the USSR. At home there is dissension and uncertainty about a number of basic vital issues that affect national stability. Meanwhile, the army is heavily committed in the nation's political and administrative life and is involved in internal security duties, which must weaken the armed forces and their preparation for the main role of defending the borders against external threats. These factors must be considered in detail.

Nationalism versus Islam

Thirty-seven years after independence, the Pakistanis are still debating the basis and character of their nationhood. Is Pakistan a Muslim nation, a Muslim majority nation, or a conglomerate of four nationalisms? Some argue that there is no such thing as a Pakistani ideology. The concept of a Muslim nation is a non-issue; Islam is a universal faith, and all its main institutions are multinational ones which cannot be confined within narrow national and geographic limits. Any attempt to do so would undermine the spirit of Islam. The concept of a Muslim nation by implication denies the existence of a Pakistani nation consisting of four nationalities because "any attempt to counterpose nations and nationalism against Muslim brotherhood is tantamount to weakening the very foundation of Muslim brotherhood."[14] Describing Pakistan as a Muslim Nation is a

> negation of the Muslim Ummat as envisaged in the Holy Quran. . . . A nation must exist within certain territorial boundaries. If it is a Pakistani Nation, then it has its boundaries. But if it is a Muslim nation then it becomes a transcendental one. In other words, any Muslims from any corner of the world can claim equal rights with us as part of this Muslim nation. Whereas

we are not even prepared to admit the Bihari Muslim of Bangladesh who claims to be Pakistani. . . . In fact, the emergence of Bangladesh is a consequence of the "Muslim" nation concept in the garb of which political and economic rights were denied to the people of East Bengal and attempts were made to destroy their historical identity."

Those who support Pakistan's ideological concepts argue that

not Islamic ideology so much as Islam itself is the lynch-pin of the State of Pakistan, and without a total commitment to Islam it will not be able to play the historical role for which it has been called into being—once the ideal identification of nation-state has been accepted, the state in its own defense tends to act as though it were a single and united nation from a cultural point of view, and if, in fact, it is not this, it must endeavor to make the facts correspond to the ideal regardless of the rights or liberty of those among its citizens who do not belong to the majority nation.[16]

While the debate continues, Islam functions at three levels within Pakistan. First, there is administrative Islam of the government; this comprises the Ministry of Religious Affairs plus a host of bureaucratic and semi-official ecclesiastical organizations. At the second level there is orthodox Islam of the ulemas (theologians) and traditionalists, which includes groups such as the Muslim League. At the third level there is militant and reformist Islam of devout laymen and fundamentalists, most of whom are young; this group includes the Jamat-i-Islami.[17] In theory, the militant and orthodox have a joint aim of establishing an Islamic society leading to an Islamic state; in practice the orthodox often collude with the government to suppress the militants.

Lacking the confidence to evolve a democratic civil-military balance, one faction of the military is tempted to rebuild Pakistan on Islamic lines. General Zia has begun implementing some fundamental Islamic reform but the majority pursue this course with little enthusiasm. In the eyes of the reformist and militants, the autocratic nature of Zia's power deprives him of Islamic legitimacy. It is fundamental to the theory of Islamic polity that there should be consent, consultation, and consensus. Hereditary monarchy and autocracy, civil or military, are both anathema to Islamic purists, even though throughout Islam's history these have been the usual forms of government. Unable or unwilling to come to terms with the basic demands of militant Islam, Pakistan has to resort both to repressing and to outbidding this element. After the seizure of the Grand Mosque in Mecca in 1979, Pakistan has come to the conclusion that the annual Haj pilgrimage could provide a background for dangerous radical ideas. Pakistan has made it difficult for people to go on a Haj by pleading a shortage of foreign currency.[18]

In Pakistan, the text or guidelines of the sermons in a mosque for the Friday service and on all important religious occasions are under official scrutiny and control. The most obvious way that bureaucratic Islam tries to outbid militant Islam is by building even more mosques, quite often financed by Saudi Arabia or Libya.[19] Another hallmark of official Islam is the concentration of Islam's outward manifestations: the projection of Islam on radio and TV, the onslaught on drinks, drugs, and pop groups, the advocacy of long dresses for girls and their separation from boys in schools. Typical, too, is the support given to missionary work (dawan). Another activity is the collection of religious taxes and titles: zakat and ushr.[20]

The Afghanistan Factor

Pakistan has allowed some three million Afghan refugees to enter their country. Their return to Afghanistan is an important issue for Pakistan, yet it is not possible without a Soviet withdrawal and political change. Pakistan has three choices: First, it could go along with the United States in wanting "to bleed the Russians white." But the Pakistanis know that the strength of the Soviet position is that the West has no leverage to influence internal developments in Afghanistan; the modernization process in that country is irreversible. Second, Pakistan could refuse to link up the Afghan issue with the wider U.S.-Soviet cold war by adhering to nonalignment rather than making Pakistan a part of any strategic consensus directed against the Soviet Union and could negotiate a withdrawal with Kabul and Moscow. Third, Pakistan could sit on the fence and get maximum aid from the United States, taking care to avoid the charge of providing military aid to the guerrillas. General Zia has opted for this last, dangerous, course.

Merely by continuing to provide sanctuary and tacit support to the guerrillas, Pakistan can be an obstacle to the Soviet pacification strategy. The Russians believe that if General Zia wants to, he can put an end to rebel bases in Pakistan. Nevertheless, the Soviets will not be provoked into attacking Pakistan. Further, sitting on the fence does not resolve the refugee problem which is causing considerable disquiet in Pakistan. The permanent presence of three million Afghans imposes a severe economic, ecological, and social burden which could endanger Pakistan's internal security and stability. Of these refugees, 100,000 are well armed and committed to fundamentalism, and they are getting increasingly involved in Pakistan's internal politics.

It would be myopic to ignore the fallout of the Afghanistan problem on Baluch nationalism. The Baluch constitute only 4 percent of the population of Pakistan, but the area of Baluchistan accounts for 42 percent of the country.[21] Even in 1975, Bhutto had charged the Soviets with fomenting Baluch separatism. He also denounced the Baluch nationalists as feudalists and set out to expropriate landowners and spread the administration into the interior. Today, the problem remains acute. There is a pro-Moscow group among the Baluch nationalists, and a section of Baluch leadership has reacted favorably to Soviet action in Afghanistan.

The Chinese Factor

Although Pakistan has no legitimate border with China, the occupied territory of Gilgit provides an entry into Sinkiang via the Mintaka and Khunjerab passes. The roads that have been built over these passes are not commercial but serve a military purpose. China's Sinkiang province has always had a long record of revolt and has never been fully integrated with the rest of China. The Muslim population of Sinkiang has closer ethnic and cultural ties with Muslims across the border in the Soviet Union. The spectacular development of Tashkent and the concentration of Soviet troops along Sinkiang's western border must exert an influence on Chinese Uighurs, Kazakh, and Kirghiz. Pakistani opposition to the Soviet Union's presence in Afghanistan encourages a Chinese belief that the roads connecting occupied Kashmir with Sinkiang will exert a favorable psychological influence on the sentiments of the Muslim population in the region.

Although the prospect of Pakistan taking on the Soviet Union militarily is improbable, the Chinese, like the Americans, want to improve the pressure points against the Soviet Union wherever possible. Thus, Pakistan, no matter how remote a pressure, serves a purpose, and the roads between China and Pakistani-occupied Kashmir not only reinforce their control over their respective areas but also act as a check on Soviet expansion in Central Asia. It is also possible to visualize circumstances when the United States would prefer to use these roads rather than the very long and vulnerable trans-China route via the north, to send vital stores to Sinkiang in an emergency. From that point of view, the roads are vital to China. The roads and Pakistani friendship with China also work against India and its ties with the USSR.

Pakistan's Military Role in West Asia

The concept of a Rapid Deployment Force (RDF) organized and equipped to move swiftly to any potential trouble spot in the world in order to back U.S. policy with military power has been debated since 1958 but was eventually rejected by the Johnson administration. Before 1979, the United States had cut off all economic and military aid to Pakistan because of their attempts to manufacture a nuclear bomb. When the

USSR entered Afghanistan, Pakistan assumed a key position in United States global strategy and became a front-line state under an overall United States strategy to contain Soviet expansion into West Asia.

In 1980 and 1981, the U.S. Army ran several military exercises to study the problems that would arise if a U.S. RDF was ordered to move into the Gulf. It was appreciated that in the event of the main threat, which is subversion and domestic turmoil, the induction of a U.S. RDF might make the situation more volatile and cause further disruption which the RDF would be meant to check. The exercise also revealed logistic weaknesses. Both these factors highlighted the need for local RDFs in addition to a U.S. force and emphasized the importance of Pakistan, from where a RDF could be moved into the Gulf very quickly. Moreover, the presence of Pakistani troops in West Asia would not be as offensive as that of U.S. soldiers. Thus, a triangular plan for safeguarding the Gulf has emerged. Saudi money, U.S. arms, and Pakistani manpower will be used to complement U.S. military power in the Gulf. Pakistan has received $3.2 billion as aid (spread over a period of six years), from October 1981. A Pakistani force is being equipped with sophisticated weapons and being organized as a local RDF which can be airlifted from Pakistan to be in position in Saudi Arabia within 24 hours.[22]

The U.S. aim is to contain the Soviet Union along a belt stretching from Pakistan to Turkey. Whereas U.S. concern for its security interests in West Asia is understandable, India is deeply affected by the induction of sophisticated arms into a neighboring state. With this concern is the fear that bases and other facilities will be provided to extraterritorial forces. There is danger that the region will be drawn into playing the superpowers' short-term game at the expense of the region's long-term interests.

Mounting Indo-Pak Tensions

Pakistan faces an inflammable internal situation. While describing the tumult within its realm as the "handwork of a few dissidents who will be dealt with severely," the authorities tend to interpret situations that are essentially political as problems of law and order. Unable to find solutions to the deepening socioeconomic, sociopolitical problems, Islamabad repeatedly claims that India has never reconciled itself to the existence of Pakistan and would like to see it weak and divided. President Zia has accused India of subversion and destabilization and of conniving with the Soviets.[23] Islamabad's reactions to India's charge of Pakistani involvement in the Akali agitation is that it is a "fib and a fake." The MRD leaders in Pakistan deny that India is involved in their agitation. Indeed, the situation would be farcical, were it not fraught with impending tragedy.[24]

f foreign intervention in South Asia are linked to the n has become a partner in U.S. strategy for West Asia med. There are some who believe that India is overreact-ne were to assume that Pakistan has no intentions of at-any increase in Pakistan's military capability requires out a matching increase in its military capability as insur-ndia is being provoked into an arms race that it cannot afford. Admittedly, every country has a right and a duty to improve its defenses against a real threat—but in Pakistan's case this is not a Soviet or Indian drive into Pakistan but is internal, political, and insurgent in nature.

There is thus no doubt that the subcontinent is in for a new arms race. At a political meeting, India's prime minister has asserted that the "clouds of war" are hovering over the Indian horizon. The Pakistani leader announces that as the chief martial law administrator, he is carrying out the will of Allah.

> There is a staggering symmetry in the politics of Pakistan and India. . . .
> Both Indira Gandhi and Zia ul-Haq have worked themselves into a position
> from which withdrawal will be humiliating, while persistence will be disas-
> trous. Fortunately . . . their people's support for another round of war is
> non-existent even if the leaders, for temporary political gain, toy with the
> idea of using the option of a provocative border incident.[25]

The Nuclear Factor

India has developed a large-caliber gun, a medium-range missile, and satellite launching capabilities. India has conducted a nuclear explosion and can, therefore, secretly fabricate a nuclear warhead for use in a missile or gun. India may have opted for a "last-wire" strategy in which it secretly manufactures nuclear weapons and—should an aggressor threaten India—it can connect the last wire and have a nuclear deterrent ready for use. Admittedly, India has pledged before the world forum that her nuclear explosion will be used entirely for peaceful purposes. But India's pledge is viewed with a measure of skepticism by Pakistanis. General Zia has also publicly pledged that Pakistan will not manufacture nuclear weapons. But does that pledge prevent Pakistan from imitating India? The pressure on Pakistan to match India's nuclear capability is compelling.

American officials have repeatedly warned Pakistan that the U.S. stand on nonproliferation does not allow the U.S. government any alternative but to stop economic aid if Pakistan continued to implement a program of reprocessing and did not conform to international safeguards. In the U.S. foreign military sales program for 1984-85, Pakistan is one of the countries listed to benefit from a liberalization of terms of financing of weapon purchases. Nevertheless, Dr. A. Q. Khan, Pakistan's top nuclear scientist, made it known in 1984 that Pakistan is years ahead of India in its uranium enrichment capability, and if the government were to decide to make the bomb, the scientists could do so.[26] Here we can see how Israel acts as a model for Pakistan. Israel has successfully adopted a strategy of ambivalence in regard to its nuclear policy. Israel has an arsenal of nuclear weapons but has never carried out a test (no longer a prerequisite for building up a nuclear arsenal). The waiver of the Symington amendment in favor of Pakistan by the Reagan administration in 1981 was a clear signal to Pakistan that the U.S. need to supply arms to the Afghan insurgents through Pakistani territory outweighed its nonproliferation objectives. Dr. Khan has not jeopardized Pakistan's arms relationship with the United States On the contrary, Pakistan is quietly challenging the United States to stop its aid by demonstrating that what Israel can do vis-à-vis the United States, it can also do on a smaller scale. So long as Pakistan does not carry out a nuclear test on its soil, it is likely to get away with its nuclear program.

Regional Cooperation and Indian Hegemony

Early in 1983, President Zia ul-Haq offered to sign a no-war pact with India. Since then, two events of importance have occurred. First, an Indo-Pakistan Commission was set up to examine how both nations can further friendship at the cultural social, economic, and political levels. Seven months after its first meeting in Islamabad, the four subcommissions that had been set up met and made limited but useful progress. Second, seven South Asian Regional Cooperation (SARC) meetings have been held. In 1983, foreign ministers attended the SARC meeting at New Delhi and mapped out parameters of the new venture. Its activities will supplement existing bilateral and multilateral arrangements, and all SARC decisions are to be taken on the basis of unanimity. Bilateral and contentious issues are to be excluded.

Despite the creditable beginnings of SARC and the Indo-Pak Commission, it is evident that the enormous differences in size and power between India and the other constituents of South Asia give rise to misgivings among its neighbors. Pakistan finds it difficult to reconcile itself to India's preeminence in South Asia; its policymakers emphasize that Pakistan can never accept such a situation.

> The Indian draws from history the strength and will needed to fulfill his grand design . . . the Indians regard themselves as the inheritors of the glory of British India. . . . Mrs. Gandhi is hostile to any power that refuses to accept India's preeminent position, and in this the chief culprit is Paki-

stan about whom the Indian Prime Minister has a fixation bordering on the pathological. . . . It was Indira Gandhi who was the architect of the upheaval of 1971. . . . which culminated in the disintegration of Pakistan.[27]

In order to bolster confidence in their two-nation theory and to reduce the advantages of India's size and power, the Pakistanis hope and plot for India to be balkanized. The Pakistanis declare that India is not one country and has never enjoyed the unity that is the hallmark of a nation state. The people who can be regarded as being potentially separatists are the Sikhs, the Dravidians (the four southern states of the peninsula), and the northeastern people who include the Nagas, Mizos, Tripura, and Assam. "If the people of the sub-continent can comprise two nations, why not three? Why not four or five or six?"[28]

Pakistan's Strategic Policy

From a consideration of the factors that have been discussed, we can discern the eight pillars upon which Pakistan has erected its strategic policy.

1. Pakistan endeavors to build up its retaliatory military capacity to punish or raise the price of invasion on both the Indian and Afghanistan frontiers.

2. On the Afghanistan issue, Pakistan will sit on the fence, placate the Russians, limit the amount of aid going across the border, and bargain for maximum aid from the United States

3. Pakistan will not explode a nuclear device for the present. Its objective will be to pursue a strategy of ambivalence and to augment its bargaining strength. It will build up a nuclear arsenal and pressure the United States so that either it continues to supply sophisticated conventional arms or Pakistan will go overtly nuclear to ensure it can deter the threats facing it in a two-front war.

4. Pakistan will endeavor to challenge and match, if not outdo, India on five fronts: diplomatic, economic, social, psychological, and military. This is Pakistan's justification for deploying the major portion of its army toward India while projecting a self-image of balancing out the Russians on the Afghanistan border.

5. Where Pakistan is unable to balance her strength against India, it will lose no opportunity to support separatist movements in India and bring in external powers in one way or the other, in the hope that this will offset the natural advantage of India's size and resources.

6. Pakistan endeavors to subdue internal upheavals sponsored by militant leftist and rightist Muslim groups by a mixture of suppression and cosmetic Islamization.

7. The military declares that it is the only binding, stabilizing force in the

country, thereby justifying its key place in the nation's political and administrative life.

8. Whereas the requirement to deal with internal law and order should warrant an overall increase in lightly armed and specially trained paramilitary forces for use in internal-security, civic, and nation-building duties, the military is not prepared to allow others to usurp its image as saviors of the nation. Therefore, the military establishment projects the internal threat as another reason to continue to increase its strength.

The Future

One of the trendier new quasi-sciences is futurology. Astrologers still earn a living because the desire to look into the future is deeply rooted in human nature, especially in troubled times. But the problems of strategic predictions are compounded by many uncertainties. Only a rash person would risk predicting the course of future events in South Asia. However, everything that is man-made is subject to change. Prudence, therefore, demands that we ask key questions and prepare for likely changes in a five-year time frame.

Will Afghanistan Continue to Be a Major Factor?

Long-term strategic aims are often tackled by short-term tactical plans. Although today Pakistan may serve America's immediate interests, this situation could change. Iran is preparing to carry out a massive ideological invasion of Muslim countries. Thousands of zealots from more than twenty Islamic countries are being trained in various Iranian cities to become "messengers of true Islam." These young men will spearhead an Islamic Shiite offensive which could split the Muslim world, leading to new schisms with incalculable consequences. The original hope that Khomeini-ism would be a religious rampart against the leftist ideologies is seen by the conservatives as an illusion; Mullahs already speak of Iran's regime as a "drift towards Islamic Marxism."[29]

Someday, the pressures of the Shiite Revolution on the Sunni regimes could be overwhelming. Under those circumstances, Pakistan may have its hands full with its own internal problems and would have little energy left to come to the rescue of the Gulf. The proposed organization of a Jordanian RDF could signify a shift in U.S. strategic perspectives and may diminish the requirement of a Pakistani force in West Asia. This in turn could reduce the need for Pakistani seaport and airfield facilities for the United States in the event of their intervention in the Gulf.

In the Reagan administration, the State Department continues to be a steadfast advocate of good relations with India, but it faces a lot of sniping from the Pentagon, which is unhappy because their Indo-U.S. strategic viewpoints differ on many global issues. Still, an improvement in Indo-U.S. relations is being encouraged at the highest levels. Yet the post-1980 Pakistan experience of dealing with the Soviet Union as an immediate neighbor has left a favorable impact on Pakistan minds. Apart from the quiet ouster from Afghanistan of Bhutto's sons, Moscow has behaved with restraint and sophistication. There is a growing body of Pakistani opinion that Moscow-Islamabad relations should not be needlessly exacerbated. It would be in Pakistan's interest if the Soviet Union is seen to be withdrawing from Afghanistan at Pakistan's behest; in the words of Agha Shahi, a former Zia official, Pakistan cannot afford to have the Afghanistan issue resolved at the superpower level, presenting Islamabad with a "second Yalta."

Is Political Change in Pakistan Imminent?

In the past, General Zia was able to manipulate public sentiment and go back on several pledges to hold elections. He may find it difficult to repeat that performance this time. He will probably have to work out an arrangement with political leaders to put an end to direct military rule. How and when Pakistani society solves the problem of its return to democracy and what changes take place in the country will be determined by many factors, but the key to power continues to be the Pakistani army. All political changes in Pakistan have so far been brought about by the armed forces, and the forthcoming one is unlikely to be an exception. Even if elections are held as promised, and the Constitution is amended to give the armed forces a supervisory role, it is not unreasonable to anticipate the emergence of a civil government that could evolve more imaginative and realistic plans for the future: avoid the dangers of a two-front confrontation, lower Pakistan's military dependence on the United States, improve relations with Afghanistan and the Soviet Union, and diminish its confrontation with India.

Will Islamization Be Intensified?

There are any number of other theological and emotional controversies within the fold of Islam that can play havoc with Pakistan's polity. It is manifest that the plan to enforce the Shariat Law is going to produce a number of problems. Social institutions cannot be created or discarded at will. The fundamentalists realize that their efforts have led to a situation where Islam is likely to become an issue of controversy rather than a factor of harmony in the country. Many are asking: "What Islamization? We had an Islamic, democratic, representative, unanimous Constitution. When the Islamic Constitution is overthrown, how can you be acting in the name of Islam? When you declare that the Shariat courts which exercise the law of God are subordinate and inferior to the verdict of Martial Law Courts, then how can you talk of serving Islam?'[30] Meanwhile, with astonishing unanimity, the various reformist movements have all arrived at the same diagnosis and cure: the Islamic state is a far-distant goal. The older Islamic parties of the world all failed because they tried to take a political shortcut to the Islamic state.[31] They tried to achieve power through political parties, manifestos, and elections. When these methods failed, they turned to violence. This is not to argue that Pakistan is turning away from religion. Far from that, religion plays a very crucial role in the life of an average Pakistani.

The object of responsible reformists is not an Islamic state but an Islamic society, to be achieved through a slow transformation by education and missionary endeavor, to convert Muslims into good Muslims.[32] When there are enough good Muslims in society, it will inevitably become an Islamic society. But until that happens, it is doubtful if the people of Pakistan would readily agree to become hostages in the hands of obscurantist mullahs and turn their backs on modern social, educational, and technological influences. It remains to be seen how far Islamization will be pushed through in practice; ways are already being found to mitigate its rigors. Meanwhile, the two-nation theory continues to distort Pakistan's perspectives, which leads Pakistan to misread India's desire for close relations and to assume that this desire is an attempt by India to denigrate Pakistan's status as an independent nation. This misperception stems from the Pakistani myth that Pakistan is an embodiment of the aspiration of the Muslims of the subcontinent.

Will Pakistan's Perceptions of India Alter?

Post-partition Indians are astonished to find influential Pakistanis expressing fear of India's "Brahmin leadership." Apparently, many Pakistani's are unaware of the radical changes in India that have created multiple power centers. New factions have arisen which have swamped the traditional power centers. Undoubtedly, caste still plays an important part in Indian politics and society, Brahmins may still carry influence in individuals, but they no longer play a group role in influencing public opinion. Regrettably, there are also many in India who know little of Pakistan, but every Indian lives among Muslim friends or neighbors. India is dotted with Muslim palaces, forts, mosques, tombs, gardens, and the graves of saints and sufis which attract millions of followers from both communities. There are few Indian arts and sciences to which the Muslims did not contribute and continue to contribute their skill. Today, millions of Indians find it incomprehensible that the Pakistanis spurn their Islamic heritage on the plea that they fear Hindu hegemony. This behavior is in complete contrast to their predecessors who, though a handful, had not only lived boldly, but also charmed and won the love and respect of the masses. If freer movement is encouraged between the two countries, then surely Pakistani youth will come to learn that in India there is a fund of goodwill mixed with curiosity toward Pakistan.

Will Kashmir Remain a Source of Friction?

Pakistani leaders every now and then harp on the Kashmir issue; the internal politics of Pakistan demands that this issue be kept alive. No party or government, civil or military, can afford to forget Kashmir at this stage in the evolution of Pakistan. Fortunately, General Zia has stated that Pakistan would continue "to argue peacefully. . . . knowing that India will not hand it over to us on a platter."[33] Nevertheless, Rajiv Gandhi has expressed his fears that Pakistan may launch an attack on India, "logically in Kashmir."[34] But this was election year in India, and the Congress (I) was bent on dethroning Farooq Abdullah, the chief minister of Kashmir. In this connection, responsible Indian politicians have proclaimed that Gandhi's statement was whipping up war hysteria. Nevertheless, it is utterly unreasonable to expect that an attempt to resolve the Kashmir dispute by force can secure for Pakistan what it has failed to obtain through three wars.

What Will Be the Challenge Facing South Asia?

South Asia is threatened by a population explosion, ignorance, and poverty. The nations of the region must modernize wisely and fast, or perish. This prediction may sound melodramatic, but if this does not happen, our children will see a decline in their quality of life during their lifetime. All regional states need to strengthen their economic base, control their population growth, display a disciplined civic sense, and evolve enlightened responsible citizens. True modernization does not have to take place at the expense of religion. The old wars of religion were bad enough. Today, competitive individualism or ant-like communism and tribal-minded nationalism are worse; all resemble each other and technology in being impersonal. So it is not surprising that the old religions are making a comeback, but with a change. Today, there is a common new spirit of mutual charity and appreciation; each of the old religions is becoming accessible, as never before, to the adherents of the other, and to human beings in search of the ultimate spiritual reality.

Independence gave Pakistan a start on the road to the Promised Land, but it will not carry Pakistan very far. The struggle for liberty has to be waged against the foes within no less than the foes without. Pakistan is a perfectly viable nation. All that it needs is a political arrangement to accommodate regional aspirations within the national framework to permit consent, consultation, and consensus. A search for ideological holy cows has so far only brought about economic disaster, political and social instability, national frustration, and martial law. Having achieved internal stability, Pakistan will turn to its regional needs. It is essential that Pakistan and India make SAARC and such agencies as the Indo-Pakistan Commission a success. If both states cannot rise above the trauma of Partition and view the past in its true perspective, they will once again lay the region open to intervention.

So What?

Let us end where we began: with history. For the past thirty-seven years, South Asia has "invited conquest." In the Indian Ocean, where once the Portuguese, Dutch, French, and British navies fought for the prize of the Indian subcontinent, today the navies of the superpowers weigh anchor. This time the "conquest" of the subcontinent will not manifest itself by a foreign occupation of the region. We should stop flattering ourselves that either of the two superpowers are interested in occupying any portion of South Asia; their strategic interests in the region are peripheral. Where once British, French, Portuguese, and Dutch armies roamed, today the KGB, CIA, and other intelligence agencies silently operate. Their aim is to safeguard their national interests. By itself this is a legitimate aim, but in the process, young nations can be subverted. Moreover, the presence of powerful foreign influences has a freezing effect on the natural evolution of developing countries. A continued confrontation between the nations of South Asia is a self-inflicted injury which results in a requirement for arms. Today, the great powers are still busy selling arms to the warring factions of South Asia very much as once the British, French, Portuguese, and the Dutch did; arms sales can be a twentieth-century form of slavery which could lead to a new type of dependency, where nations become pawns in a struggle between the superpowers.[35]

History records that superstition, obscurantism, rituals, and fanaticism often marred Indo-Aryan, Indo-Muslim, and Anglo-Indian cultures of the past for long periods. These evils are not the monopoly of any single race or religion. In fact religion has always been overvalued by humans as a political force: Roman Catholicism was unable to unify Catholic France and Spain; Islam could not unify West Asia nor the two wings of Pakistan. It is doubtful that the Christian Irish could be expected to share a common view on Ireland. We would do well to recognize that when Babar fought at Panipat, it was Muslim who fought Muslim; in 1971, it was Muslim who fought Muslim in East Pakistan. Whereas Pan-Arabism, not religion, could unite Syria, Iraq, and Saudi Arabia, religion is not a solid basis upon which to construct a confederation of nations. Nevertheless, it is surprising how, even today, many Indians and Pakistanis have yet not recognized or understood why Akbar succeeded and others failed, and the sources from which the former drew his inspiration as a statesman. Pakistan cannot be overwhelmed from without unless it has first destroyed itself from within.

NOTES

1. Christianity came to India before it arrived in Rome.
2. All dates are A.D.
3. In the case of the Sikhs, for example, Guru Nanak chose a Muslim as one of his principal companions and incorporated the major part of the basic concepts of Islam in his hymns. It was Akbar who granted the site of the Golden Temple at Amritsar.
4. Today there are more Muslims living in India than in Pakistan.
5. This view is a mirror image of the attitude of those in the West who denounce détente as appeasement of Communism.
6. In 1949, the Han Chinese were only 6 percent of the population. By 1973 they constituted 35 percent and numbered 3.5 million out of a total of 10 million. Today, the Han constitute 45 percent of the population; they have reduced the other nationalities in the region to a minority status. In 1978, China tried to set up a Muslim Republic of Pamir in the Wakhan Corridor and the Badakhshan regions of Afghanistan, adjoining Sinkiang and the Pakistani-occupied terrritory of Kashmir. The attempt was foiled by the Afghans.
7. Protestantism found real political backing against the power of the Roman Catholic church in rulers like Henry VIII. Also, the birth of protest against the Roman orthodoxy came together with the growing phenomenon of mercantile capitalism. Neither process really affected Islam.
8. Shahid Burki, *Pakistan under Bhutto* (New York: Macmillan, 1980).
9. Mr. Mahbub-ul-Haq, chief economist in the Pakistan Planning Commission in a speech in 1968.
10. $2.1 billion in 1980-81 or about 94 percent of export earnings.
11. A 2.5 percent per annum tax levied on savings to make collections for social welfare programs.
12. A levy on farm produce income.
13. See Stephen Philip Cohen, *The Pakistan Army* (Berkeley and Los Angeles: University of California Press, 1984).
14. Ghous Baksh Bizenjo, former governor of Baluchistan and leader of the National Democratic Party.
15. Akbar V. Mustikhan.

16.   A. K. Brohi, Pakistan's minister of law and parliamentary affairs in 1978.
17.   In fundamental Islam there is no separation between religion and politics; the truly devout Muslim politician is committed to work ultimately for the Islamic state, with an Islamic society as the first step.
18.   This act is one of the five Pillars of Islam. A few lucky ones are now selected at random by computer.
19.   The militant tend to regard Saudi Arabia with tolerant scorn and to declare Libya's Islamic "Revolution" to be shallow and foolish.
20.   However, even critics have admitted that the administrative efficiency of the collection and distribution of the Zakat Fund is one of the redeeming features of General Zia's drive for Islamization.
21.   The Iranian Baluchis form a mere 2 percent of the population of Iran, and the area inhabited by them is much smaller than that of Baluchistan.
22.   The U.S. RDF—now termed Centcom, Central Command—will move to rear bases in Egypt, Israel, Sudan, and Somalia from where they can be moved forward to any trouble spot in the Gulf; their heavy guns and tanks are now located on roll-on-roll-off ships at Diego Garcia.
23.   *Sunday Telegraph* (London), February 19, 1984.
24.   S. N. Chopra, "Indo-Pak Relations," *Probe* (New Delhi), December 1983.
25.   Ibid.
26.   In an interview as reported in *Nawai-Waqt* (Lahore), February 9, 1984.
27.   Lieutenant General A. I. Akram (ret.), President, Institute of Regional Studies, Islamabad, in a series of articles entitled "Shadows over South Asia," in *The Muslim* (Islamabad), January 1984.
28.   Ibid.
29.   The similarity between Khomeini-ism and Marxism is striking. The Mostazafeen (dispossessed) replace the proletariat, while the bourgeoisie appear as the mustikhareen (rich). The former's jihad (holy war) against the latter recalls the Marxist concept of class struggle. In Khomeini's jame-e-towhidt (unitarian society) there would be "no government, no classes and no oppression."
30.   Benazir Bhutto, in an interview in *India Today* (New Delhi), February 15, 1984.
31.   The Masjumi in Indonesia, PAS in Malaysia, the Muslim League in Pakistan and Bangladesh, the Moslem Brotherhood in the Arab world.
32.   A good Muslim is one who, in particular, does not succumb to such evils of modern life as corruption and consumerism.
33.   In an interview in *Impact* (London), January 1984.
34.   In an interview reported in the *Financial Times* (London), February 6, 1984.
35.   Whereas economic aid to nations of the Third World in 1980 averaged $20 million, they purchased $18.3 billion worth of arms and signed contracts for another $41 billion for future deliveries.(I) has a 5-fold strategy: a publicity campaign to dub the J & K Government as pro-Pakistani; to encour-

age dissidence and weaken Abdullah's party from within; to provoke a rift within Abdullah's family so that his followers are split into two feuding camps; to engineer law and order problems in the state to justify eventual Central action; to force Farooq to confine himself to J & K and prevent him from taking hold of administrative decisions. *India Today* (New Delhi), February 15, 1984.

6

The Peace Option for Pakistan?

M. B. Naqvi

Pakistan-India relations are in a perpetual state of strain. Indian politicians and defense officials claim to see a threat from Pakistan, whose acquisition of military equipment from the United States is said to endanger India. The process of normalization proceeds at a snail's pace, if at all. Whatever dialogue exists is taken up by mutual recrimination. Military incidents and tensions rise.

From Pakistan's perspective, it seems altogether too one-sided. Pakistan seems to be bending over backward to reassure India that it has no war-like designs. Pakistan's readiness to proceed with normalization at a quicker pace is supposed to be clear to all. Yet the Indian leadership seems to have certain ulterior motives for putting pressure on Pakistan.

What will result is impossible to say. But it is in such circumstances that India and Pakistan have earlier stumbled into war. Unless peace-making efforts are undertaken by those in power in both countries, the familiar old dynamic of India-Pakistan relations will keep these countries on a downhill course.

Pakistani Security Perceptions

Pakistani reactions to this situation are varied, of course. Many people have noted with alarm the growth of a negative element in India: the strengthening of Indian chauvinism.[1] However, there is also a widespread feeling that another war on the subcontinent would not be in Pakistan's interests.[2] Perhaps for the first time, some people see the need for adopting a policy of peace and friendship toward India. For those who favor economic and cultural progress in both countries, this rather new climate of opinion in Pakistan provides a good basis for peace-loving elements in both India and Pakistan to build upon. It is true that this new and more peaceable attitude has not found expression in a visible form, such as a peace movement, but it is there nonetheless.

Yet, Pakistanis still face the question: Why are the Indians stoking the old fires of animosity, and why are they keeping up pressure on Pakistan? Insofar as the acquisition of American arms is concerned, the Indian position has become ridiculous. American experts have said that even after they have received all the agreed-upon arms, the balance of power between Pakistan and India will not be significantly changed.[3] The Indian experts, I believe, concur. If this is so, the position becomes untenable for both sides. For India to protest is making much of little. For Pakistan to continue to acquire weapons is downright silly. What is the point of acquiring armaments at 14 percent interest if they will not significantly enhance military capabilities vis-à-vis India—the only country with which war is ever contemplated. Today's policy is irrational because it enrages and yet does not effectively deter India. Either Pakistan must choose to keep up with India's increasing capabilities— which means the effort must actually change the existing balance of power in its favor—or it should change its India policy, lock, stock, and barrel.

The question however remains: Why is India objecting so strenuously to a Pakistan military policy that does not exist? Adequate reasons have to be found for it. Of course, one does not know what Pakistani officials are doing, except that they claim to be sure on two counts: India does not intend to invade Pakistan, but if it does, they shall teach it a lesson it shall not forget.[4] In modern states, however, official assessments are not enough; nonofficial ones have to do their own work.

Pakistanis attribute several motivations to the Indians. There is the hardy perennial: The Indians have not actually accepted the 1947 partition, and they will undo Pakistan as and when they can. The present tension is a projection of this mentality.[5] There are variations of this view: India is not doing away with Pakistan altogether but hurting and weakening it by any and all possible means, including promoting disintegration or occupation of parts of Pakistan.

Second, many Pakistan pragmatists think that the Indians are not necessarily spoiling for a war. They may be keeping controlled pressure on the Pakistan government in order to force it to adopt a policy of which India approves. Not all of these eminent people are clear about which particular policy the Indians want Islamabad to adopt, largely because in such situations precise demands are not formally made; they are hinted at or implied.[6]

The third is an explanation formulated after a few long-out-of-date meetings with Indian officials and nonofficials in 1981 and some in 1983 and through occasional glimpses of Indian newspapers. It starts from the precariousness of Pakistan's position vis-à-vis Afghanistan. The Indians appear to believe that unless Pakistan performs a U-turn in its Afghanistan policy, the Soviet Union and Afghanistan would before long start doing terrible things; even if an outright invasion is unlikely, they can insidiously promote disintegration in Pakistan or otherwise hurt it.[7]

Such action may conceivably mean that large parts of Pakistan can become quite like Afghanistan. Recent comments by observers in Washington strengthen this reaction of the Russians to the enhanced American aid to Afghan *mujahiddin*. This was an old Indian expectation and was not acceptable to India, or so it asserted. The Indian government therefore has to do something to preempt the Russians. What form the Indian action would or could take was not made clear, but naturally it will have to be decisive enough to achieve what it sets out to do.

Fourth, there is a loudly expressed view in India that India is a democracy and wishes to have friendship with the people of Pakistan. The latter are deprived of a legitimate representative government. Democratic India cannot enter into a long-term arrangement on major issues with a dictatorial government in Islamabad behind the back of the Pakistani people. India had better wait until Pakistan has a democratic government. This view seems to be shared by circles close to the Indian government. But is this the policy of India? Few in India would answer that with an emphatic yes.

A fifth explanation of Indian policy is not a variation on the theme of democracy but is advanced by the same sort of people. They say that India's national interests demand that no superpower should become intimately involved in the South Asian subcontinent. Pakistan's Afghanistan policy provides an occasion and scope for the superpowers to intervene in Pakistan. India cannot countenance this, and it follows that India should do something to prevent it, although the details are seldom spelled out.

One other circumstance is relevant. The Indian government (and many people who support it) has expressed its sympathies for Pakistan's opposition parties. Indeed, it is possible to discern two policies being followed by Indian democracy vis-à-vis Pakistan. One policy is the more-or-less diplomatically correct policy of cautious friendship at the government level. The other policy is toward the Pakistani people, wherein Indian officials, displaying a certain amount of distance from the Islamabad government, convey to the people of Pakistan a message of long-term friendship. For a big country to adopt a more-or-less hostile policy toward the government and to show friendship to its people is an intimation of hostile action.[8]

A point may be made in passing. A war releases innumerable forces, not all of them calculable in advance. Another war, no matter on what issue or for what purpose, would be a tragic development; South Asia might never be the same again. It would be a terrible gamble from which hardly anyone would benefit.

Pakistan's Security Strategies

What Pakistan should do about its situation is difficult to determine. The absence of a national consensus over Afghanistan is a terrible handicap. The government's policy on Afghanistan is not shared by many sectors of the public, although to be fair, the sort of people who support the government also support its Afghanistan policy. But among the politically articulate sector the government remains under heavy criticism. This sector would like Islamabad to recognize the Afghan government and to make peace with it, in order to ensure both stabilization within Afghanistan and the return of the three million Afghan refugees.

A number of far-reaching constitutional changes have been introduced by the Pakistan president, Gen. Muhammad Zia ul-Haq, one in which he has held a referendum on a curiously worded question about his Islamization plan, an affirmative answer to which implies a mandate for him to continue to rule for another five years. Armed with this mandate, Zia held general elections to the national and provincial legislatures on an ad hoc basis, subsequently restored parts of the 1973 Constitution, extensively amended the Constitution on his own strongly questioned authority, took a fresh oath of office under that amended Constitution, and appointed a prime minister. The powers of the prime minister, particularly in relation to the president, remain unclear and a subject of much controversy. Despite the changes, nothing of substance seems to have been altered; a search for the locus of power reveals it still to be with the President and his armed-forces constituency.

All observers predict that the basic policies of Pakistan will remain unchanged, especially those vis-à-vis Afghanistan, the United States and India; even the personal handling of them will remain undisturbed. The chances of a political upheaval, the avoidance of which was the aim of the above civilianization exercise, not only remains a distinct possibility but may have become a strong probability in view of the highly contentious nature of the new civilian system. Most political commentators have called it a bogus democracy; some have called it martial law in mufti. To the extent that this prognostication may be even partially correct, it increases the vulnerability of the Pakistani authorities to increasing external pressures because they lack the vitality of a truly representative democracy. Indeed the frustrated and long suppressed hopes of democratic freedoms that continue to be denied in practice by a nominally democratic regime may lead to frequent disorders and more open expressions of disaffection, giving an opening, conceivably, to the Soviets to play their Baluch and Pathan nationality cards.

The regional situation is relevant here. Three wars between India and Pakistan have already taken place in thirty-seven years, and the fourth looms on the horizon. Against Indian wishes, Pakistan has cultivated distant great powers; its relations first with the United States and later with China and now with conservative Islamic countries in Southwest Asia have tended to enable the West to become involved in South Asian affairs—on the hopeful supposition that it would be to Pakistan's advantage.

Pakistan's efforts to secure powerful friends have met with indifferent success, whereas India has been able to build a big war machine. Pakistan's relations with the United States have seen many ups and downs, indeed more downs than ups, so much so that not many Pakistanis have been willing to trust the United States.[9]

Starting with 1953-54, Pak-U.S. relations were on a rising curve until October 1962, when the whole relationship virtually came crashing down. The October 1962 India-China war demonstrated that South Asia was an area where a genuine correspondence of long-range interests between the two superpowers existed.[10] Both superpowers wanted India as a bulwark against China and were ready to cooperate in building up India militarily. The bottom was knocked out of Pakistan's foreign policy. Those who advocate resuscitating the old Pak-U.S. relationship should ask and answer two questions: First, have the superpower interests toward South Asia as a whole changed? Second, can Pakistan, while regarding India as its main security threat, rely on U.S. support against India? The same hard-headed questions apply to China. Although Sino-Pakistan friendship has survived, its basis has, in a subtle way, undergone a change. China now actually subscribes to the Russo-American goal of keeping South Asia out of big-power rivalries and is trying to repair the damaged Sino-Indian relationship.[11] Insofar as Pakistani fascination with the Islamic block is concerned, no great power except India seems to take it seriously. The lack of independence and military strength of the Muslim countries of Southwest Asia, quite apart from their basic orientation toward the Arab-Israel dispute, determine that this is no more than a political mirage: Pakistan certainly cannot bank on these countries for anything if the United States does not approve of these countries helping Pakistan. That is partly because the Indians have done their own public-relations work with these Arab states and partly because common sense prevents any Arab country from committing itself on

India-Pakistan disputes. Other major powers like Britain, France, Germany, Australia, and Japan, find no other option but to concur and support Russo-American détente in South Asia. That leaves Pakistan as the odd man out.

Pakistan and Afghanistan

The Afghanistan issue has to be seen in the context of this long-term correlation of forces in South Asia, the region to which Afghanistan actually belongs. Insofar as this particular country is concerned, a few elementary facts must be remembered. By the mid 1960s, it had become clear that the United States had written off Afghanistan as an area of Soviet influence. Second, after the Saur revolution a treaty between Afghanistan and the Soviet Union was signed, after which Brezhnev declared that Afghanistan had irreversibly become a member of the socialist camp; henceforward the Brezhnev doctrine would apply to it. The Soviet army entered Afghanistan in the closing days of 1979 after these firm declarations.

Despite the exigencies of the Afghan *mujahiddin* struggle against the Karmal regime and their Russian friends, two things are abundantly clear. First, the Soviet army cannot be dislodged from Afghanistan by military means; sober military assessments by all major powers seem to support this conclusion, propaganda about Russian losses notwithstanding. Second, unless a political settlement acceptable to the Soviet Union is reached, the latter will stay put in Afghanistan. At present, the chances of such a settlement are very small because Pakistan demands the Russian departure from, and a representative government in, Kabul and also supports the *mujahiddin* cause.

A solution along the lines of the June 1983 effort involves a total stoppage of all aid reaching the Afghan *mujahiddin,* and possibly the strengthening of the Karmal government. Moreover, international guarantees, including American and Chinese ones, that are acceptable to the Russians have to be provided so that the internal situation in Afghanistan can be stabilized to Russia's satisfaction. But there is a snag: Iran is not only to be a signatory but must, like Pakistan, cooperate with a Kabul government that the Russians approve. Nothing of the kind can be expected from the present Tehran government. Thus in the short to the medium term, the Russians are unlikely to start packing their bags. What happens after a change in Tehran is anybody's guess, depending upon the nature of the change. In sum, the Russian presence in Afghanistan has to be accepted as a fact of life; it translates into the simple proposition that Afghanistan is now an integral part of the Soviet power system which stretches from Torkham to the Kamachatka peninsula in the northeast, and the Oder Neisse Line to the west.

There is no indication that the Americans are likely to do anything concrete about Afghanistan; what they do covertly can be, at most, a mere extension of what they are already doing. They can only use Afghanistan as an anti-Soviet propaganda stick, which is neither here nor there in hard terms.[12]

But the Russian presence in Afghanistan has great significance in two separate contexts. Afghanistan is only a few minutes flying time from important Pakistani targets, and less than 300 nautical miles from the Hormuz Straits, which has one significance in relation to South Asia and another in relation to Southwest Asia, particularly the oil-producing states of the Persian Gulf. Although there is no kind of consensus among the superpowers over Southwest Asia, there is one over South Asia, although it is somewhat the worse for wear. The détente over South Asia has survived many vicissitudes, but the latest American initiatives of increasing supplies to the *mujahiddin* seem to be putting a strain on it, as far as the consequences for Pakistan are concerned. These initiatives include the official confirmation by both President Anwar Sadat and the White House that they were sending military equipment to Afghan *mujahiddin*. The 1978-79 upheaval in Iran has also significantly changed the outlook for the Persian Gulf. With the Americans out of Iran, the situation in the area has become very unstable: the RDF and naval buildup around the Hormuz Straits by the United States have been countered by the Soviets in kind, and the tension is almost palpable. In addition, the old uncertainties in the Gulf area have been multiplied by the Iraq-Iran war. The stakes of both superpowers have increased. Southwest Asia is one of those areas where a third world war can start.

Choices for Pakistan

It is against this background that Pakistan has to chart a course. It must remember its isolation in basic terms of the détente in the subcontinent between the superpowers. Pakistan faces danger from two sides: India and Afghanistan (where the Russians can be heard growling).

Yet the institutions necessary to have a policy and a national consensus are in a shambles. Despite the changes made in March 1985, the country is still, at bottom, governed by the armed forces. Although elected institutions have been nominally restored, political parties and human rights of the citizens remain suppressed. Promises are galore, but hard action to enable people to feel free is conspicuous by its absence. The country still has no acceptable national policy. This is more poignant insofar as Afghanistan is concerned. There is continuing polarization between the still-powerful president and the new democratic setup that is seen as his civilian facade on the one hand and the long-established political element on the other. This is the strongest argument for a peace policy vis-à-vis both India and Afghanistan.

Pakistanis think that the Indian government is set on a course that may result in war.[13] If a war does come, it will have to be fought. But that is not a policy. It is sometimes said that weak and small countries cannot afford to have a foreign policy. They can only react. This is despair and moral cowardice. Let Pakistan have the courage to formulate a long-range peace policy toward India; peace with others will follow.

There is virtual consensus over the desired policy toward the superpowers: nonalignment, free of any tilt toward anyone in particular. Pakistan must, therefore, steer clear of all security arrangements with others.

Our attitude toward the burning questions next door needs to be defined. Pakistan's stance so far has heightened the hostility of Afghanistan, the Soviet Union, and, at one remove, India, a hostility that Pakistan can do without. Pakistan needs to pick up the threads of a political solution from where the United Nations, Afghanistan, Pakistan, and USSR left off in June 1983. The chief roadblock—refusal to recognize the Kabul regime—needs to be removed. The first object should be to begin to return the Afghan refugees. Realistically, both Islamabad and the present regime in Kabul not only have to work out the modalities of the huge operation, but have actively to cooperate. The insistence on a change in Afghanistan—an Islamic and nonaligned Afghanistan with a representative government—has been formulated in terms that are redolent of the Indian formulation for the East Pakistan refugees in 1971;[14] India could do so because it was certain of its ability to ensure the refugees' return, in "honor and freedom." On the contrary, even the continuance of the insurgency so close to Pakistani borders is a serious threat to the latter's security. Stabilization of the situation in Afghanistan is in Pakistan's interest. It would only be a nuisance and a mild embarrassment to its American friends if Pakistan were to recast its Afghanistan policy; U.S. vital interests are not engaged.

Not only will Pakistan safeguard its own security by cultivating friendly cooperation with Afghanistan and Soviet Union, it will also encourage Afghanistan's external independence and possibly nonalignment, preferably drawing it into the new web of friendship halfheartedly woven: SAARC. The social system or regime in Afghanistan or the Soviet Union should be totally irrelevant here.

The region centering on the Persian Gulf, chiefly focused on the Hormuz Straits, is a major flashpoint. Pakistan should keep out of that complication altogether. Its response to the proposal of reviving the RCD seems rather risky because of the uncertainties of Iran's situation and its deep involvement in other crises. For one thing, Iran's war with Iraq has entered a more dangerous phase. However, thanks to the peculiar orientation of Pakistan's Pan-Islamic sentiment, Islamabad is more liable to get involved in security arrangements with the oil-bearing Persian Gulf Arab states. That would be dangerous and make it vulnerable to Russian pressure, because the Gulf security arrangements are aimed against the Soviet Union and enjoy unlimited American support. Indeed, the Rapid Deployment Force (RDF) was conceived only to operate in the USSR and in Iran. The Soviet media are already accusing Pakistan of becoming involved with the RDF arrangements. Pakistan cannot afford to let such suspicions be aroused, much less confirmed.

To the north, the situation is relatively comfortable. Pakistan's friendship with China is likely to endure. The Chinese do not expect the Pakistanis to become involved in any of their problems or disputes. The only difficulty is that, in contrast, Pakistanis frequently expect China to get involved in their disputes. To be fair to the Chinese, it must be realized that, faced as they are with tremendous military problems with the Soviet Union, with which they have a 4,000-mile border, an extremely complicated situation obtains in Northeast Asia, and the unpredictable future policy of Japan bears out the view that the fundamental Chinese interest in South Asia is to see tranquility and stability.

The really difficult problem for Pakistan concerns relations with India and the rest of South Asia. Two assumptions and drives have characterized Pakistan's relations with India. Pakistanis instinctively feel that they should be taken as seriously and considered as important as the Indians by the rest of the world. It is a legacy of pre-independence India's Muslim politics: to be equal in importance to the Hindus. This tendency is one source of the Pakistan-India rivalry that spawned the arms race between them soon after independence. This wholly unabated rivalry can result in another war, just as it caused earlier ones. The task now should be to reverse this trend, terribly strong though it is.

Conclusion: Pakistan's Options and Peace

There are two ways to stop an arms race: in one, both sides agree to reduce or dispense with their armament-acquisition programs and agree to some specific force levels; in the second, one side decides to end the race by opting out of it. The former approach has, so far, never worked in history. The twentieth century has seen any number of disarmament conferences. None of them has succeeded. Pakistan has offered a subcontinental version of the MBFR talks. India is not interested and points out that it is a much larger country, with interests other than Pakistan. India is worried over the arms race in the Indian Ocean, and there is the old dispute with China. So long as other threats endure, New Delhi finds no basis for any particular force equation with Pakistan: it is averse to the very idea of linking its force levels with Pakistan, no matter at what level. What then is Pakistan to do?

Pakistan has two options: First, it can, in a huff, continue the arms race and let events take their course. Secondly, it can untie the Gordian knot by unilateral action. In the latter event, it should decide to reduce drastically its own defense establishment and budget. It should let India squander even more of its own resources on its armed forces. This may appear to be a radical approach, but is the only practical way of ending the arms race.

The notion that peace can be preserved by balance of power is unproven. No balance of power has ever been stable or has preserved peace. All peace interregnums were a result of a bewilderingly large number of specific causes and circumstances. Balance of power, indeed, never lasts beyond a given moment. The effort to balance someone else's real or imagined power always sparks off an arms race that goes on intensifying by its very logic. Wars result, sooner or later.

But the idea of unilateralism is thought to be somewhat looney; only cranks are thought to be capable of advocating it. Although European examples now abound and unilateralism is now in high intellectual fashion, the idea is still startling in Pakistan. Will not the stronger country immediately overrun us as soon as we reduce our force levels? The answer, with certain assumptions, is yes, but no with others.

Let us first take the case of India's other neighbors: Nepal, Bhutan, Maldives, Sri Lanka, and Bangladesh. Each of them is militarily much weaker than Pakistan, but none feels as insecure. One reason why India does not take any of them by assault is that none of them is in competition or an arms race with India. Does this not show that weapons do not give security? Pakistan should be more secure than Nepal. Why is the situation the other way round? We cannot forget that the ultimate guarantors of a country's security are its people. It is their will to stay free that ensures their freedom. There is no reason to believe that India or any other nation can enslave Pakistan if its people do not want to be enslaved. With neighbors such as Pakistan's—India, the Soviet Union, and China—the idea of arming to ensure security is inherently unrealistic. It is far safer, more realistic, and appropriate to cut down wasteful expenditure on a war machine that does not produce security. The resources saved can be utilized for more productive purposes. The more it improves the quality of life of its people, the stronger Pakistan will become.

Once the arms race is behind them, Pakistan's relationship with India becomes manageable, although still not easy. There would still be difficulties. To begin with, India's very size, resources, and strength make it an awesome giant. India's armed forces pose a question for others: what does it want to do with its 1.2 million soldiers and their modern equipment? As long as India does not give a satisfactory reply, it will continue to constitute a problem.

A relationship with India should have two objectives: it must be peaceful, and it should promote the economic progress of both parties. There are also other worries. India has a highly developed heavy industrial base that is operating at most at only 50 percent of capacity. This is an even more serious threat to others than its huge armed forces. The experience of the interwar period in Europe, especially that of Germany, has proven that a semipermanently underutilized heavy industrial capacity tends to militarization and an aggressive military posture. Japan's experience in the same period was similar, and although the forces behind Italian militarization were somewhat different, they were qualitatively of the same kind. This possibility is why all of India's neighbors want guarantees that their relationship with India will be free of all pressures. Every non-Indian in South Asia wants elaborate economic and cultural cooperative arrangements in which the Indians can be committed to a procedure of deciding by unanimity. It is significant that the Indians are anxious to keep all their disputes with their neighbors, except the Maldives, purely bilateral, while the others wish them to be tackled in whatever multilateral forum possible, which was why Bangladesh proposed a South Asian forum. It is also symptomatic that India's initial reaction was unsympathetic, although this response was later modified. A peace policy has to emphasize economic and cultural cooperation in South Asia through SAARC and make it the central point of foreign and other policies. Let SAARC be developed into a tight economic community with proper and realistic safeguards for all, such as the European Economic Community provides to, for instance, Luxembourg or Belgium.

Once the India-Pakistan arms race comes to an end, political harmony within South Asia, buttressed by wide-ranging economic cooperation, should be easy to achieve. The Indian objective of keeping the great powers out of South Asia would then be acceptable to all, including the great powers themselves. It is to be hoped that the SAARC arrangements will achieve a development pace that will keep India's heavy industries peacefully and optimally employed for the benefit of all. India's big military establishment in that situation would be an inexplicable oddity. In all likelihood it would be scaled down, because SAARC should by then be absorbing everybody's full energy. A huge and wasteful expenditure on irrelevant war preparations cannot long survive in a stable peace situation.

The way to tackle the problem of India's oversized war preparations is to adopt a twofold policy. On the one hand, Pakistan should seize the moral high ground by unilaterally opting out of a ruinous arms race. On the other, it should mount a strong propaganda campaign on the need to preserve peace (in fact, promoting a proper peace movement, with connections to peace movements elsewhere) and press for closer economic and cultural cooperation in South Asia in a way that would also seek eventually to incorporate Afghanistan into the South Asian system. That is the way to preserve peace, national freedom, and equality in South Asia.

There are quite a few specific things Pakistan can do if it adopts a thoroughgoing peace policy. First, it should request India to use its good offices in both Kabul and Moscow. Pakistan should coordinate its Afghanistan policy with India, work to coopt India into the OIC, lift the ban on private sector trade, give India most-favored nation treatment in trade, and respond positively to Indian suggestions for easier travel and cultural exchanges. Indeed, Pakistan can unilaterally lift all discriminatory treatment of Indian visitors.

Pakistan's friendship with America may seem to be incompatible with this new policy. In the narrow, short-term sense it is; the Reagan Administration will probably react angrily, but many in the United States can be expected to see the long-term benefits of a South Asian system that reduces Indo-Pakistani antagonism and stabilizes the huge mass of humanity and resources in this region. That would help anchor a volatile Asia. The success of SAARC would have a beneficial impact on Southwest and Southeast Asia alike; which would be welcome, in different ways, to all the major powers.

NOTES

1. See A. T. Chaudhri, *Dawn* (Karachi), January 28, 1984, "Two Faces of Indo-Pakistan Ties," and *The Pakistan Times* (editorial), January 12, 1984, "What Are India's Intentions?"
2. See the Indian writer A. G. Noorani, "Politics of National Security," *Indian Express*, December 29, 1983.
3. PPI story in *Dawn*, January 4, 1984, "India has nothing to fear from Pakistan—U.S. Expert View." A PPI story in *Dawn*, May 13, 1984, about Vice President Bush's visit to India and Pakistan carried a Reuters story to the effect that Bush assured India that U.S. arms do not disturb the Indo-Pakistan balance of power.

4. It would be invidious to choose from the all-too-numerous pronouncements of the Pakistan Defense Minister and other defense officials dealing with the defense preparedness of the Pakistan armed forces.

5. M. A. Akhyar's weekly column "Current Topics" in *Daily Business Recorder*, November 11, 1983, "Of the Goddess of War and Peace."

6. *Morning News* (Karachi) editorial of January 6, 1984, "Indira's War Song."

7. "Indira's Hegemonistic Designs" by Dr. Ghulam Mustafa Chaudhry in *Pakistan Times*, October 30, 1983. The India writer Rajendra Sareen is the greatest exponent of this view.

8. Ibid. Also see the Pakistan foreign minister, Sahibzada Yaqub Khan, quoted in *Business Record*, November 6, 1983. This is how the late Mrs. Gandhi's many statements were interpreted in Pakistan, especially those on Sind (during the MRD's 1983 struggle) and those in sympathy with Nusrat Bhutto and Benazir Bhutto.

9. A. M. Asghar Khan's statement in *The Muslim* (Islamabad), March 20, 1985.

10. Both superpowers simultaneously offered aid to India against China, and India accepted in 1962; Nehru even requested a U.S. nuclear umbrella.

11. This change in the Chinese stance can be traced to the statement issued by the Chinese foreign minister welcoming the Indo-Pakistan agreement of April 1974 reached at Delhi, if not earlier.

12. This is a point that a number of Pakistani commentators, including this writer, have repeatedly made.

13. See my article, "Our Foreign Policy Assumptions, Motivations and Frustrations" in the *Pakistan Observer*, July 18, 1966, and "Is Foreign Policy the Criterion" in the same newspaper, March 23, 1966.

14. Mrs. Gandhi, the Indian Premier, and Jagjivan Ram, the Defense Minister, repeatedly emphasized throughout most of 1971 that the aim of the Indian policy was to enable the refugees from East Pakistan to go back in peace and honor.

7

American Policy in South Asia: Interests and Objectives

Pervaiz Iqbal Cheema

To a South Asian, American policy in the region appears inconsistent, confused, and reactive rather than calculated, long term, and innovative. While the confusion is influenced by regional dynamics, the inconsistency in the policy is also the product of internal American factors, including periodic changes in administrations. Washington has not properly gauged the intensity of the rivalry between the major states of South Asia. It views Indo-Pakistan relations from a global perspective, disregarding the aspirations of regional actors. The reactive aspect of the policy is not only derivative from global considerations, but has something to do with the American puritanical streak, its reactive enthusiasm to "do something immediately" without considering the long-term implications and the psyche of the people involved in the target area. Massive enthusiasm, initially exhibited, often subsides with the passage of time as the realization of long-term and other considerations sinks in.

Thus, shifting perceptions of global and regional interests coupled with negligible interest in the aspirations of regional states have not only affected the durability of existing relations and led to their periodic rearrangement, but have also produced a long chain of actions and reactions. While most of its actions and reactions were congruent with global considerations, the periodic modification of America's regional policy to suit its global pursuits appeared to local states as a confused policy, lacking clarity and coherence in its declaratory and operational dimensions. For local states, America's regional policy was far more important than its global pursuits. This chapter identifies and examines American interests and objectives as pursued by its policy formulators.

American Interests

A nation's vital interests are those interests for which it is prepared to undertake a serious economic, political, and military action irrespective of the cost involved.[1] Preservation of such interests is accorded so high a priority that even military action is regarded as a legitimate act. Perhaps that is why aggression has often been justified by its perpetrator as absolutely necessary for the security of the nation. However, it needs to be mentioned here that a superpower's perception of threat is not merely confined to an attack on its homeland, but may include threats that are much more distant in space. A regional power is primarily concerned with the threat that entails an attack on home territories. Given the existing nuclear arsenal possessed by the superpowers, an attack on the homeland of one by the other would actually amount to the destruction of both. Thus, such an eventuality is highly unlikely.

However, threats to the sources of important raw material, supply lines, and allies could constitute a threat that warrants a firm response from a superpower. The nature and degree of response depends on the thinking of the incumbent administration. The agreed response is then translated into what is commonly referred to as strategic objectives which, in fact, are more specific goals calculated to serve those vital interests.[2] Different leaders contrive different policies in order to serve those goals.

South Asia has always remained an area of peripheral and derivative interest to United States. There is little by way of resources that America obtains from the region which is crucial to its economy. Neither American investments nor the volume of trade with the region is substantial enough to make the area an important partner; the main consideration governing its South Asian policy stems from global pursuits and interests. The area's importance has fluctuated in rhythm with the shifts in America's global policies. Put simply, the major American interest was and still is (in modified form) to prevent the absorption of the area into the communists' orbit. The early thrust was against advancing communism in general; later, the emphasis was confined to Soviet expansionism after the Sino-American rapprochement. Linked with it has been (and still is) the American interest in retaining assured access to the strategically important Gulf region. The Soviet invasion of Afghanistan and a revolution in Iran have given new life to the threat to choke off oil supplies to the West. Other important American concerns include the maintenance of regional stability, preventing the spread of nuclear proliferation and the preservation of economic and commercial interests. In many ways the economic and commercial interests were and still are of secondary importance as far as South Asia is concerned.

American Involvement

The initial American involvement in Asia was primarily the product of its global policy of the containment of communism. The emergence of communist China in 1949, coupled with professed Soviet intentions of internationalizing communism, led many Americans to believe that without Western assistance Asian nationalism might not be an impediment to expanding communism. In congruence with its containment policy, the Americans sponsored a system of security alliances on the periphery of the communist world. They were willing to sign up for their team all those players who exhibited some interest in checking the onward march of communism. They did not bother to analyze closely the factors and compulsions of these regional players. Each local participant had his own set of reasons for closer association with America.[3]

A sense of insecurity and helplessness during Pakistan's early years pushed that country into the arms of the Americans. Without giving much thought to its immediate geopolitical realities, Pakistan joined SEATO and CENTO in order to balance the perceived Indian threat and to acquire much needed economic and military assistance. The Americans accepted Pakistan's participation in their collective security arrangement without properly comprehending the nature and intensity of the deep-rooted Indo-Pakistan hostility. Although both Pakistan and the United States went into the alliance with a view to serve their own national interests, neither fully understood the implications and consequences of an alliance between unequal partners. The Americans never contemplated the use of U.S.-supplied equipment or U.S. forces against India. The Pakistanis, on the other hand, expected that the Americans would not only extend full diplomatic support to Pakistan's case on Kashmir but would also actively back Pakistan in the event of a war with India. Although a little on the high side, Pakistani expectations were somewhat natural because Pakistanis thought that the Americans were not only fully conscious of the Indian threat to Pakistan's security but also realized that this had been the main factor in Pakistan's decision to join the Western camp.[4] Pakistan may have been naive in this, but its naivety was probably due to a lack of experience in diplomacy. Perhaps the Americans were just as naive: their experience as world policemen was limited. They were not able to judge the implications of an alliance between a superpower and a small power that was deeply enmeshed in a local conflict.

Pakistan benefited from its association with the United States in many ways. The association not only yielded much desired economic and military assistance but also infused confidence and psychological security against the perceived Indian threat. Similarly, the Americans gained from their association with Pakistan. Not only did they enlist Pakistan's support in establishing both the northern and southern tiers of their defense alliance system, they were able to maintain continuity in it, Pakistan being physically located at a point where the alliance systems converged geographically. "In addition, the United States received certain specific privileges from Pakistan, such as facilities for launching high altitude reconnaissance aircraft over Soviet or Chinese territories—significant privileges in the era before spy satellites."[5]

The Indian reaction to the U.S.-Pakistan military relationship was strong and angry. Nehru accused America of introducing the Cold War into the region. Irritated at the Eisenhower-Dulles policy, India moved closer to the Soviets, hoping to balance the American presence. Despite the American interpretation of nonalignment as "immoral," the incumbent U.S. administration thought fit to keep India assured of American friendship and readiness to provide military assistance.[6] Obviously the major American objective in this was to slow down or stop the Indian drift toward the Soviets. Thus, economic aid continued to pour into India on a much bigger scale than that allocated for Pakistan.[7] This aid enabled India to allocate its own resources toward military requirements and to pursue successfully its policy of nonalignment, earning worldwide prestige as a truly independent country—whereas Pakistan was dubbed a subservient state.

But America's soft policy toward India did not check the Chinese, did not balance Soviet influence in India, nor did it convince India of America's sincere wish to work for peace in the area. New Delhi regarded the U.S. security relationship with Pakistan as destabilizing. The 1956 Hungarian crisis clearly demonstrated the Indian bias in favor of the Socialist bloc. Although Indian and U.S. views converged on Suez, the Indian attitude over the Hungarian crisis lacked the bite reflected in its Suez policy. America chose to ignore the duality in Indian policy, and economic cooperation continued to grow. In 1959 the Americans and the Pakistanis signed a bilateral agreement to which Nehru reacted strongly. The American response to Nehru was to provide immediate assurances to India that the agreement was entirely governed by the "Eisenhower Doctrine," which only covered aggression from communist countries.

The advent of the Kennedy administration registered a major change in America's India policy. Not only did the new administration accept nonalignment as an operative principle of international relations, it admired democratic India (as against militarily governed Pakistan). Because of the efforts of India's friends in the Kennedy administration, a much better understanding developed rather quickly. Apart from the new administration's tilt toward India, other international developments and advancements in technology further paved the way for a closer association of the two countries. With the advent of reconnaissance satellites and ICBMs (which reduced the importance of advanced military bases), the Sino-Soviet rift, and the Sino-Indian border war, the Americans began to see India as a counterpoise to China.

To allay Ayub's expressed apprehensions, the Kennedy administration gave assurances that before extending military aid to India, Pakistan would be consulted.[8] However, when the time came, the Americans bypassed this promise to an ally and rushed military aid to neutral India. Even the Indian "police action" in Goa in December 1961 and the subsequent resentment expressed by the Indians over American support for Portugal was not allowed to stand in the way of the American decision to provide military aid to India.[9] The way the Americans seized the opportunity to befriend India gave birth to feelings in Pakistan that it was India that was regarded as the main prize in South Asia and that Pakistan was being used as a balancing lever. Such feelings were further exacerbated when the Americans decided to impose an arms embargo after the 1965 Indo-Pakistan war.

Perhaps the most intriguing thing about the American reaction to the Sino-Indian war was that its enthusiasm to help India was much more pronounced than the reactions of India's friends within the nonaligned world. The Soviets were initially ambiguous, but later on they openly supported India. The only reaction which reflected a sense of urgency was that of the Americans. The resultant attitude of the Indians toward America mellowed and softened. The Indian attitude toward the presence of America's Seventh Fleet in the Indian Ocean become one of unconcern.

The Indo-Pakistan Wars and the United States

In September 1965 a second Indo-Pakistan war broke out and lasted for seventeen days. This conflict presented the Americans with an acute dilemma. One of the combatants was an ally, the other was a state that they were striving to win over. The United States decided not to get involved in a regional crisis that was not of direct concern to them. Not only did the war confirm India's fears that American-supplied military hardware would be used against them, but the policy of neutrality disillusioned the Pakistanis, who were a little too hopeful of American active support. It made the Pakistanis painfully aware that their "long nourished American equalizer" would not be available in time of crisis.[10] The disillusionment spread when the Americans announced an arms embargo. Most Pakistanis interpreted the action as favoring India. Whereas Pakistan was entirely dependent upon U.S. arms, India's sources of arms procurement were diversified, and her reliance on American arms was less than 10 percent of her total dependence on external arms suppliers. Although Washington probably wanted to pursue an evenhanded policy, the Pakistanis interpreted the move as aimed against Pakistan and as a betrayal of the alliance partnership. The war forced Pakistan to reappraise its foreign policy and moved her closer to the Chinese. The Chinese option opened up for the Pakistanis after the 1962 Sino-Indian clash, and since then, the Chinese had cultivated the Pakistanis. Although Chinese support for Pakistan in the 1965 war was materially insignificant, its vociferous denunciation of India invoked friendly responses among the Pakistanis.

With the increasing American involvement in Vietnam, the importance of South Asia gradually declined. The spotlight did not focus on South Asia until the invasion of Afghanistan by the Soviets in 1979 except for a brief period in the 1970s. The Indo-Pak war of 1971 attracted American attention, and this time the United States played a role somewhat similar to that of the Chinese in the 1965 war (except that the United States ordered one of its aircraft carriers to move into the Bay of Bengal). The *Enterprise* mission was seen in Pakistan as nothing more than a symbolic gesture; clearly, it could not prevent the dismemberment of Pakistan. Because of known Soviet involvement and support for India in the 1971 war, the American move fell far below Pakistan's expectations. Apart from adopting a relatively hard posture with regard to India, the Americans had decided to settle on a policy geared not to prevent the dismemberment of Pakistan but to save West Pakistan's anticipated disintegration.[11] This convinced the Pakistanis that they were no more than a pawn in a chess game—and the loss of a single pawn never amounts to the loss of the game. Thus, Pakistani disenchantment, which started in the aftermath of the 1962 Sino-Indian border war, reached its climax in 1971. Viewed within the context of the support the Soviets have given the Indians over the years, and the three major letdowns by the Americans, Pakistani bitterness is not surprising. Pakistan paid a heavy price for its alignment policy with the United States; not only did it antagonize the Soviet Union and many Arab states, but it also provided India with a means of wriggling out of her commitments on Kashmir.

The dispatch of the Enterprise carrier task force to the war region neither satisfied the Pakistanis nor deterred the Indians or the Soviets. For the Pakistanis, the action was "too little," came "too late," and could not prevent the dismemberment of Pakistan.[12] As far as India was concerned, the American move not only tarnished its image but also helped the Indian government to strengthen further its ties with the Soviets. Viewed within the context of America's global objective of checking expanding Soviet influence, the move made no sense. Not only had the

USSR and India already signed a treaty of friendship just before the war, but Nixon himself was convinced that India had become aligned with the Soviets.[13] The logical course of action would have been to undertake a major action to deter both the Soviets and the Indians from dismembering Pakistan.

Most American analysts tend to interpret the Enterprise mission as a move to woo China.[14] Since South Asia was a high Chinese priority and the Chinese were apprehensive about expanding Soviet influence in the area, the Americans felt compelled to demonstrate some sort of support for China's friend, Pakistan. Three factors seems to have influenced the decision to send the task force. First, the Americans were then engaged in establishing relations with the Chinese and felt an acute need to assure the Chinese that they were prepared to strengthen their ally, Pakistan, against Russia's ally, India.[15] Second, the United States intended to communicate to its prospective friend how it treated its allies and how dependable it was.[16] Third, Nixon was not only annoyed over Mrs. Gandhi's duplicitous attitude but was also angered by the Soviets' hard line and wanted to convey to the Soviets that if they were not going to restrain India, the Americans might have to undertake tougher action.[17] It seems that the American gesture was primarily intended to communicate to the Chinese the desire to have some kind of working relationship with China. It was neither genuinely oriented to save Pakistan's dismemberment nor to upgrade reliance on America. Once again the Americans ignored the sensitivities of the local states and undertook an action that was "derivative of U.S. interest elsewhere."[18]

The Nuclear Issue

During much of the 1970s, American relations with the major states of South Asia did not register any improvement. Not only did the Americans lack a clear perception of their interests, especially in the light of emerging new politico-military realities in the area, but they were still deeply involved in Vietnam. The 1971 war consolidated Mrs. Gandhi's position as virtual empress of India and also contributed substantively to the rise of Zulfiqar Ali Bhutto to power in a truncated Pakistan. Realizing the futility of a one-sided approach and the cost of heavy reliance upon American support, Bhutto decided to pursue a more diverse foreign policy, a policy of bilateralism that entailed an evenhanded approach vis-à-vis all the major powers. This was actually initiated under Ayub's regime but was more vigorously applied by Bhutto.[19] Consequently, Pakistan not only left SEATO and the Commonwealth but also managed a marginal improvement in its relations with the Soviets.

U.S. relations with India had already touched the lowest point as a result of the American role in the 1971 crisis. They remained strained until March 1977, when Morarji Desai was elected Prime Minister of India. Many in the United States were unhappy with the Emergency in India (1975-77). Although this "eclipse of democracy in India" was not subjected to official American comment, the media in the United States unleashed a vehement criticism which, in turn, provoked the wrath of Mrs. Gandhi.[20] With the advent of the Janata government, relations with America began to stabilize.

Relations with Pakistan further deteriorated over the issue of the nuclear reprocessing plant. After the Indian nuclear explosion in May 1974, Bhutto angrily remarked that the Pakistanis would "eat grass" if necessary to match the Indian nuclear capability. Two years later, Bhutto signed an agreement with France to purchase a nuclear reprocessing plant. Bhutto's expressed determination, coupled with the above mentioned deal, was interpreted in America as Pakistan's move to becoming a nuclear power.[21]

After the signing of the agreement, both Pakistan and France were subjected to strong pressures to cancel the deal. Believing the media stories that were the product of a systematic campaign to malign Pakistan, and disregarding Pakistan's repeated assurances (i) that it had no intention of making an "Islamic bomb," and (ii) that its modest program was meant for plowshare purposes, the Carter administration took a strong stand against Pakistan. Again, this was part of American global policy to check nuclear proliferation. Had a similar policy been applied to India, perhaps Pakistani bitterness would not have intensified. Under the U.S. nonproliferation law of 1978, India was ineligible to receive nuclear fuel from the United States on two grounds: it had not signed the NPT and it would not allow full-scope safeguards on the operations of all its plants. Yet the American president thought fit to overrule the Nuclear Regulatory Commission and even won senatorial backing for shipment of fuel to India. Predictably the Pakistanis vociferously questioned the dual policies of the United States in South Asia.

Neither India nor Pakistan has signed the NPT, as both intend to keep their nuclear option open. India feels that the NPT is a discriminatory treaty and that it cannot afford to be a signatory because of the China factor; Pakistan is not going to sign the NPT until India does. On the other hand, the Americans are committed to cutting off not only nuclear assistance but also economic and military aid, inclusive of military sales credits to any recipient country that refuses to accept IAEA's full safeguards.[22] However, the Americans have thrice deviated from their position: first, when Carter supported the shipment of fuel to India; second, just before the signing of an economic aid-cum-military sales package between the United States and Pakistan, when the administration secured an exemption for Pakistan from the Symington amendment;[23] third, when Reagan persuaded France to provide nuclear fuel to India after Mrs. Gandhi's U.S. visit in 1983. However, it is possible that the last instance of deviation could have been influenced by the moral obligations of the Americans emanating from the 1964 agreement with India, when the United States committed itself to a thirty-year supply of fuel for the Tarapur nuclear plant. The passage of the 1978 non-proliferation act without provision to meet previous commitments amounts to another instance of American betrayal. Disregarding treaty commitments with smaller countries reflects not only the arrogance of power but also a confusion and incoherence in American policies.

The Afghanistan Crisis

The advent of the Iranian revolution and the Soviet invasion of Afghanistan fueled the long-standing western fear of Soviet expansionism and gave an acute sense of urgency to the need to respond adequately to both those dangerous developments. A low-profile American policy in the region was abandoned. The immediate American reaction was not only to condemn vociferously the Soviet move and to refuse to ratify SALT II, but also to try to establish a new relationship with a Pakistan that (in U.S. eyes) had become a "frontline state."

A stream of academics, journalists, and officials have visited Pakistan during the last five years, somewhat reminiscent of the flood of officials who tried to assure Ayub Khan (after the 1962 Sino-Indian war) of America's sincerity. Despite the magnitude of the security threat emanating from Afghanistan, the Pakistanis, fully aware of geopolitical realities, have demonstrated courage and forbearance and have pursued a cautious path in their dealings with the Americans. Although Pakistan's caution is commendable, it may not have produced the expected dividends. Not only has the recent Pak-American aid-cum-sales package failed to enhance Pakistan's security, the Americans have kept to themselves the control of aid on a yearly basis. Compared to recent Indo-Soviet deals, the Pak-American deal with its veto clause reflects America's distrust of Pakistan. The situation as it stands today seems thus: the Americans are anxious to strengthen Pakistan's defense capabilities in order to raise Soviet costs if they decide to invade Pakistan. Yet they do not trust Pakistan and feel that if the Soviet threat does not materialize, then Pakistan might use American-supplied equipment in some undesired direction. Part of the distrust stems from past experience with Pakistan, but part of it is the product of a conscious effort not to annoy India too much.

For most Pakistanis the Indian reaction to the Afghanistan situation was disappointing. Compared to India's reaction to America's $3.2 billion aid package for Pakistan, its response to superpower aggression against a fellow nonaligned state was negligible and reflective of a dilemma. Being heavily indebted to Soviet support (political, economic, diplomatic, and military) and being their only reliable noncommunist friend, India was confronted with an extremely unpleasant choice: to condemn aggression would produce Soviet anger (and weaken some profitable links), but to condone it would tarnish India's own image. India chose not to condemn the Soviets and tried to repay its massive debt, incurred over the years, by accepting the Soviet interpretation of the situation in Afghanistan.[24] It is alleged in some quarters in India that the Indian government concentrated on a diplomatic effort to defuse the situation and reportedly conveyed to the Soviets its uneasiness.[25] However, once the urgency and tension generated by the invasion subsided, India softened toward the Afghan situation and even revived the Indian-Afghan Joint Commission that had been put on the shelf after the Marxist takeover in 1978.[26]

The initial American reaction was strong and impressive, but this enthusiasm has gradually subsided as other issues have come into play. Apart from focusing upon the aid program and encouraging the Geneva parleys to secure a feasible solution, America reverted to its routine for dealing with crises that do not have a high priority. Thus, assertions of American concern for Pakistan's security appear from time to time—motivated mainly by Pakistan's strategic location at the mouth of the oil-rich Gulf.[27]

Conclusion

Ironically, no country has contributed as much as America to the economic growth and the military strength of South Asian countries, yet recognition of America's part in this remains somewhat elusive. Perhaps the major reason lies in reactively oriented American policies toward South Asia. American regional policy moves from one end of the spectrum to the other in congruence with global and regional developments, rather than being based on a well-calculated, long-term regional policy. While the major concern of the Americans in the region has been to check the onward march of communism and to contain Soviet expansionism, the main objective of Pakistan has been to ward off the Indian threat (the threat from Afghanistan is a recent development). The Indian preoccupation has been to strengthen itself to the extent that it can easily cope with perceived threats emanating from China and Pakistan.

Just as Stalin was unable to comprehend Pakistan's drift toward what he referred to as the colonialist and imperialist West, American policy makers have rarely been able to understand, particularly in the past, the conflictual cobweb of South Asia. While befriending Pakistan, they have made every effort not to annoy India. Perhaps that is why, on many occasions, the Americans sent senior officials to sound out the Indians before undertaking a certain course of action vis-à-vis Pakistan. What they often failed to realize was that such moves hurt the United States in Pakistan. They also failed to understand that any effort to strengthen Pakistan leads to a strong Indian reaction.

Although the major American concern has been and still is to deny the region to the Soviets, American policies have not been able to prevent the Soviets from making substantial inroads. While Soviet influence in the area has gradually increased, American influence has remained somewhat peripheral despite enormous doses of aid. Continued Indo-Pakistan hostility baffles and overwhelms the Americans. Ultimately, the American contribution toward the peace and stability of South Asian has not been as great as it should have been. However, the situation has now radically changed. Not only does Pakistan acknowledge the eminent Indian position in the region, but it has also made many positive overtures to lessen the intensity of incumbent distrust. In addition, efforts to work out a regional cooperative organization could further solidify the existing trend.

Compared to a shifting American policy, the Soviets and the Chinese have been extremely consistent in their approach to South Asia. What American policymakers need to learn is the significance of consistency. Consistency strengthens credibility. The United States must apply a well-thought-out policy to an area and then develop calculated moves geared to attaining U.S. objectives, rather than always reacting to unexpected events and sudden developments. Admittedly, reactive moves may at times be necessary, but the United States should not lose sight of long term regional objectives. A lesson can be learned from Chinese and Soviet policies: despite the dramatic changes in the international and regional environments, Moscow's support for India and Afghanistan has remained essentially unaltered, and Chinese relations with Pakistan have continued to grow.[28]

Given the prevailing winds in South Asia, America can undertake many positive measures to enhance not only its stature and credibility but also to strengthen the area's stability. It should formulate its long-term objectives in South Asia, maintaining a certain amount of consistency. It should support, as it has been, the ongoing process of Indo-Pakistan normalization and regional cooperation. This détente is the key to the emergence of a regional framework. It could eventually result in the establishment of an effective regional association and a significant reduction in tension. One way to approach this objective is to channel all future aid through a collective regional framework. If the aid is attractive enough, the chances are that the regional countries will accelerate their efforts to evolve the desired regional organization. Despite the impressive progress made by most of the area countries, assistance (economic and military) is still welcomed. Nonparticipation by one or two countries need not destroy such an arrangement.

Apart from encouraging Indo-Pakistan normalization, the United States could also play a crucial role (with the Pakistanis) in normalizing Sino-Indian relations. In fact, the triangular normalization among China, India, and Pakistan is perhaps the most positive answer to the needs of the area. It could also reduce the chances of nuclear proliferation. China's quiet encouragement of Pakistani efforts to mend fences with India reflects its desire to improve relations with India. Admittedly, triangular normalization is a difficult task, not only in view of Soviet investments in the area and their rivalry with China, but also because of the solidified distrust between India and Pakistan.[29] However, efforts toward this goal could produce dividends beyond the expectations of most Americans. The leaderships in the three countries involved seem to be receptive to the idea. Pakistan, being the smallest of these countries, seems relatively more active, perhaps because it recognizes existing realities in the area and has a strong desire for peace and stability in the region.

Finally, the U.S.-Pakistan security relationship needs to be maintained, not only because of Pakistan's proximity to the Strait of Hormuz and the useful role Pakistan can play in the security of the Gulf (coupled with its courageous stance against Soviet aggression in Afghanistan), but also because that relationship generates a sense of security among the people of Pakistan, which, in turn, strengthens the government's determination to carry forward the process of normalization with India. Pakistan neither hopes to be a threat to India, in view of the existing power differentials, nor could it ever be a deterrent to the Soviets. Cognizant of operative geopolitical realities, Pakistan's policies reflect the desire not to engage India in another futile clash. Pakistan's restrained attitude toward the Afghan crisis seems to illustrate its peaceful intent. At the same time, India has to avoid exaggerating the threat emanating from Pakistan's security relationship with the United States. However, if India should cater to Soviet objectives in the area, then Pakistan's anxieties and apprehensions will continue at a high level. And if this happens, then the Americans should recognize that their policy of drawing India some distance away from the Soviet Union has failed.

NOTES

1. For a detailed analysis of vital interests, see Bernard Brodie, "Vital Interests: By Whom and How Determined," in F. N. Trager and P. S. Kronenberg, eds., *National Security and American Society* (Lawrence: University Press of Kansas, 1973), pp. 63-67.

2. See Richard Cronin, "United States Interests, Objectives, and Policy Options in Southwest Asia," in Shirin Tahir-Kheli, ed., *U.S. Strategic Interest in Southwest Asia* (New York: Praeger, 1982).

3. See T. B. Millar, "America's Alliances: Asia," in *America's Security in the 1980s Part II*, Adelphi Paper No. 174 (London: International Institute for Strategic Studies, 1982), pp. 28-29.

4. See National Security Council Paper, *U.S. Policy towards South Asia,* NSC 5617 (Dec. 7, 1956), p. 6.

5. Rodney W. Jones, "Mending Relations with Pakistan," in *The Washington Quarterly*, 4 (Spring 1981), 20.

6. India had been authorized to obtain reimbursable U.S. military assistance under section 106 of the Mutual Security Act of 1954 as amended. By September 30, 1956, India had purchased $34,108,283 of equipment, of which $28,853,450 had been delivered almost immediately. See NSC 5617, p. 33.

7. During the years 1955-65 India received $10.5 billion, whereas Pakistan merely received $2.5 billion. However, if calculated on a per-capita basis, it May turn out that Pakistan has received relatively more than India. See Shirin Tahir-Kheli, *The United States and Pakistan: The Evolution of an Influence Relationship* (New York: Praeger, 1982), p. 155.

8. M. A. Khan, *Friends Not Masters* (London: Oxford University Press, 1962), p. 145.

9. India's forcible occupation of Goa was vehemently criticized in almost all Western countries. The liberal friends of India in the United States were also extremely critical of Indian aggression, and they expressed their resentment in rather harsh tones. India, on the other hand, was somewhat shocked initially at the Western attitude and then launched a wave of bitter anti-American criticism. See Norman D. Palmer, *South Asia and United States Policy* (Boston: Houghton Mifflin, 1966), p. 23. See G. W. Choudhury, *India, Pakistan, Bangladesh, and the Major Powers* (New York: The Free Press, 1975), p. 107.

10. Thomas P. Thornton, "South Asia and the Great Powers," in *World Affairs,* 132 (March 1970), 352.

11. See Henry Kissinger, *White House Years* (Boston: Little, Brown, 1979), pp. 842-918.

12. W. H. Wriggins, "United States Relations with South Asia," a paper written for the Eighth European Conference on Modern South Asian Studies, Tallberg (Sweden, July 2-8, 1983).

13. Richard M. Nixon, *The Memoirs of Richard Nixon* (New York: Warner Books, 1978), pp. 650-59.

14. See L. I. Rudolph and S. H. Rudolph, "The Coordination of Complexity in South Asia," in L. I. Rudolph and S. H. Rudolph, eds., *The Regional Imperative: The Administration of U.S. Foreign Policy towards South Asian States under Presidents Nixon and Johnson* (Atlantic Highlands: Humanities Press, 1980), pp. 42-45. See articles in the same volume by Stephen Philip Cohen, Gerald A. Heeger, Stanley A. Kochanek, and Christopher Van Hollen. See also Van Hollen, "The Tilt Policy Revisited: Nixon-Kissinger Geopolitics and South Asia" in *Asia Survey*, 20 (April 1980), 339-61, and Kissinger, *White House Years*, pp. 842-918.

15. Rudolph and Rudolph, *Coordination of Complexity*, pp. 43-44.

16. Ibid.

17. Nixon, *Memoirs*, pp. 650-59.

18. Wriggins, "United States Relations."

19. Z. A. Bhutto, "Bilateralism: New Direction" in *Pakistan Horizon*, 29 (1976): 3-79.

20. See Norman D. Palmer, "The United States and South Asia: The Carter and Reagan Administration," in L. Ziring, ed., *The Subcontinent in World Politics* (New York: Praeger, 1982), p. 225.

21. See P. I. Cheema, "Pakistan's Quest for Nuclear Technology," in the *Australian Outlook*, 34 (August 1980), 188-90.

22. There is one exception to this general rule. If the president of the United States decides that the termination of such aid would seriously jeopardize America's vital interests or certifies that the country in question has assured him that it will not acquire or develop nuclear weapons or assist other nations in doing so, then the aid could be continued. However, if, within thirty days after the receipt of such certification the Congress adopts a concurrent resolution stating in substance that the Congress disapproves the furnishing of assistance pursuant to the certification, upon their adoption of that resolution the certification shall cease to be effective and all deliveries of assistance furnished under the authority of that certification shall be suspended immediately. Presidents still could continue the flow of aid even after the adoption of such resolution, but only for thirty days and that would have to provide another certification stating that immediate termination of aid would be detrimental to the national security. See sections 699 and 670 of the Foreign Assistance Act of 1961, as amended in *Legislation on Foreign Relations through 1981* (Washington: U.S. Government Printing Office, 1982), pp. 177-81.

23. The Symington Amendment forbade U.S. assistance except food aid to countries that pursued nuclear enrichment technology and refused to give assurances that they were not developing nuclear weapons. See *Keesing's*

Contemporary Archives (July 6, 1979), p. 29701; (Sept. 11, 1981), p. 31074; (Sept. 17, 1982), p. 31707.

24. Suyit Mansingh, "United States-India Relations: Problems and Prospects," *India Quarterly,* 36 (July-Dec., 1980): 268-70.
25. Ibid.
26. A. de Riencourt, "India and Pakistan in the Shadow of Afghanistan," in *Foreign Affairs,* 61 (Winter 1982-83): 434.
27. See, for example, *Hearings before the Committee on Foreign Relations,* U.S. Senate, 97th Congress, 1st Session (March 24, 1981, March 31, 1981).
28. P. I. Cheema, "Pakistan's Security Problems," in K. J. Newman, ed., *Pakistan: 35 Years after Independence* (Hamburg: German-Pakistan Forum, 1983), pp. 188-207.
29. Ibid., pp. 183-207.

8

U.S. Policy in South Asia

Selig S. Harrison

The central objective of American policy in South Asia should be the promotion of improved relations between India and Pakistan as part of the larger evolution of a South Asian cooperative regional organization. At the same time, the United States can effectively pursue this objective only if it maintains a detached posture toward the military rivalry between New Delhi and Islamabad.

This position need not preclude all military and militarily related sales to India and Pakistan, but it would dictate an extremely selective and restrained approach toward such sales comparable to the policy pursued by Washington between 1965 and 1981. The United States may confront specific situations, such as the Chinese invasion of India in 1962 or the Soviet occupation of Afghanistan in 1979, which may justify carefully circumscribed sales of military equipment for temporary periods to either India or Pakistan or both. But such sales should not be made if they would serve primarily to improve the position of either country in the Indo-Pakistan military rivalry (e.g., the sale of 155-mm howitzers to Pakistan for use in plains warfare against India, as against 105-mm howitzers, which would be more useful in mountain warfare along the Afghan frontier). Above all, the United States should seek to avoid becoming the principal military supplier to either country. American policy should encourage the diversification of military procurement by both India and Pakistan as part of a larger effort to minimize the present polarization of the subcontinent along the lines of the American-Soviet and Sino-Soviet rivalries.

The task of defining the limits of American involvement is not an easy one. To suggest the direction of my thinking, a detached policy would not rule out selling C-130s to India or providing a sophisticated, one-directional radar network to Pakistan for the Afghan frontier. It would also permit the commercial sale of high technology with defense applications to both countries under the same security criteria and ground rules.

The commitments already made to Pakistan for the sale of F-16s and other India-focused weaponry would be honored, but new commitments would be prohibited. For such commitments would only exacerbate the existing tension between India and Pakistan and would be completely incompatible with the objective of promoting regional cooperation.

Apart from marginal military sales consistent with the maintenance of a detached posture, the United States should emphasize positive economic assistance and trade policies toward both India and Pakistan, including support for infrastructural assistance to Pakistan to improve roads, airfields, and other military-related facilities in areas bordering Afghanistan. Such economic support would assist both countries in maintaining military establishments consistent with their size and economic strength. Just as economic assistance to India in past years has released funds for military spending, so economic assistance to Pakistan is also a form of security assistance. The difference is that military spending must be justified when it is made possible by economic assistance within the internal battle of the budget in a country. In contrast, when the United States provides grant or concessional military aid to a country, it intervenes on the side of a military elite in the battle of the budget. To be sure, the United States affects internal power relationships within other countries in extending one form of economic aid as against another. By its nature, however, economic development leads to the eventual diffusion of some of the benefits of external economic support, while military assistance tends to give disproportionate power to military elites in the internal economic and political power struggles of other countries.

American military assistance has had a powerful impact on Pakistani domestic politics during the past three decades. The impact of U.S. military aid grants on the interplay between Pakistan elite groups not only gave the military an edge over civil service and political factions, it also strengthened and hardened the dominant position of West Pakistan over the numerically superior eastern wing. The social base of the Pakistani armed forces has been overwhelmingly Punjabi. Moreover, the Punjabi-dominated military juntas that controlled Pakistan before 1972 worked hand in hand with narrowly based business groups that were also similarly centered in the western wing. American military aid grants have helped to give the ruling military-business leadership its entrenched position in the West, and this in turn encouraged the unyielding response of the Ayub and Yahya regimes in the face of an increasingly determined Bengali posture.

It might very well be that military rule would have come to Pakistan in one way or another, whatever the United States had done, and that the eventual collapse of the partition settlement was preordained by the inherent anomaly of a state so diverse and so geographically truncated. However, the inevitability of a total East-West rupture must remain a moot point, and one of the crucial factors to be considered in speculation on this issue is the interaction between autonomy demands in the Eastern and Western wings.[1] Under military-dominated regimes, Bengali autonomy demands posed a direct threat to the ruling power groups, since concessions to autonomy in the East would have intensified Pushtun and Baluchi demands in the West. By contrast, given a looser, federal pattern in the West and a more broadly based power structure, Bengali, Pathan, and Baluchi interests would have been mutually reinforcing. The struggle in the West was closely divided in the fifties between advocates of a federal compromise and the "one-unit" setup finally adopted. In the absence of U.S. arms aid, some form of accommodation might well have evolved between a less intransigent military hierarchy and other West Pakistani elite groups. Even after a decade of the Ayub Khan regime, there was a powerful surge of unified action among Bengali, Pushtun, and Baluchi groups during the stormy interval of relative political freedom spanning the last months of Ayub and the Yahya Khan coup.

In the present context of Pakistani politics, American over-identification with the Zia ul-Haq regime as a result of the resumption of American military aid by the Reagan administration has again complicated the resolution of Pakistan's internal power rivalries by aligning the United States on the side of the military in its struggle with the bureaucracy and with civilian political forces. The fact that the military is now more clearly Punjabi dominated than ever before has meant that the United States is also aligned with a repressive majority in its confrontation with self-conscious ethnic minorities.

Although a variety of factors have contributed to American military assistance policies in South Asia, one of the governing American motives behind these policies in the case of Pakistan has been a conscious desire to support the rise of military regimes as a means of getting concrete U.S. military benefits. Since Pakistan, like India, is characterized by an underlying climate of Third World nationalism, civilian regimes would have been reluctant to permit the installation of the electronic intelligence facilities that the Ayub regime permitted in Peshawar from 1958 to 1967. Similarly, the Zia regime has been attractive to Washington not only in the context of hypothetical contingencies in the Gulf but also as a possible partner in the ongoing task of monitoring Soviet submarine activity in the northern Indian Ocean.

Some Pakistanis, such as Pervaiz Iqbal Cheema, have criticized the United States for its tendency to define its interests in South Asia primarily in relation to the superpower conflict and for its resulting insensitivity

to the depth of Indo-Pakistani tensions.[2] Pointing to the divergence between Pakistani and American perceptions of their security relationship
during the fifties and sixties, he calls for a new type of American aid relationship with Pakistan in which the United States defines its objectives as
the promotion of an Indo-Pakistan balance. He advises India not to "ex-
aggerate" the threat posed by American aid. As his analysis implicitly
suggests, however, Indo-Pakistan tensions do not have much to do with
any transitory assessment of the military balance by one side or the
other. These tensions are a function of a continuing struggle over the
terms of the power relationship between the Hindu majority and the
Moslem minority that has been taking place for centuries in the subcontinent. It is not fear of Pakistan that explains the Indian reaction to the
F-16s. Rather, it is the Indian belief that the United States is interfering
in the evolution of what New Delhi regards as a natural balance of power
in South Asia.

Indian leaders are confident of their ability to subdue Pakistan in any
protracted conflict and do not believe that Islamabad would launch an
all-out frontal attack. Their concern has been that Pakistan, armed with
a highly sophisticated attack aircraft such as the F-16, might engage in
more limited military provocations, forcing New Delhi to pay an unac-
ceptably high price in order to enforce its military superiority.

New Delhi is seeking to achieve unchallengeable dominance over Pakistan for historically rooted psychological and political reasons that lie beyond the scope of this chapter. Cheema candidly acknowledges that, for
its part, Pakistan has attempted since its inception to obtain sophisticated military equipment from the United States in order to improve its
balance of military power with India, albeit periodically cloaking this objective in the guise of other security objectives. The experience of the
past three decades has demonstrated that the Indo-Pakistan rivalry is
propelled by primordial indigenous forces beyond the control or management of Washington, and the United States should henceforth maintain a scrupulous detachment from this rivalry.

In my view, American policy in South Asia during the decades ahead
should be designed to promote three critical, interrelated security objectives, to which other security objectives should be subordinated:

1. *An improvement in American relations with India that would reverse the present drift to de facto Indo-Soviet military collaboration in
the Indian Ocean.* Such an improvement would not be possible in the
context of continued U.S. sales of sophisticated military equipment to
Pakistan, even if the United States were to offer to sell comparable
equipment to India.

Should the United States enlarge its military support of Pakistan, Indian hostility to the American presence in the Indian Ocean would be likely to grow, together with Indian reliance on Soviet support for Indian naval development. By contrast, an American policy sensitive to Indian power aspirations would provide a favorable environment for the continued use of Diego Garcia, if such a policy were accompanied by arms limitation negotiations designed to achieve greater symmetry in the levels of U.S. and Soviet deployments in the Indian Ocean.

So far, New Delhi has carefully stopped short of de facto military collaboration with Moscow, but it would be unwise to assume that such restraint will continue to govern Indian policy regardless of the nature of U.S. policies toward Pakistan. An atmosphere of xenophobic resentment is now building up among the key military and political figures who could have a major voice in shaping New Delhi's regional military role in the decades ahead. Given continuing provocations in the form of multiplying American weapons aid to Islamabad, in time this atmosphere could lead to a variety of punitive, anti-American moves in the Indian Ocean designed to limit the American military presence or to harass American forces in their use of existing facilities, including Diego Garcia.

Even if the United States were to taper off its military sales to Islamabad, New Delhi would no doubt continue to make significant military purchases from the Soviet Union. But this would not, in itself, be adverse to American interests in the context of a detached American posture toward the subcontinent in which a more compatible Indo-American relationship would be developing side by side with continuing Indo-Soviet links. What makes the growing Indo-Soviet military relationship worrisome is not the resulting degree of Indian dependence on Moscow. India has retained considerable freedom of action, offsetting its Soviet dependence with increasing arms purchases from Western countries. Close Indo-Soviet ties would become menacing to the United States only if Washington continues to array itself against Indian regional ambitions, prompting an Indian desire to retaliate in its own perceived interests.

2. *A political settlement in Afghanistan that would lead to the reduction and eventual withdrawal of Soviet combat forces while, at the same time, precluding or limiting the establishment of operational Soviet strategic bases there.* At present, the Soviet air bases at Bagram, Kabul, Qandahar, and Shindand have runways long enough to receive a limited number of Bison bombers and other long-range strategic aircraft, but these facilities were built before the occupation with earlier Soviet and American economic and military aid. Most American and other western intelligence sources agree that Moscow has not yet taken the variety of steps that would be necessary to equip its Afghan air bases to support

large numbers of strategic aircraft on long stopovers (e.g., substantially lengthened the runways, substantially expanded petroleum storage facilities and built new hardstands for parking reserve squadrons). Instead, Soviet efforts to improve these bases have been primarily tailored to make them more effective as counter-insurgency bases for helicopters and tactical fighter aircraft used against the *Mujahiddin.*

The objective of forestalling the establishment of strategic bases in Afghanistan would be undermined by further escalation of the Afghan conflict. If the present escalation should continue, together with a growing polarization of Afghan political forces, Moscow would be likely to intensify its efforts to make Afghanistan a South Asian Mongolia governed by a monolithic Communist elite. This would necessitate an indefinite military occupation, which would no doubt be accompanied, in time, by the development of strategic bases. American interests would be better served by a negotiated settlement based on acceptance of a Finland-style security relationship between the Soviet Union and a less monolithic client regime in Kabul. Such a relationship is implicitly envisaged in the United Nations draft agreement on Afghanistan currently under discussion between U.N. Secretary General Perez De Cuellar and the governments of Pakistan, Afghanistan, the United States, and the Soviet Union.

Pakistan's security would be greatly enhanced by an Afghan settlement. Should the conflict escalate, Soviet retaliatory pressures on Pakistan are likely to intensify. Already, as an accompaniment to its support of the U.N. negotiations on Afghanistan, Moscow has made thinly veiled threats to destabilize the Zia regime if Islamabad continues to cooperate with the United States, China, and Middle Eastern countries in channeling weapons aid to the *Mujahiddin.*

3. *The denial of Arabian Sea ports and other coastal facilities in Baluchistan and Sind to the Soviet navy and air force.* Moscow would be most tempted to seek and most likely to obtain such facilities as an accompaniment to the balkanization of Pakistan.

The emergence of an increasingly militant Sindhi separatist movement since 1983 has emphasized the built-in conflict between dominant Punjabi and *muhajir* (immigrant) elites and the non-Punjabi ethnic groups indigenous to the areas that have made up Pakistan. At present, the non-Punjabi minorities are not receiving substantial Soviet support, but the danger of a Soviet dismemberment strategy is growing as the Pakistani political crisis sharpens. American support for the Zia ul-Haq regime has emboldened Zia to reject meaningful compromise with his opponents and is progressively driving opposition elements into an anti-American and pro-Soviet stance.

American interests in Pakistan would be best served by a compromise between moderate leaders of the minorities who favor the continuance of Pakistan, restructured along confederal lines, and moderates in the Punjabi-muhajir elites who recognize increasingly that Pakistan faces a serious threat of balkanization.

Zia's effort in 1985 to legitimize his regime by holding tightly controlled elections did not represent a significant step toward such a compromise. The central government would have a stronger grip than ever over the provinces under the postelection governmental structure ordained by Zia. Even a return to more genuinely participatory political life under the 1973 Constitution would not bring political stability to Pakistan unless the Constitution were amended to incorporate safeguards barring the central government from forcibly ousting an elected provincial government unilaterally, as Bhutto did in 1973.

In my view, such safeguards against arbitrary central government intervention are more critical to the minorities than the much-discussed issue of the division of powers between Islamabad and the provinces. The minorities are concerned not only with the substance of autonomy but also with the feeling of autonomy. This psychological factor explains why they attach so much importance to the safeguards issue. It also underlies their emphasis on the need for a linguistic redemarcation of provincial boundaries that would give each of them majority control over a specific territory, together with explicit constitutional recognition of their distinctive ethnic identities.

A constitutional compromise in Pakistan could well set in motion an overall process of improvement in the South Asian security environment. It would not only neutralize the climate of militant separatism in Baluchistan and Sind that now offers such a tempting invitation to Moscow but would also strengthen the forces in Pakistan seeking a political settlement in Afghanistan. An Afghan settlement would, in turn, help to forestall Soviet adoption of a balkanization strategy. Finally, in the context of a more representative government in Islamabad and Pakistan's moderation of its role as a front-line state, the prospects for a relaxation of Indo-Pakistani tensions would be greatly improved.

NOTES

1. See my analysis in *The Widening Gulf: Asian Nationalism and American Policy* (New York: Free Press, 1978), pp. 274-76.
2. See P. I. Cheema, "American Policy in South Asia: Interests and Objectives," Chapter 7 of this book.

9

U.S. Policy and South Asia: The Decision-Making Dimension

R. R. Subramaniam

A unique feature of the American government is that powers are exercised by separate executive, legislative, and judicial branches. In practice, however, the powers and influences of the three are not equal—especially in foreign policy matters. Throughout American history, the judiciary has been content to play a passive role in the foreign policy process. The Supreme Court forcefully upheld the exercise of executive power in foreign relations; this point was underscored by its verdict in the Chadha case of July 1983, when the power of Congress to veto presidential decisions was weakened. This ruling had a clear bearing on future congressional actions, especially with regard to nuclear nonproliferation issues.

The growing congressional militancy in the area of nuclear nonproliferation, which culminated in the framing of the U.S. Nuclear Nonproliferation Act (NNPA) of March 10, 1978, does not seem to have ebbed in its enthusiasm. The Reagan administration's foreign policy has put a much greater emphasis on combating Sovietism worldwide than on curbing nuclear proliferation. Since the president is mainly in charge of U.S. foreign policy, congressional powers have been inadequate to thwart the White House in deciding how the United States can carry out specific programs such as nuclear proliferation or arms aid. In the cases of Carter and Reagan, the White House's decision regarding nuclear or arms export to South Asia has prevailed. Of course, a major element of the decision-making process is the ability of the president to work collaboratively with Congress. It needs to be pointed out that several misperceptions continue to cloud the thinking about India in both the executive and the legislative branches of the government. In the post-Indira Gandhi phase, such misperceptions may change. Apart from India's relationship with the Soviet Union, the principal adversary of the United States, it is the capabilities and intentions of India, especially after the nuclear detonation of May 1974, that have continued to shape Washington's attitudes toward New Delhi. This was the case in the Carter administration, less so in the Reagan administration. However, as the new prime minister, Rajiv Gandhi appears to be veering toward Nehru's disarmament policy at the global level.

Because India and the United States are both democratic states, it would seem that by this criterion alone the formulation of a policy aimed at strengthening the relations between the two countries would be a natural corollary. However, for the United States, in its pursuit of global or grand strategic objectives, the critical determinants of policy formulation have been the Soviet Union, Europe, Japan, and the Middle East. Since the seventies, China has also become a factor in U.S. strategic policy. When nuclear proliferation became an issue of major concern, as it did during the Carter administration, India by virtue of its nuclear detonation became, albeit temporarily, a front-burner issue. Subsequent developments like the Soviet intervention in Afghanistan brought Pakistan to the "front line." Through this development an opportunity was provided to Pakistan to improve its relationship with the United States.

The policy of nonalignment which President Zia ul-Haq of Pakistan is following today seems consistent with the goals of the United States. The Indian version of it by contrast had been perceived by policymakers in Washington as tilting toward the Soviets. Rajiv Gandhi may correct that tilt. Pakistan has sought to draw the United States, as a superpower, into its regional interactions with its adversary, India, through the earlier "new Cold War" attitudes of President Reagan. If, however, President Reagan were to achieve arms control agreements with the Soviets in his second term, this could prove to be a positive factor for Rajiv Gandhi's disarmament initiatives launched at the Six Nation Summit in New Delhi in January 1985.

In the past, Pakistan's participation in U.S.-sponsored anticommunist pacts like CENTO (aimed at the USSR) and SEATO (aimed at China) enabled it to obtain military hardware. This was at a time when Nehru sought to restructure a subcontinent free of the superpowers. Rajiv Gandhi, too, may strive for that. These attempts were sharply set back when the Sino-Indian war broke out in October 1962. Subsequent developments led to the bettering of Sino-Pakistan relations and rendered Pakistan's participation in SEATO irrelevant. The gravitation of Islamabad toward Beijing in the early sixties actually weakened the U.S. position in South Asia. But in the early seventies it was Pakistan that strengthened U.S. relations with China, although gaining little advantage for itself. It took the Indo-Pakistan War of 1971 to restructure South Asia and establish India as the dominant regional military power.

America's fading military connection with Pakistan was resuscitated only a decade later, when Reagan's anti-Sovietism opened a window of military opportunity for Islamabad. In a stricter sense, one should say that after the Soviets intervened in Afghanistan, it was Zbigniew Brzezinski, Carter's national security advisor, who sought to reaffirm U.S. ties with Pakistan through the 1959 Bilateral Agreement.[1] Less than a year before the intervention, President Carter had used the provisions of the Symington-Glenn amendment to the Foreign Assistance Act to impose economic sanctions against Pakistan on the basis of intelligence reports that Islamabad was constructing an unsafeguarded enrichment plant.[2] Following the Afghan developments, White House officials were preparing legislation to lift the ban that the amendment had imposed on military and economic assistance to Pakistan. This decision of the Carter administration was to activate a set of processes that the Reagan administration, with its anti-Soviet posture, further pursued to pave the way for the sale of forty high performance aircraft, F-16s (possibly with Saudi funds) as well as for a $3.2 billion military and economic aid package that was to be spread over five years. This agreement between Islamabad and Washington was announced in Islamabad on June 11, 1982, by former Under Secretary of State James Buckley on his visit to Pakistan. Before this visit, in his address to the Karachi Institute for International Affairs, the Indian foreign minister had stressed the need for Pakistan to procure arms for legitimate self-defense. However, F-16s could be used for offensive strikes against India, although the American rationale for supplying them was that they would be used for air defense against intruding Soviet MiG aircraft from Afghanistan.

One issue had continued to dominate American military policy in South Asia: the transfer of weapons, and this type of policy underwent a significant change during the period from 1977 to 1979, when President Carter pursued a policy that ensured that offensive arms would not be introduced into regions of tension.[3] It is for this reason that Islamabad could not procure the offensive ground attack A-7 aircraft, even though the military leaders are believed to have been willing to trade this against the procurement of a reprocessing plant, especially during Zulfiqar Ali Bhutto's tenure.[4]

For New Delhi, the F-16s appeared to signal the renewal of the American commitment, one that appeared to have been weakened somewhat by Carter's emphasis on nuclear nonproliferation. In the past, military rulers in Pakistan have often sought to emphasize the intraregional dimensions of its regional dispute with India over Kashmir. This strategy does not seem to have worked in Pakistan's favor in any of its wars with its neighbors. The present leadership has sought to jibe with the Reagan administration's anti-Soviet policies, and once again hoped to neutralize

India's relationship with the Soviet Union. Pakistan's initial efforts to integrate itself into a broader "strategic consensus" involving U.S. interventionary forces in the Gulf do not seem to have borne fruit. At best, one sees an American approval for Pakistani military brigades in Saudi Arabia, as well as a major reversal of Carter's nonproliferation decisions. These decisions appeared to have had a braking effect on Washington's military relationship with Islamabad because of the involvement of the Soviet Union in the region. The decision to release that brake may have been greatly influenced by the academic staff of the National Security Council in both the Carter and Reagan administrations.

The decision-making processes in the American government are the product of several interacting institutions, both in the executive and the legislative branches. Brecher has observed, "A decision is made by an individual or individuals or a group authorized by the political system to act within a prescribed sphere of external behavior."[5] Following Brecher, one may say that in the case of nuclear proliferation and arms transfer policy, the individual attitudes of Carter and Reagan have had a large bearing on the application of the said policy to South Asia.

To date, most process-related analyses that relate to arms control focus on either Congress or substantive issues or negotiations. Jimmy Carter was one of those rare presidents who had a genuine interest in the subject of nuclear proliferation. A major issue that confronts all American presidents is the effective coordination, management, and integration of overall arms control, defense, and foreign policy. Those responsible for framing a national security policy within the establishment often perceive arms control processes to be inimical to their interests. When these interests predominate and the executive achieves little by way of arms control, the congressmen who seek an arms control record focus their attention on nuclear weapons proliferation.

When the Carter administration took office in January 1977, it had four basic objectives:

1. To focus its nonproliferation efforts on the dangers of the fuel cycle and to attempt to remove political incentives through diplomatic channels.
2. To use the time created by imposing a domestic moratorium on plutonium reprocessing to build an international regime so that the fuel cycle was immune to proliferation abuse.
3. To reestablish U.S. dominance as a supplier of nuclear materials.
4. To discourage commercial reprocessing, both at home and abroad.

The task force constituted to fit together the pieces of a new and embracing nonproliferation policy was duly formed under the auspices of the

NSC, and was headed by Dr. Joseph Nye of the U.S. Department of State. It was officially designated to prepare the Presidential Review Memorandum No. 15 (PRM-15). This interagency group drew its membership from several parts of the executive bureaucracy. A representative of the Nuclear Regulatory Commission (NRC) was given observer status in order to facilitate communication between the regulatory agency and the executive branch. The PRM-15 study was launched in late January 1977 as an independent review, with a presidentially decreed deadline of March 21. Purists in the Carter administration pushed for an absolutist position. They wanted the administration to come down hard on the allies (Western Europe and Japan) as well as on the intransigents (India and Pakistan). They recommended measures such as an embargo on low enriched uranium (LEU) fuel to coerce foreign governments that had a nuclear relationship with the United States into shelving their reprocessing plans.

The moderate view, as represented by Joseph Nye's state department team, foresaw the dangers of Washington overreaching itself. They warned against threats of drastic U.S. action (a cut-off of enrichment services). Instead, they wanted an earnest diplomatic effort to push for agreement on stricter export ground rules and voluntary postponement on plutonium recycling. In the end, PRM-15 left open the question of how tough a line the United States should take on foreign reprocessing and on what terms, if any, the administration would find reprocessing acceptable. That issue was slated to be at the top of the agenda for the meeting of the NSC Policy Review Committee that would decide the matter as part of its job in sanctioning official administration nonproliferation policy.

The forum for deciding the reprocessing question was the Policy Review Committee. The members of the committee were National Security Advisor Zbigniew Brzezinski, Secretary of Defense Harold Brown, CIA Director Stansfield Turner, ACDA Director Paul Warnke, and NRC Chairman Marcus Rowden. The State Department was represented by Warren Christopher, Deputy Assistant Secretary of State, and Joseph Nye. The attempt to re-negotiate the 1963 Indo-U.S. Agreement on Cooperation of Civil Uses of Atomic Energy epitomized the problem of winning acceptance of the administration's new export conditions. India's position tried the skill and patience of the Carter administration's officials. It also led to a breach in the administration's relations with the NRC. On April 20, 1978, the NRC, on a tie vote, rejected India's license application for the export of seventeen tons of enriched uranium needed for fueling the Tarapur Atomic Power Station (TAPS). In doing so, the commission rejected the recommendation of the State Department that the license be approved on a one-time basis, so as not to disrupt its delicate diplomatic attempts to nudge New Delhi away from a recalcitrant position opposing the new U.S. terms of export.

NRC Commissioner Victor Gilinsky, who served in both the Carter and the Reagan administrations, had a position on the nuclear proliferation issue that may be characterized as hostile to India. Having opposed the sale of enriched uranium to TAPS in the past, he has written articles in several prominent newspapers opposing the sale of spare parts—the one contentious issue that remains in the nuclear relationship between India and the United States, now that France has replaced the United States as a supplier of enriched uranium for TAPS (as per the agreement reached between President Reagan and Indira Gandhi in Washington in July 1982). Richard Kennedy, the ambassador-at-large for nonproliferation affairs in the Reagan administration had argued in 1978 that "the law did not intend this Commission to rule on foreign policy."[6]

This particular area of American foreign policy, namely nuclear proliferation, illustrates how (in the case of South Asia) the U.S. decision-making apparatus displays a lack of effective coordination between the generalists concerned with global issues and the regional experts who are concerned with South Asia, as well as lack of balance between global, regional, and bilateral factors. Senator Stuart Symington once compared the policy planning, decision-making, and program execution in the nuclear area of U.S. foreign policy to a "battle royal" with many contestants. In the executive branch of the government alone, the decision-making process spans twenty-one different federal agencies and councils.[7] Often enough it is the State Department that takes the lead in the negotiations of nuclear agreements. If, however, the export in question involves hardware, for example, spare parts for the Tarapur Atomic Power Station, then a major decision-making role is assumed either by the Department of Commerce or the Nuclear Regulatory Commission to consider the implications for nuclear proliferation. The issuance of licenses for export of heavy water to Argentina and hot isostatic presses to South Africa by the Commerce Department in 1983, only indicated how no agency in the United States government concerned with nuclear proliferation is effectively coordinated in the process.

Disorganization on nuclear issues does not appear to be confined to the executive. It exists in Congress as well, since the subject is divided among at least nineteen committees in the House and the Senate. Many of these Committees have overlapping interests. Congressional committees, such as the Senate Government Operations Committee and several subcommittees of the Senate Foreign Relations Committee, have regularly held open hearings and initiated legislation on nuclear export and nonproliferation policy. In particular, it is the Subcommittee on Energy Nuclear Proliferation and Government Processes of the Senate Committee on Governmental Affairs that has provided a vehicle for the legislative arm to monitor the executive's nonproliferation record.

Senator Charles Percy, then the chairman of this subcommittee, was to observe on November 19, 1981 that "I will continue to call for hearings on this topic [nuclear proliferation] until this subcommittee perceives that our nation has awakened to the seriousness of the problem." The proliferation of nuclear weapons and the capacity to make them by certain nations had been regarded by many members of the Congress to be the principal danger of the nuclear era. Since the end of World War II, both the executive and the legislative branches of the United States government have helped devise and carry out policies aimed at preventing proliferation. Congressional involvement in shaping nonproliferation policies has been characterized by periods of intense interest (as during the Carter administration) interspersed by periods of little visible activity (as appears to be the case during the present Reagan phase). The institutions most directly concerned with nonproliferation include the Atomic Energy Commission and its successors, the Energy Research and Development Administration, the Department of Energy, and the Nuclear Regulatory Commission, and the Arms Control and Disarmament Agency. Congress had mandated U.S. nonproliferation policies in the Atomic Energy Act of 1946, and those that now appear in the Atomic Energy Act of 1954, as subsequently amended.

Arthur Schlesinger's concept of the "imperial presidency" cast Congress as a subordinate in international affairs, especially in issues of arms control and nonproliferation. In the past decade, however, especially after the Indian detonation in May 1974, it is Congress that has taken an almost theological approach toward nonproliferation issues. By the end of the 94th Congress in 1976, a spirit of doubt and distrust about proliferation prevailed. It was this atmosphere that was responsible for the delay in issuing nuclear export licenses. India was a particular victim of this delay. The year the Carter administration assumed office, 1977, was one of the most tumultuous for U.S. nonproliferation policies. The Nuclear Energy Policy Study Group (made up of leading intellectuals, some from the eastern liberal establishment and sponsored by Ford and MITRE) performed a study and in 1977 issued a report entitled *Nuclear Power: Issues and Choices* which called for strong nonproliferation measures. This report was to have a strong influence on President Carter, and it came at a time when the Congress, largely guided by the aims of Senators Percy and Glenn, was working on comprehensive nonproliferation legislation aimed at creating the Nuclear Nonproliferation Act.

On April 7, 1977, President Carter delivered a speech titled "Nuclear

Power and Foreign Policy'' in which he revealed his plans to end domestic production of plutonium. He also called on other nations to join the United States in halting the use of plutonium for nuclear fuel. Other Carter proposals that were relevant to South Asia included a call for all nations to adopt a voluntary moratorium on the sale or purchase of enrichment or reprocessing plants (retroactively applied to such agreements as those between France and Pakistan) and to make no new commitments of nuclear technology or fuel to countries that refuse to forego nuclear explosives, to refrain from national nuclear reprocessing, and to place all their nuclear facilities under IAEA safeguards.

The attempt by the Carter administration to apply these requirements retroactively was resisted by India, which felt that domestic legislation such as the NNPA could not be used to negate an international contract of the kind to which India and the United States had agreed in the 1963 civilian nuclear agreement. In the case of Pakistan, the NNPA ceased to have any effect because the American supply of enriched uranium to the Pakistan Research Reactor (PARR) in Islamabad had ceased well before the NNPA came into effect. What was relevant, however, was the connection of the Symington-Glenn Amendment to the Foreign Assistance Act of 1961. On July 22, 1977, Congress sent to the president the International Security Assistance Act of 1977, which was also an amendment to the Foreign Assistance Act. It added a section to cut off funds under the International Security Assistance Act or the Arms Export Control Act to any country that delivered nuclear enrichment equipment, materials, or technology to any other country, unless two conditions were met before delivery. First, the supplying and receiving countries had to agree to place all such items upon delivery under multilateral auspices and management when available; second, the recipient country had to agree with the IAEA to place all such items and also all nuclear fuel and facilities in the country under IAEA safeguards. The president might continue to furnish prohibited assistance if he certified in writing to Congress that the termination would have serious adverse effects on vital U.S. interests and that he had received reliable assurances that the country in question will not acquire or develop nuclear weapons or assist other nations in doing so. The bill also specifies procedures for Senate action on any joint resolution to terminate or restrict such assistance.

As for reprocessing, the bill added a new section that also provided for cutting off funds specified above to any country that 1) delivered nuclear reprocessing equipment, materials, or technology to any other country, or 2) received such equipment, materials, or technology from any other country (except for the transfer of reprocessing equipment associated with the investigation, under international evaluation programs in which the United States participates, of technologies that are alternatives to pure plutonium reprocessing), or 3) is not a nuclear-weapons state under the NPT and detonated a nuclear explosive. The president might continue to furnish such assistance if he certified in writing to Congress that the termination of such assistance would be prejudicial to the common achievement of U.S. nonproliferation objectives or would otherwise jeopardize national security. The bill also specified Senate action on any joint resolution to terminate or restrict the assistance.

On September 21, 1982, the *New York Times* reported that Pakistan had been aided by China to develop a capacity to enrich uranium for weapons use. (This news report emanated from sources in Washington, and since the media in the United States are an important gauge of the mood in the American foreign policy process, the report carried some weight in India). Then, on December 18, 1982, Senator Glenn sought further assurances from the executive that the F-16s that were being transferred to Pakistan would not be in violation of American nonproliferation guidelines. Strictly speaking, he sought a further amendment to the Arms Export Act which would prevent re-transfer of American sophisticated arms to China, which was believed to have been aiding Pakistan in the development of nuclear weapons. There appears to be no conclusive proof that China was doing this, and the powerful media such as the *New York Times* and the *Washington Post* have contributed in no uncertain terms to this obvious connection (from New Delhi's perspective) being a reality. [Ed. note: Similar concerns were raised in August 1985, on the occasion of the signing of a civilian nuclear agreement with China which includes verbal assurances concerning China's assistance to potential nuclear proliferators.]

One other irony of the decision process is that the Office of International Security Affairs (ISA) in the Pentagon (which mirrors the Bureau of Politico-Military Affairs of the State Department) does not seem to be unduly concerned with the nuclear weapons proliferation issue. [Ed. note: Since this was written, a small but expert group focusing on nonproliferation was established in ISA.] Even when it raised objections to the transfer of forty F-16s with advanced radar (ALR-69) to Pakistan, the considerations had more to do with technology leakage to the Soviet Union than with Pakistani acquisition of a nuclear weapons capability. The diplomacy of both Kissinger and Brzezinski and of recent directors of the Politico-Military Bureau in the State Department favored a trade-off between conventional weapons and nuclear acquisition. Former U.S. Secretary of State Alexander Haig spoke of the need to "whet Pakistan's nuclear appetite" in January 1981, when the Reagan administration entered office.

Because it pursued a global anti-Soviet philosophy, the Reagan administration found a strategic utility in Pakistan, which borders Soviet occupied Afghanistan. However, the perceptions of the military leadership in Islamabad of its role in a larger U.S. framework, aimed at combating the Soviet Union in the oil-rich Gulf, may have been exaggerated. The Pakistanis envisioned the emergence of a strategic relationship with the United States which would mirror that of Israel and Japan. If the military leadership in Islamabad misjudges the extent of U.S. commitment to Pakistan security, another war may result with India. Surprisingly, the United States and the Soviet Union share the same goal with regard to nuclear proliferation, although the major decision-making bodies in the Reagan administration do not seem to attach to it the primacy that the Soviet Union does. Soviet propaganda aimed at India has recently made the charge that the United States has enhanced the development of a Pakistani nuclear weapons capability. Washington has strongly denied this charge. The government of Rajiv Gandhi appears to be adopting a posture on nuclear disarmament that does not differentiate between the USSR and the United States. Hence, charges of such nature by Moscow are unlikely to influence the views of New Delhi. One might argue that stopping the nuclear proliferation process in South Asia is from Washington's perspective inconsistent with its goal of stopping Soviet thrusts beyond Afghanistan. Although the thinking that prevails among some of the NSC staff may endorse such a position, there is no evidence that either the State Department or the Congress would adopt it. The thesis that a nuclearized South Asia would be stable, which has been suggested by Kenneth M. Waltz, is shared by almost no one else, either in the executive or the legislature.[8]

The American decision-making process on foreign policy varies according to the type of administration in the White House, but most administrations attempt to manage events that are essentially regional through global perspectives. The failure of several administrations to restructure globally framed policies to suit regional requirements has been most evident in South Asia. The U.S. reaction to events in South Asia is based on its perceptions of the USSR and China, two states that border the region.

It is India, with its large population and industrial infrastructure, that has the *capacity* to re-structure events in the subcontinent. New Delhi's perceptions of regionality are not shared by its smaller neighbors, which perceive the doctrine of regionality to be synonymous with hegemony. The force that could shape the emergence of a SAARC, free of the superpowers, is continually vitiated by these suspicions. American strategic interests in the Persian Gulf have been threatened by the Soviet intervention in Afghanistan; since these interests continue to operate, the expansion of U.S. military facilities in Diego Garcia will proceed apace. These decisions evolve from contingency plans created in the Pentagon. Whether or not they are created in consultation with the State Department remains unclear.

Some American scholars, experts on South Asia and on military matters that impinge on the region, have argued in favor of the creation of a separate South Asian Affairs Bureau in the State Department, headed by an Assistant Secretary of State for South Asian affairs dealing with India, Pakistan, Bangladesh, Nepal, and Sri Lanka.[9] The argument in favor of this proposal is the growing importance of South Asia. A separate bureau would enable a clearer coordination of the complexities of the region. Since Pakistan is an important factor for U.S. interests in the Gulf, splitting Pakistan from the South Asian region and including it in a policy grouping that could coordinate more effectively with the NSC would seem to avoid duplication.[10] Under the existing state of affairs, the Assistant Secretary of State in charge of both the Near East and South Asia has relatively easy access to the Secretary of State, because the developments in the Near East affect U.S. interests.

In this regard, arms transfer decisions that aim to preserve regional stability should be authorized by Congress only on the condition that these weapons will not be used against India. Such a codification would go a long way in removing some of the misunderstandings that arise whenever American arms are transferred to Islamabad. Whether influence can be brought to bear on Islamabad to accept such an agreement remains an open question. Amid reports in the media that Pakistan was receiving nuclear weapon designs from China, Senator Glenn, who has led the crusade against nuclear proliferation, introduced an amendment to the Arms Export Control Act that would ensure that there would be no re-transfer of the U.S. F-16s supplied to Pakistan to any third country.[11] Such a re-transfer clause also exists (with regard to enrichment and reprocessing technology) in the amended Foreign Assistance Act. There is no reason why a similar agreement cannot be codified which stipulates the non-use of American arms against countries not considered hostile to U.S. interests.

Conclusion

Nuclear proliferation and arms aid are two issues that will continue to occupy the concerns of American foreign policymakers; only the emphasis of one over the other, or the linkage of one with the other, is determined at a policy level by the motivations and attitudes of the president. Several institutions that participate in the decision-making process proceed from divergent positions. For example, the Arms Control and Disarmament Agency and Congress now favor the creation of a comprehensive sanctions regime in order to thwart nuclear proliferation, especially in South Asia. On the other hand, in institutions like the NSC and the Pentagon, one discerns a need to use arms transfers provided there is no leakage of military technology to the Soviet Union. This inconsistency in the decision-making process is but a natural consequence of the nature of the actors and the vested interests that are involved.

The foreign policy of the Reagan administration has been greatly influenced by such men as NSC advisor Robert MacFarlane, and Assistant Secretary of Defense Richard Perle.[12] Few of these people could be characterized as experts in either the nonproliferation or arms transfers field. Their policies emanated from deep suspicions about the Soviet Union, and because the Soviet Union is a major factor in South Asia, such thinking is likely to persist: the ripples of their anti-Soviet ideology will be felt in South Asia through 1988. A major reversal of American arms transfers policy—which allows for licensed production of U.S. military equipment in India—seems unlikely at the present stage: what one sees instead is an increased military presence in Diego Garcia guided by a strategy of encircling the Soviet Union with a U.S. presence from Pakistan to Sri Lanka. The immediate corollary of this strategy will be an enhanced Indo-Soviet military relationship.

U.S. decision making for South Asia should seek to enhance regional cooperation, although the present defense-dominated posture of the Reagan administration hardly seems geared for that kind of policy. [Ed. note: After this chapter was completed, the United States sent two special emissaries to India and Pakistan in September 1985, Donald Fortier of the NSC staff and Michael Armacost, Undersecretary of State for Political Affairs. Newspaper reports indicate that Fortier and Armacost were to discuss a number of bilateral and multilateral issues with Rajiv Gandhi and Zia ul-Haq, and were especially supportive of Indo-Pakistani dialogue on nuclear and security matters. (*New York Times*, September 13, 1985)] What seems to be in the future is increased superpower tensions in the southern belly of the Indian Ocean.

NOTES

1. Christopher Van Hollen, "Leaning on Pakistan," *Foreign Policy* (Spring 1980): 35-50.
2. Dr. A. Q. Khan, the initiator of the project, has claimed that the enriched uranium plant is now operational. He has been quoted as saying that, given

the green signal, he could now produce atomic weapons. Of course President Zia ul-Haq has denied any such intentions. See *New York Times*, February 10, 1984.

3. Stephen Philip Cohen, "South Asia and U.S. Military Policy." Report prepared for the Commission on the Organization of the Government for the Conduct of Foreign Policy (Washington, Spring 1975).

4. Shirin Tahir Kheli, "Proxies and Allies: The Case of Iran and Pakistan," *Orbis*, 22, No. 2 (Summer): 368-69.

5. Michael Brecher, *The Foreign Policy System of Israel: Setting, Images, Process* (New Haven, Conn.: Yale University Press, 1972), p. 374.

6. Michael Brenner, *Nuclear Power and Nonproliferation: The Re-making of U.S. Policy* (New York: Cambridge University Press, 1981), pp. 116-32.

7. Stuart Symington, "The Washington Nuclear Mess," *International Security* 1, No. 3 (Winter 1977): 72.

8. Ed. note: Waltz's views on proliferation have been influential in South Asia and elsewhere. See Kenneth M. Waltz, "What Will the Spread of Nuclear Weapons Do to the World?" in J. K. King, ed., *International Political Effects of the Spread of Nuclear Weapons* (Washington, D.C.: Government Printing Office, April 1979). Also see K. Subrahmanyam, ed., *Nuclear Proliferation and International Security* (New Delhi: Institute for Defense Studies and Analyses, 1985), pp. 18-19, and Shai Feldman, *Israeli Nuclear Deterrence* (New York: Columbia University Press, 1982).

9. See the remarks by Stephen Philip Cohen, Congressman Stephen Solarz, and Selig Harrison in "Soviet Policy in Asia," *Hearings before the subcommittee on Asian and Pacific Affairs of the Committee on Foreign Affairs, House of Representatives* (July 28, 1983), p. 317.

10. See Dan Haendel, *The Process of Priority Formulation: U.S. Foreign Policy in the Indo-Pakistan War of 1971* (Boulder, Colo.: Westview Press, 1977), pp. 142-81.

11. Senator Glenn introduced an amendment to the Arms Export Act that specified such a requirement. See *Congressional Record* (December 18, 1982).

12. Leslie Gelb, *New York Times*, March 12, 1984.

10

The United States and South Asia: Policy and Process

William J. Barnds

The dispersion of power among the executive, legislative, and judicial branches of government is a unique feature of the American system of government, although the executive and to a lesser extent the legislative branches are the key actors in the field of foreign affairs. However, there are both trends and cycles in the relative political strength of the executive and legislative branches. The cycles normally grow out of the relative strength and proclivities of individual presidents and congressional leaders, or of the successes or failures of the executive in handling the normal foreign policy challenges it faces year by year. The longer-term trends grow out of more fundamental misjudgments or errors of one branch or the other, or out of basic changes in the international scene.

Thus the leadership of President Franklin Delano Roosevelt in responding to the challenge of the Axis powers, and the reluctance of Congress to face up to the dangers posed by the Germans and the Japanese followed by the widespread American conviction that the Cold War required a centralized decision-making authority, resulted in a period of presidential domination of U.S. foreign policy. Even though Congress initially supported U.S. involvement in Vietnam, the fact that it later took the lead in challenging Presidents Johnson and Nixon on Vietnam led to a sharp rise in congressional power during the 1970s. In short, a major shift in power usually results from a historic mistake by one branch or the other. It is still too early to be confident that the ascendancy of the legislative branch has ended. The Chadha decision declaring the congressional veto unconstitutional points in that direction. However, the Reagan administration's foreign and defense policies, which many Americans regard as an overcorrection of the weakness of the Carter administration, may result in increased congressional assertiveness through its ultimate control of the purse strings.

The United States has also had considerable difficulty in integrating its global and regional security policies. This traditional problem has been complicated by the need to integrate such policies with newer concerns such as nonproliferation, terrorism, narcotics, and human rights, not to speak of the higher priority that must be accorded economic considerations in view of the more competitive international environment facing the United States.

American policy toward South Asia over the past decade or so provides an excellent case study of all of these problems; to understand them, it is useful to go back a bit further in time. The initial U.S.-Pakistani alliance came to an end for most practical purposes during the 1965 Indo-Pakistani war, when the United States halted arms shipments to both Pakistan and India. This action had a much greater impact on Pakistan than on India because the former was far more dependent upon the United States than the latter. Between the 1965 war and the Soviet invasion of Afghanistan, the U.S. government had no South Asian security policy as such—except not to get involved in such matters under normal circumstances. Its role during the 1971 Indo-Pakistani war—initially cutting off nearly all aid to Pakistan, but at the last minute sending the Enterprise task force into the Bay of Bengal—was basically a function of the Nixon-Kissinger approach to China. Apparently, they thought that failure to take (or threaten) action against India after it invaded East Pakistan would indicate to China that the United States was a paper tiger, but neither Nixon nor Kissinger has ever explained satisfactorily why making impotent threats would have a more favorable impact on the Chinese leaders than standing aside.

Once Indian predominance on the subcontinent was established, the United States accepted it and made no attempt to play a significant direct role in South Asian security affairs. This was partly because the United States was preoccupied elsewhere, but also because of a growing American conviction that the nationalism of the Afro-Asian states would prevent them from subordinating themselves to the USSR. The ruptures in Soviet relations with Egypt, Ghana, and Indonesia were often cited as evidence for this conclusion. Moreover, détente with the USSR reduced concern over Soviet expansionism.

By the mid-1970s new issues had been added to the American agenda. Nonproliferation, especially in the wake of India's 1974 nuclear explosion and Pakistan's attempt to develop a nuclear capability, gave a higher priority to the U.S. government's policy toward South Asia. Since the United States was not actively involved nor deeply concerned with South Asian security issues at the time, this created no immediate dilemmas between conflicting objectives. Although there were differences in emphasis between Congress and the executive, both branches favored a strong nuclear nonproliferation act, although the executive and the Senate Foreign Relations Committee toned down the version that emerged from the Senate Government Operations Committee. The conflicts over nonproliferation policy within the executive were due as much to conflicting views of different departments as to deficiencies in the coordinating mechanism. Generalists and regionalists, as well as those concerned primarily with a particular issue—be it nonproliferation, human rights, or narcotics—will frequently be in conflict no matter how sound the coordinating mechanism is, because they assign different weights to different issues and goals.

It is interesting that different laws relating to nuclear nonproliferation have caused problems in U.S. relations with India and Pakistan. The Nuclear Nonproliferation Act of 1978, which covers the exports of nuclear fuel, equipment, and technology, brought the United States into conflict with India because it forbids the export of such materials to non-nuclear weapons states unless the recipient country agrees to take certain actions, such as accepting full-scope safeguards. India's refusal to do so is well known, and even though the fuel issue was resolved when France agreed to replace the United States as the supplier, the issue of spare parts to Tarapur has periodically strained Indo-American relations. The president has the authority to waive the restrictions on such exports without fear of a congressional veto since the Chadha case, but the political costs in terms of his relations with Congress would be high in view of the reports that during 1983-84 India undertook some preparations for a second nuclear test, although such actions do not necessarily indicate that India had made a decision to explode another nuclear device.

The law that created the initial problem in U.S.-Pakistan relations is the 1976 Symington Amendment to the Foreign Assistance Act of 1961. The Symington and Glenn amendments are now separate amendments that deal with the importation of enrichment and reprocessing equipment respectively. The Symington amendment originally covered both reprocessing and enrichment equipment. There is no logical reason to differentiate between the dangers of proliferation via the enrichment rather than the reprocessing route, although there is less need to test an explosive made with highly enriched uranium than one made with plutonium to be confident it will actually explode. But Senator John Glenn thought reprocessing presented the greatest danger, and in 1977 he proposed his amendment, which prohibited aid to a country even if it accepted full-scope safeguards. However, the supporters of the Glenn amendment judged that they could not get the votes to set standards for waivers involving reprocessing equipment that are as strict as had been written into law in the Symington amendment for imports of enrichment equipment, and so allowed the President greater flexibility to waive a halt in aid. It was the importation of enrichment equipment by Pakistan that caused the United States to cut off all foreign assistance—except PL-480—to Pakistan early in 1979.

This was the situation when the Soviet invasion of Afghanistan took place in December 1979. President Carter's offer to seek legislation allowing him to waive the requirement of the Symington amendment and to provide $200 million in economic and $200 million in military aid to Pakistan over a two-year period eventually came to naught when President Zia rejected such aid in his famous "peanuts" remark, for the amounts were too small and the duration of the relationship too uncertain to attract Pakistan. (This episode demonstrates that it is normally better to wait to be asked for assistance than to offer it overeagerly to another country). Yet it is important to note that even those with a strong interest in nonproliferation—such as Senator Glenn—felt that nonproliferation had to be subordinated to meet the challenge involved in the Soviet invasion of a nonaligned Third World country, and they were willing to support a waiver for Pakistan.

The administration had to seek legislation for such a new relationship, however, not only to obtain the funds for the six-year $3.2 billion program (half economic and half military) it sought, but because Pakistan's continued efforts to develop a nuclear enrichment capability made it essential either to change the Symington amendment or to establish the right to waive it. Thus Congress was in a strong position when the administration made its formal request for the program in September 1981.

There was widespread agreement in Congress on two points as the program underwent examination. The first was that the cutting off of aid in 1979 had not been successful in causing Pakistan to halt its nuclear development efforts. The second was that Pakistan faced a serious security threat with the Soviets in Afghanistan. Even those Americans who felt that the earlier U.S.-Pakistani alliance had been a mistake believed that military aid was appropriate in the 1980s because Pakistan now faced a genuine security threat from the USSR, although it was recognized that Pakistan still gave first priority to defense against India.[1] There was uncertainty, however, about the amounts and types of military assistance Pakistan required. The main difference was between the administration and some key members of Congress, especially in the House of Representatives, over whether the F-16 was really the appropriate aircraft for Pakistan. Some members felt Pakistan would be better served by a larger number of less expensive and less sophisticated aircraft, while others were concerned about the impact that sending F-16s would have on Indo-

Pakistani and Indo-American relations. A motion of disapproval (the congressional veto, which had not yet been declared unconstitutional) of the F-16 sale failed to win a majority by a single vote in the House Foreign Affairs Committee. Even if it had won, it probably would not have been passed by the full House—and certainly not by the Senate.

The key issue during congressional consideration, however, was how to change the law regarding nonproliferation so that Pakistan would be eligible for foreign assistance. The administration wanted a simple waiver for Pakistan, but that had limited support in Congress. Virtually everyone would have liked to have agreed to supply aid in return for a Pakistani agreement to halt its nuclear development efforts, but few thought Pakistan would accept such terms in view of India's nuclear capabilities, especially since such terms would have had to be made public. Serious thought was given to changing the law to require the president to halt aid to any country that manufactured a nuclear explosive device. However, several problems—especially that of defining the specific point at which an explosive device was "manufactured" — made apparent the shortcomings of such an approach. Finally, the barrier was set at the explosion of a nuclear device as the most feasible compromise solution.

It is interesting to note that the House and Senate each arrived at the same decision in their separate deliberations, but they proposed different U.S. responses in the event of a nuclear explosion. The Senate version of the bill contained an absolute ban on aid to any country, while the House version mandated a similar halt to aid, but allowed the President to waive the termination if he found that an end to aid would "jeopardize the common defense and security." However, such a presidential waiver was subject to a congressional veto by a majority of both houses of Congress rather than by the two-thirds vote required by the original Symington and Glenn amendments. The eventual compromise required a halt to all aid to a country conducting a nuclear explosion, but gave the president power to waive the termination for thirty days. If Congress did not affirmatively approve continued aid within this period, the termination became permanent.

Finally, it should be noted that the major military aid program for Pakistan proposed by the Reagan administration was accepted with little opposition by the Democratic-controlled House of Representatives as well as the Republican-controlled Senate, and that its continued funding over the next few years has created very little controversy. Many Indians have found this hard to understand, in view of the unsuccessful outcome of the earlier U.S.-Pakistani security relationship. The difficulty for those with doubts about the wisdom of the new U.S. link with Pakistan, however, was that Indian policy seemed to offer no alternative option.

India's strong objections to the modest Carter program made it seem as though New Delhi had no sense of proportion about what might create a threat to its security, so its objections to the larger Reagan program won few supporters. Moreover, India's later statements calling for the removal of foreign troops from Afghanistan (without naming the Soviet Union) never overcame the adverse impact of its initial statement at the United Nations, which was made just after the Soviet invasion of Afghanistan. And New Delhi's continued reluctance to acknowledge that the Soviet occupation of Afghanistan has created a serious security threat to the region has made it virtually impossible for any American to gain support for a policy that gives top priority in the subcontinent to India.

There is, of course, no assurance that the present American approach to South Asia will succeed. The United States faces the difficult task of providing enough arms to Pakistan to give it the strength and confidence to withstand the Soviets in Afghanistan, but not so many—or such sophisticated—arms as to cause either Pakistan or India to act unwisely toward each other and bring about a new war on the subcontinent. Nor is it at all certain that providing large-scale economic aid and a substantial supply of conventional weapons will cause Pakistan to refrain from developing a nuclear weapons arsenal, although Pakistan—like India—has said that it has no intention of following such a course. Only time will tell, and the crucial decisions affecting South Asian security will be made by India and Pakistan, not the United States.

NOTES

1. See the testimony of Selig Harrison before the House Foreign Affairs Committee's Subcommittee on International Security and Scientific Affairs, on International Economic Policy and Trade, and on Asian and Pacific Affairs, Sept. 22, 1981, *Security and Economic Assistance to Pakistan* (Washington, D.C.: U.S. Government Printing Office, 1982), pp. 139-79.

Part Two

Four Visions of the Future

11

Security and Stability
in South Asia

Lt. General A. I. Akram

Stability in the Third World, particularly South Asia, has political overtones. Its study is deeply subjective and depends on one's point of view. However, the importance of stability as a source of strength leading to greater security is widely acknowledged.

Security also has many facets: the land and the people, the government and its ideology, external and internal forces, and political, military, economic, physical, and psychological dimensions. Just as varied are the threats to security. In this chapter we shall consider security to be a matter of safeguarding the national integrity of the state (or states) in the region against foreign military aggression. The part played in foreign aggression by nonmilitary measures directed at internal targets (subversion, economic pressure, political blackmail) is acknowledged, but it is outside the scope of this chapter.

The threat to the security of a state comes from across the land border of that state. The potential enemy is the neighbor, only the neighbor, and always the neighbor; every neighbor is a potential enemy, provided there is a clash of interest grave enough to make acceptable the waging of war with its attendant horror and destruction. The neighbor may be a single state or, in case of group security, a group of neighboring states joined in a common purpose against a common adversary. Moreover, the defender's plans and preparations are founded not on the intentions of the neighbor but on his capability, for intentions can be concealed or changed overnight, whereas capability takes years to develop and cannot be concealed. Thus a threat to our national integrity comes from any neighboring state that has an actual or potential clash of interest with us and that possesses the capability of attacking us.

When we study South Asia, we are really looking at India and Pakistan, for these are the protagonists of the subcontinent. When these two countries are at peace with each other, South Asia by and large is at peace. If the two countries have troubled relations, South Asia is uneasy. When the two fight, South Asia trembles. Other powers of South Asia—five in number—have no external security problems and no threat from any neighbor (except possibly from India). India and Pakistan determine in their war and peace the present and the future of the region.

In their perception of threat, India and Pakistan see external enemies and are enemies to each other. At times one of them appears to combine with a third power to create a greater threat to the other. We will examine this situation and go on to analyze the implications of various potential threats, concluding with a discussion of measures required to meet those threats.

Development of Threat Perception

At the time of partition, India and Pakistan saw each other as the enemy and the only enemy. There was no one else to threaten the states of South Asia. This situation originated in the pre-partition hostility between Hindus and Muslims. It was confirmed by the Kashmir War of 1948 and further strengthened by the confrontations of 1950 and 1951 when war was narrowly averted. Pakistan then realized how serious the threat from India was to its national integrity.

Pakistan turned to the West in quest of allies who could strengthen its defense capability. This led to Pakistan becoming a member of CENTO, which it joined along with its Muslim brothers in Iran and Turkey, to defend its region against aggression from outside. The West was concerned with the threat of communist aggression against the so-called free world; Pakistan was primarily concerned with its own defense against any aggressor, no matter from which side he came. It was inconceivable that Pakistan should use weapons acquired from America for the defense of only its northwestern border while its national integrity was being threatened from the east.

Enter the Chinese

So things remained until the Sino-Indian War of 1962, which opened India's eyes to the danger from the north. India turned to the Western powers for arms, forgetting its earlier stand on neutralism and on keeping the world powers out of the subcontinent. The West readily provided arms for the defense of India, which India as readily accepted.

India now perceived itself as under threat from two directions: Pakistan in the west and China in the north. The Chinese threat was exaggerated in Indian minds (and still is) because China has no claim upon In-

dian territory, the boundary dispute between the two powers in Ladakh
and NEFA (Arunachal Pradesh) notwithstanding. There can be no invasion of the Gangetic plain from the north, but the psychological impact
of the Chinese threat, often exploited by Indian politicians, remains
strong.

Between the Sino-Indian war and the coming of the Russians, India
and Pakistan fought two wars, in 1965 and 1971. The first war was a
draw, although claims of victory were made by both sides, but the second
was a victory for India, which was able to wrest the eastern wing from
Pakistan and help create of it the new state of Bangladesh. These two
wars clarified the perception and strengthened the conviction in both
countries that Enemy Number One was the other.

Enter the Russians

The next alteration in the South Asian threat perception came with
the military intervention by Soviet forces in Afghanistan at the end of
1979, the reasons for which will be taken up later. Whatever the causes of
this invasion, it placed the Soviets in occupation of a country whose
southwestern borders are only 300 miles from the Persian Gulf, a region
on which depends the long-term survival of Western Europe and Japan.

The implications of the move need to be further elucidated. The Soviets are very skillful in making the indirect approach and always outflank
their adversaries, militarily and politically. Since a direct move to the
Persian Gulf is fraught with danger and may force a clash of arms with
the United States, the USSR can approach the Gulf through Pakistan,
getting to the coast of the Arabian Sea where they could establish themselves at the vital ports of Pasni and Gwadar, a stone's throw from the
Persian Gulf.

The Role of Pakistan

It was this threat to the Western alliance which brought the United
States to the realization that a strong Pakistan would discourage an adventure by forces hostile to the West. Pakistan responded for purely national reasons, and a mutuality of interests between Pakistan and the
United States led to the revival of the 1959 security arrangement under
which Pakistan now receives $3.2 billion, of which about half is a loan
for military sales at 14 percent interest.

So far as Pakistan is concerned, its primary requirement is to strength-
en itself in order to defend its national integrity against an aggressor, regardless of the direction from which that aggressor comes. It is not joining a military alliance or entering into a military pact. It is not giving
military bases to foreign powers nor compromising its principles, either

of sovereignty or of nonalignment. If, as a result of Pakistan's ability to defend itself and keep hostile forces out of its territory, the West gains more security for itself, so much the better.

To sum up, the threat perception in South Asia is as follows: Pakistan finds itself confronted by India, possibly aided by its ally, the USSR, India finds herself confronted by Pakistan, possibly helped by its friends, the United States and China. The fact that none of these three giants is likely to get directly involved in an Indo-Pakistan war is of little consequence. Threats exist in the minds of the threatened and are based on the possibility of aggression rather than its certainty or even probability.

India and Pakistan

The main cause of the conflict between the two main powers of South Asia lies in the images that they have of themselves and of the other, images that have existed since before partition and of which both peoples are prisoners.

Soon after partition, Pandit Nehru proclaimed that the new India was a successor of British India and inherited the mantle of glory that the British had worn. India would therefore play a great role in the world, starting with South Asia, of course. Nehru was fully supported by the Indian people, newly awakened to freedom and proud of the great cultural heritage of their past.

Nehru's dream of greatness could not be translated into reality because of the opposition of the other states of South Asia, which were mistrustful of Indian designs. These states resisted India's attempts to play a dominant role in South Asia, but they eventually submitted because they were not strong enough to withstand Indian pressure. Pakistan, however, remained adamant; it would not acknowledge India as preeminent or dominant. Pakistan was also conscious of a role. It had emerged in the world as the largest Muslim state of the time and dedicated itself to serving and fighting for Muslim interests everywhere. Pakistan spoke of parity with India, the difference in size between the two notwithstanding.

Pakistan thus became an obstacle in India's march to greatness. If Pakistan would not accept India as a great power, the rest of the world was not likely to do so either. Pakistan had to be removed from the path of the Indian march to glory, but Pakistan had no intention of being so removed. This led the two countries on a collision course, and they collided again and again.

They are still on the same collision course, in spite of the reduction in size of Pakistan, which is partly compensated for by the internal weakening and disruption within India and the rise of divisive elements in that country. This state of affairs is likely to continue so long as India retains its designs of hegemony over South Asia, preeminence in Asia, and a great power role in the world.

Obstacles to Peace

With this as the main cause of the conflict between the two powers of South Asia, we come to the obstacles that this conflict has created which are at the same time the causes of further conflicts. In other words, they are both cause and effect: they feed the conflict and are in turn fed by it. These obstacles are (a) hostility, and (b) resort to arms.

The two nations have a mental state of such hostility toward each other that they are unable even to get through to each other. Whenever one side makes a proposal for the improvement of relations, the other side is convinced that it is a trick or trap. The two sides will irritate each other, take pleasure in each other's discomfiture, sling mud at each other; this attitude is getting harder and sharper with time.

Both sides are quick on the draw, taking to arms at the slightest pretext. They regard the use of arms as the first resort, not the last. Irritations occur in other parts of the world too, which lead to diplomatic tension or dissatisfaction, but in South Asia irritations very quickly deteriorate into a clash of arms. We take to battle like a duck to water. The result is that enormous resources are wasted in armaments and armed forces to the detriment of development. Finally, the superpowers are drawn into these conflicts, which is not necessarily in the best interests of the region.

Military Balance

The concept of military balance is rather vague and does not lend itself to easy definition. It depends on many factors, for example, military vulnerability and military effectiveness, and it cannot be reduced to a simple equation of size, as the Indians claim. They say that they must have larger armed forces than Pakistan because they are so much bigger in size in terms of geographical mass (four times as big) and population (eight times).

Size is not relevant to the issue of military balance. If it were, the USSR, with a geographical mass two and a half times that of the United States, would need armed forces two and a half times as big, which is absurd. And if it were a matter of population, then China would have to have armed forces four times as big as the Soviet Union, which is equally absurd. This is a matter neither of geographical size nor of the population of a country. Military balance is relevant to the degree of threat to which the countries involved in the balance are exposed.

India is four times bigger than Pakistan in terms of geographical mass, but half of that country, the peninsula lying south of the Mahanadi and Narmada rivers, can be excluded from the comparison because it is totally free of military threat. There has never been an invasion of India across the east or west coasts of the peninsula. The odd naval battle fought by the Portuguese off the west coast and the naval contest in the Indian Ocean between the English and the French for the prize of India do not constitute an invasion of India proper. And because Pakistan has no means whatever of landing forces on the Indian peninsula, we can safely say that half of India is entirely safe from attack. This leaves the continental mass of India north of the Narmada and the Mahanadi rivers, which is only twice the size of Pakistan.

The Threats to India and Pakistan

Now we have to assess the threat to this continental part of India. There is a threat from the north, from China, but this is more psychological than real. The Himalayas just cannot become a great battlefield. The Indian military knows this, and for this reason they are converting some of their ten mountain divisions into normal infantry divisions for operations against Pakistan. If there is a threat from the north, it is a very limited one.

India has no threat in the east from Burma or from Bangladesh. Bangladesh is unlikely to become a David to the Indian Goliath. Even if, for the sake of argument, we accept that in the future there may be some possibility of military action in the east, India does not need more than a handful of divisions to deal with that contingency.

Geographically, the only threat to India is from the west, where lies Pakistan. This seems absurd, in view of the difference in size and resources between the two countries, but India having fought three wars with Pakistan, a fourth one is not inconceivable. This is, however, the main threat, and this is what we must bear in mind when we speak of military balance between the two countries.

Now let us look at Pakistan. This country is exposed to attack along most of its border. To the east lies India, a past enemy. To the northwest lies Afghanistan, with which Pakistan has had trouble off and on ever since Pakistan came into being and which is now being stiffened by the presence of eleven Soviet divisions. This puts Pakistan in the terrible military predicament of a possible war on two fronts. To the south lies the Arabian Sea, whose coast is open to Indian attack. India could land forces almost anywhere and may already have planned to do so, for the Indians have the naval and air strength required for such a landing. The only parts of Pakistan that are free of threat are the very small part in the north where it has a common frontier with a faithful friend, China, and a small part in the west facing brotherly Iran.

The Correct Balance

It is in this context that we must examine the question of military balance: who is threatened by whom, from which direction, by how much force, and with what combination of hostile forces? India has the advantage of being under threat (albeit an imaginary one) only from Pakistan, which is a much smaller neighbor. If India has much larger armed forces than it needs for purely defensive purpose, it could only be to meet more ambitious aims than just the defense of its territory.

There is much more to the question of military balance, including factors that we do not have the time to examine. However, it is certain that a military balance must be based on threat perception and vulnerability, not on the physical size of the countries concerned. Such a balance implies that each adversary knows that if it starts a war it will receive unacceptable punishment from the other. Thus, if there is a correct military balance between two possible adversaries, it guarantees peace, for it discourages both of them from indulging in military adventure.

Keeping in mind the state of threat and vulnerability, if the Indian armed forces were to be not more than half again as big as Pakistan's, we could say that there is a reasonable balance in South Asia.

The Nuclear Factor

A great deal is known about the nuclear programs of India and Pakistan. An enormous amount of publicity has been directed at the two countries, mainly by the Western press, and in this, Pakistan has been the victim of a stream of vicious propaganda. We will not go into the details of the propaganda to prove its falsity, nor need we go into the actual position of nuclear development in India and Pakistan, for that is quite well known. We will take the present nuclear situation as it exists and go on from there.

Although India is ahead of Pakistan and has already exploded a nuclear device, both countries have fairly advanced nuclear development programs and, let us face it, both are capable of making the bomb. The fact that it will be a crude weapon does not alter that position. Neither side has a bomb at the moment, their mutual suspicions notwithstanding, but each side has that capability.

Because of this, the nuclear factor has become a part of the security threat and there are fears in both countries that the other might steal a march and have a nuclear weapon ready for use before the other has done anything about it. This fear is aggravated by the hawks on both sides, particularly in India, who keep pressing the government to acquire nuclear weapons. Most of these warmongers are chairbound strategists with little idea of the complexity of a nuclear weapons program and the enormous expenditure and time required to establish the kind of infrastructure that is necessary for full scale nuclear war.

There is little realization of the fact that once launched on a nuclear weapons program, we cross the nuclear weapons threshold, and there will be no holding us back. India and Pakistan will be swept on by the irresistible tide of nuclear compulsion to become full-scale nuclear powers. Thus, perhaps by the end of the century we could say that we have achieved nuclear deterrence, but that might have to be at the expense of mass starvation in South Asia, for such a nuclear weapons program would inflict irreparable damage, perhaps destruction, on the economy of the two countries.

A peculiar situation in the nuclear equation between India and Pakistan is that they need the weapon only against each other. If India makes the bomb, Pakistan will follow suit, and vice versa. If neither makes the bomb, neither needs it. The two countries are under no nuclear threat from any third power. The only people who will derive satisfaction from a nuclear weapons program are the megalomaniacs who see in the bomb an instrument of global greatness.

Since mutual suspicion exists between India and Pakistan no matter how unlikely the threat, there is a case for a joint study and a joint commitment to the peaceful development of nuclear energy, not only for cooperation between the two countries but also to eliminate the threat of nuclear weapons from the subcontinent. India and Pakistan should work together in the field of nuclear energy to the benefit of both countries and of a nuclear-free South Asia.

Impact of External Powers

The Regional Quartet

In broad terms, the India-Pakistan equation is shaped by the actions and attitudes of a quartet of powers: the USSR, China, India, and Pakistan. There are other powers too which have some effect on South Asia, like the United States (discussed below) and Bangladesh, which is emerging as a friend of Pakistan and China; but subcontinental relations are chiefly determined by the quartet. To put the equation in its simplest form: it is the USSR and India vs. China and Pakistan, although there is no treaty between China and Pakistan.

The Soviet-Indian link is based on hostility between India and Pakistan, India and China, and China and the USSR. The Pakistan-China tie is supported, although not entirely governed, by this hostility. The state of relations between India and Pakistan has already been explained. The hostility between China and the USSR is deep-rooted and draws its strength not only from a historical conflict which is almost 300 years old, but also from the rivalry that exists between the two giants as leaders of the communist world.

Soviet-Indian friendship is founded entirely on self-interest. Each is using the other. India uses the Soviet Union to gain strength for itself and to be able to pose a strong threat to China, while at the same time exerting pressure on Pakistan to accede to India's demands. The Soviet Union uses India as a counterweight to China and is happy to keep the present tension alive between India and China, and India and Pakistan. Should these troubles end and the underlying disputes be solved amicably, the Soviets will not be so important to India.

The strained relations between Pakistan and the Soviet Union are not the result of any basic hostility between the two, since there are no grounds for such hostility. In this equation Pakistan has been the aggrieved party and has every right to complain about this superpower drawing red circles around its cities, using its veto at the United Nations in support of India (and against Pakistan), and posing various other kinds of threats against it. Pakistan would wish to be friends with the big giant of the north, if only the Soviets would stop arming and supporting India against Pakistan and stop putting on its shoulders the burden of three million Afghan refugees. All this could end, and they could be good neighbors.

Pakistan's friendship with China is something unusual because it does not depend solely on joint hostility towards India. The two countries have supported each other for a generation in the spirit of loyal friendship rather than material gain, and should there be an improvement in the hostile relations that India has with both of them, the Pakistan-China equation would remain unchanged.

Enter the Americans

The United States is not a regional power and is not directly involved in South Asian affairs, but as a superpower it is engaged with the Soviet Union in an unrelenting contest for the body and soul of the Third World. Both are striving for the resources of the Third World, bases in the Third World, and the minds of the people of the Third World. India and Pakistan are pieces on their giant chess board.

Pakistan has a security agreement with the United States, signed in 1959. According to the agreement, the United States regards Pakistan's sovereignty and independence as vital to its national interests and promises to come to its aid in case its sovereignty and independence are threatened by a third power. For the last many years this agreement had been a dead letter, but the revolution in Iran and the Soviet invasion of Afghanistan changed all that. The latter operation has brought Russian forces to within 500 kilometers of the Persian Gulf (the free world's major source of oil) and the warm waters of the Arabian Sea (where Soviet naval bases might be located).

Seeing this threat to their vital interests, the Americans sought to revive the agreement of 1959. They offered to sell Pakistan weapons and equipment under an economic aid and military sales program that would enable Pakistan to defend itself against external aggression. Thus, it is not love, but rather a mutuality of interest which has drawn Pakistan and America together.

The Need for the Superpowers

Today the superpowers are coming in for a great deal of abuse in South Asia and are blamed for everything that goes wrong. India and Pakistan are adept at pinning the blame on each other or on third parties instead of acknowledging it themselves. While the presence of superpower influence in South Asia works in the interest of the superpowers and even to the detriment of South Asia, it should not be forgotten that India and Pakistan invited the superpowers in.

It was Pakistan's fear of India and of India's rising hegemony in the fifties that led Pakistan to turn to the West, to sign a security arrangement with the United States and enter SEATO and CENTO. In this way Pakistan drew the Americans into the subcontinent. On the other hand, when in August 1971 India had finalized its plans for the invasion of East Pakistan and the dismemberment of the country, it entered into a Treaty of Peace, Friendship, and Cooperation with the Soviet Union, drawing the Soviets into South Asia.

As a matter of interest, in spite of Indian denials, the Indo-Soviet Friendship Treaty has a military clause. According to Article IX, "In the event that any of the parties is attacked or threatened with attack, the high Contracting Parties will immediately start mutual consultations with a view to eliminating this threat and taking appropriate effective measures to ensure peace and security for their countries." It was a similar Soviet-Afghan treaty that facilitated the Soviet invasion of Afghanistan.

The Soviets in Afghanistan

The Progress of Events

In December 1979 the Soviet Union invaded Afghanistan and advanced progressively to take control of the entire country. During this period Soviet forces have been built up to something like 110,000 troops, adequately supported by air and logistical forces, against whom is arrayed the bulk of the Afghan population. A fiercely independent nation is fighting back in guerrilla actions and disputing with the Soviets and their Afghan puppets even their control of the cities. In fact, only the cities and the highways are under the control, such as it is, of the Soviets.

The impact of Soviet intervention in Afghanistan has been felt beyond the Afghan borders. Pakistan has been flooded with three million refugees—a very heavy burden for a poor country to carry—whose maintenance costs Pakistan almost a $2 million a day and imposes a grave social and ecological strain. In fact, the biggest problem in Pakistan today is how to lighten this load and get the refugees back to Afghanistan.

There have been talks in the past to solve the Afghanistan problem. There have been indirect talks with the Kabul regime, because Pakistan does not recognize the Afghan government and will not speak directly to it. In these talks attempts have been made to achieve a political solution to enable Afghanistan to exist once again as a free, nonaligned, sovereign state, as it has been in the past.

Pakistan has based its stand on four principles:

(a) the complete withdrawal of all foreign forces from Afghanistan;

(b) the return of the Afghan refugees to their homes in safety and honor;

(c) affirmation of Afghanistan as an Islamic, nonaligned, sovereign state; and

(d) the right of the Afghan people to choose their own government.

So far the talks have not achieved the desired results, and the deadlock continues. The fighting in Afghanistan also continues unabated, with the courage and resolution of the freedom fighters undiminished. Thus, the Soviets are no closer to their goal of fully subjugating this turbulent land. The pain is felt mainly by the Afghans and by Pakistan, which must care for the Afghan refugees on its soil.

Pakistan has been under some pressure from the Soviet Union to hold direct talks with the Karmal regime, but it has refused to do so. This follows a resolution of the Islamic Conference that no Muslim state will have anything to do with the Karmal regime. Moreover, a move to have direct talks with this regime will only have the effect of legitimizing it and giving it greater strength, without any assurance that fruitful results will follow.

The Causes

There are several causes usually offered to explain the Soviet invasion of Afghanistan, and it is not necessary for us to choose one of them as the cause. Very often such undertakings have several causes, each of which can justify, in whole or in part, a particular course of action. We should accept all these factors as possible collective causes of the invasion. Basically these factors are:

— The course of Russian imperial expansion over the last 400 years. Imperial expansion may sound odd in describing the actions of Communists, but these people are Russians, and it is possible that they have discarded one type of expansionism (imperial) for another (Communist).

— The old Russian desire to get to warm waters. This has been in the Russian mind for 200 years.

— Nearness to the Persian Gulf, through which flows the oil on which the free world depends. Without this oil, Western Europe would suffer terribly, and Japan would collapse like a house of cards, no matter what measures may be taken to provide reserves against future shortages. There are those who deny that this is a motivating factor on the grounds that the Soviets do not need oil, as they have enough of their own. The point here is not their need for oil, but the enormous advantage that they gain by denying this vital commodity to their opponents.

— The battle for the minds of the Third World. In this battle, whichever superpower gains an advantage over the other, gains ascendancy in the minds of the Third World.

— The power vacuum in Afghanistan (in terms of internal dynamics). As usually happens, such a vacuum attracts forces from outside. In this case, it attracted Soviet forces from across the Amu river.

— The Islamic revolution in Iran and its possible impact on deeply Islamic Afghanistan, which in turn could affect the Islamic republics of the USSR.

There are apologists who would have us believe that none of these causes is relevant and that the Soviet Union entered Afghanistan as a purely defensive measure because it fears encirclement and the possible presence of American forces close to its southern borders. This is most unconvincing. There is no danger whatsoever to the Soviet Union from Afghan territory. First, it is inconceivable that any Afghan government would allow American bases on its territory when even Pakistan, a pro-Western power, has refused to give bases to the United States. Second, an American strategist would have to be out of his mind to put missiles and other weapons, including nuclear weapons, on bases in Afghanistan where their protection would be nearly impossible and where they could be destroyed at ease by Soviet countermeasures. To do so at the cost of billions of dollars, when the job can be done better and more cheaply by U.S. nuclear submarines prowling the Arabian Sea, does not make sense. Perhaps that is why the Americans have more than once indicated that Afghanistan is outside their sphere of interest. The question of the Russians feeling vulnerable on their southern flank is not worthy of serious consideration.

It needs to be emphasized that of all the reasons that could have led the Soviets into Afghanistan, the most vital, and from the Western point of view the most dangerous, is their nearness to the Gulf. From the southwest corner of Afghanistan, the Soviets are only 300 miles from the Straits of Hormuz, through which flows 30 percent of Western Europe's requirement of oil and more than 60 percent of Japan's. It is conceivable that in the future, in a moment of inaction or disarray or weakness, when a Western response is unlikely, the Soviets could maneuver to get to the Gulf and turn off the oil taps, which would put out the lights in Europe and Japan. Whether the West will launch a nuclear offensive against Moscow on that account is highly debatable.

Russian Methods

It is possible to discern clear trends in the methods that the Russians use to achieve their political aims around the globe. Here are three of them:

— *Steadfastness of Purpose.* The Russians never change or give up an aim. They may defer it; they may even carry out a tactical withdrawal and display an apparent abondonment of the aim, but they will take it up again when conditions are suitable and will pursue it until it has been fully achieved. They will not abandon the aim.

— *The Indirect Approach.* The Russians will not take on an adversary head-on. They will deal with military adversaries by political maneuvers. They will achieve political objectives through economic pressures. They will defeat an enemy by internal subversion and disruption. Even when forced to tackle a military adversary by military means, they will outflank him rather than launch a frontal attack.

The Russians will not tackle NATO by attacking on the central front, but by subversion, by peace movements, by turning off the flow of oil through the Gulf which would lead to a collapse of NATO. Similarly, they will not take the Gulf by marching straight towards the Straits of Hormuz but by approaching it indirectly, perhaps via Pakistan. A Russian presence at the vital Pakistani ports of Pasni and Gwadar would be sufficient to cause a near-paralysis in the Western alliance.

— *Use Others.* Whenever possible the Russians will use others to do their dirty work for them. They used the North Koreans in Korea to tackle the Western powers and discredit them. They used the North Vietnamese in Vietnam to wear down the Americans and give them a bloody nose. They used the Cubans in Angola and in Ethiopia and the South Yemenis at the southern tip of the Arabian peninsula. They also used the Ethiopians against the Somalis.

As for Afghanistan, the Soviets could not very well ask the Cubans to come halfway around the world to fight for them in a country which was just across the river from Soviet Asia. Here the Russians had to go in themselves, sustained by the erroneous belief that the operation would be a pushover. Seeing how the operation has gone in Afghanistan, the Russians may well wish they had asked the Cubans in to do the job!

It may be farfetched to assert that in the case of the Indo-Pakistan war of 1971, the Soviet Union also used India as a proxy to punish Pakistan for bringing the United States and China together and for its close relations with China. Others maintain that it was the Indians who used the Russians to neutralize the Chinese and prevent them from hampering India's seizure of East Pakistan. (As a matter of interest, the Soviet Deputy Foreign Minister was present in India throughout that war.)

Be that as it may, it would be in Soviet interests to weaken Pakistan's resistance to such a degree that it could put up no opposition to Russian moves in Southwest Asia, particularly the Persian Gulf and the Arabian Sea. The Russians could view with approval an Indian invasion of Pakistan designed to render it incapable of resisting a Russian move through its territory. They could even assist the Indians in such a campaign by operations designed to tie down Pakistan's forces on the western front. And if India will do this job, regardless of its own national aim, it is a matter of semantics whether we call it a "proxy" of the Soviet Union or not.

What should be clear is that Pakistan's successful opposition to Soviet moves aimed at the Persian Gulf or the Arabian Sea depends on its retaining a credible and effective military capability. Any power that weakens that capability serves Soviet interests; any power that strengthens that capability thwarts Soviet designs.

Danger to India

Unfortunately, the present government in India has failed to realize the danger posed to the integrity of India by the presence of aggressive Soviet forces in Afghanistan. In a geopolitical sense, the Khyber Pass is the frontier of South Asia and not of Pakistan alone, and history has shown that any aggressor who crosses the Khyber Pass does not stop until he has reached the plains of Panipat, a little short of Delhi. The danger to Pakistan is a danger to India itself, and any damage suffered by Pakistan from the Soviet and Afghan forces would be damaging to Indian interests.

Should Pakistan be so weakened and its integrity so shaken that it finds itself under occupation by Soviet troops, the danger from that will not be to the Gulf alone but also to India. Delhi will then be horrified to find that Russia as its neighbor, like all neighbors, will be a potential enemy.

The danger to South Asia would be considerably lessened if India and Pakistan worked together in dealing with the Afghan problem. If, instead of condoning the role of the Russians in Afghanistan, India openly condemned it, joining Pakistan and most of the world in this matter, and if Delhi used its considerable influence with Moscow to bring about a withdrawal of Soviet forces from that embattled country so that the Afghan refugees could go home in safety and honor, that would be a great achievement not only for India but also for the region as a whole. It is fair to hope that South Asia's long-term interests will achieve more prominence in Indian thinking in the future than they have done in the past. Meanwhile, the pressure of the world on the Soviet Union must continue.

Regional Stability

Like everything else in this world of perpetual change and turmoil, stability must also be seen and measured in relative terms. When we view South Asia in this context, it seems far more stable than the other regions around it, like the Horn of Africa, the Middle East, the Gulf, and Indo-China. Even while carrying out a continental comparison, things look more cheerful here than in the African continent and in Latin America. It is a region in which interstate peace, however fragile and tenuous, has held since 1971. This is no mean achievement.

There are many reasons for South Asian stability, and other comparable regions lack these or do not possess them to the same degree. Despite the trauma of colonization, the historical fact of remaining under a single imperial system has given the South Asian states a similar institutional infrastructure, similar elite outlook, common languages, and shared administrative, economic, and educational systems. By and large South Asian societies are, by Afro-Asian standards, open, and regional democratic impulses are strong. Endemic poverty and a lopsided income distribution notwithstanding, no society in South Asia is at the threshold of a revolution.

Since India is the largest geopolitical entity of South Asia, its internal political, economic, and sociocultural stability adds to the general stability of South Asia. However, lately there are signs that the Indian political system is under pressure, if not siege. The other societies in South Asia are also passing through a critical phase of political transition, in which the search for a more stable and viable system is being vigorously pursued, albeit with a local, ideological flavor. It is hoped that the ancient wisdom of South Asia will prevail, and each state will be able to work out its salvation without an attempt by any neighboring state, however powerful, to impose its model on one pretext or the other.

There is a direct linkage between the internal stability and the economic performance of these states. A few consecutive poor harvests can lead to political upheaval, and the stability of South Asia is primarily dependent upon its economic performance. The media revolution, a good thing in itself, adds not only to the aspirations but also to the frustrations of the masses. It is time that the elite of South Asia address themselves to economic development wholeheartedly and on a priority basis.

Communal violence and ethnic, cultural, and linguistic chauvinism are endemic to the South Asian scene. Lately these ugly tendencies have shown an unfortunate upsurge which is a constant source of instability in the region. The peculiarities of South Asia are such that social violence in one place acts like a volcanic eruption, and its tremors are felt far and wide. The containment of social violence is going to be a difficult proposition for each state in the coming decade.

South Asian states still have unresolved territorial, boundary, and economic disputes like the sharing of waters and trade and transit routes, which affect the stability of interstate relations. Yet, given wisdom and goodwill, there is no reason to believe that these disputes cannot be settled amicably for the good of the states concerned and of South Asia as a whole.

Conclusion

South Asia has a glorious future, one that assures peace, stability, and prosperity for all seven of its members. It is perfectly reasonable to imagine a state of affairs as follows, say in the late eighties:

(a) India and Pakistan are at peace—a real, durable peace between two good, friendly neighbors.

(b) The armed forces of the two states have been much reduced in size and face outward. They are no longer needed against each other.

(c) India and Pakistan, the major powers of South Asia, backed by the remaining five nations, stand together, and the world knows that when it touches one, it touches the other.

(d) There is complete nuclear cooperation between India and Pakistan, with nuclear scientists of the two countries working together as partners in a joint venture.

(e) As a result of the reduction in defense expenditure and the channeling of savings into development, there is a notable improvement in the standard of living and the quality of life in South Asia.

We are far from that paradise, but progress can be made in that direction, starting with the removal of tensions within the region. It is noteworthy that of the seven sisters of South Asia, the smaller six have no problems among themselves, but each has problems with India—problems, disputes, misunderstandings, disagreements, call them what you will. (Even tiny Maldives nearly clashed with India in 1982 over the island of Minicoy.) All the problems and tensions felt by the six are related to India which, at least for the moment, stands as an obstacle to better intraregional relations. As the largest (and most problem-causing) state of South Asia, India must take the initiative to ease tension in the region, to reassure its smaller neighbors, and to move with them toward that paradise. With India lies the key.

That, however, is for the future to unveil. For the present the security situation in South Asia forms a triangle, the sides of which are:

(a) *India vs. Pakistan.* India and Pakistan feel threatened by each other. In fact they are Enemy Number One in their mutual threat perception.

(b) *India vs. China.* India feels threatened by China to the north, although this threat is more psychological than real. Moreover, India sees the possibility of collusion between China and Pakistan (and even America) against India.

(c) *Pakistan vs. Soviet Union.* Pakistan feels threatened by the Soviet forces in Afghanistan, aided by what remains of the Afghan army. Pakistan also fears collusion between the Russians and the Indians and considers an India aggression as possibly the act of a proxy serving the interests of the USSR.

This situation calls for measures which fall in two categories. The first of these is to defuse the tension and remove the threat that looms in South Asia. The second is to meet that threat head-on and deter aggression by one's own preparedness.

In order to defuse the threat, the following measures are required:

(a) *India: Pakistan.* The two countries should sign a No-War Pact, to be followed by a Friendship Treaty. There should be military talks aimed at reducing the armed forces of the two countries to such an extent that they cease to be a potential threat to each other. This process can be continued until both India and Pakistan begin to face outward in their defense instead of facing each other. Peaceful nuclear cooperation, along with making South Asia a nuclear-free zone, would be essential for defusing the threat.

(b) *India: China.* Talks must proceed to solve the border issue. The matter is not complex, and there is no need to let it drag on.

(c) *Pakistan: USSR.* A political solution to the Afghanistan problem must be found, one that will result in the withdrawal of Soviet forces from Afghanistan and the safe and honorable return of Afghan refugees to their country. Until such a solution is achieved, world pressure against the Soviet Union must continue. Pakistan needs the help of the West in dealing with the situation. Should India also throw in her lot with Pakistan, this would achieve even more rapid results, for the good of both countries.

If it is not possible to remove the threat by the above measures, the only way to prevent aggression is for the countries in question to be strong enough to deal with such aggression. As for Pakistan, it must receive help from the free world to defend its national integrity against all possible aggressors, which include India and the Soviets in Afghanistan.

12

India and Pakistan: We Know the Past; Must We Live in It?

Jagat S. Mehta

It is a perversity of our times that diplomacy is more and more backward-looking. We expend our skills and energy on explanations, rationalizations, accusations, domestically oriented populism, and external propaganda, and much less on understanding and persuasion between sovereign nations. Historical evidence is used selectively and becomes an oppression of worst-case scenarios. The extent of the irrelevance of history and the lessons we can learn escapes us, and our problems are avoidably perpetuated.

The Indian subcontinent has a long history before and through British hegemony. Considering the circumstances of the partition, it was to be expected that post-independence relations between India and Pakistan were going to be difficult. Throughout these decades there has been a running conflict between the independent dynamics of regional politics and the globalism of the superpowers. The superpowers alternated between indifference and conflict management, partisan involvement and exasperation, and the regional powers oscillated between dependence on and independence from outside powers. In varying measure, every country was guilty of inaccurate contemporaneous judgment, but these were compounded by the intertwining of the two dynamics. Only the Soviet Union emerged with net political gains beyond what might have been anticipated at the end of World War II, and that, too, largely because windows of opportunity were opened to her. But after Afghanistan, even the USSR must have had agonizing regrets.

1947-1965: South Asian Conflict and the Cold War

Without going over the entire history in detail, it is worth recalling some milestones in this story of misperceptions.

We all know that before India and Pakistan could settle down to their independence, the two countries became locked in a military and diplomatic confrontation over Kashmir.[1] The expectation was that these two dominions would remain economically dependent and politically pliant like the white dominions in the Commonwealth. Pakistan's case concerning Kashmir and the Anglo-American attitude toward it were fundamentally an extrapolation of the pre-independence rationale of religion determining the frontiers of the new dominions. India argued that legally valid frontiers have the sanctity of international law against all forms of intervention. However, despite a sense of disappointment with Anglo-American attitudes, India's relations with the West remained generally warm and trusting. In 1949 India decided to remain in the Commonwealth, and Nehru expressed fulsome admiration for and gratitude to the American democracy during his first visit to the United States in the same year. Despite the known admiration of Nehru for Soviet civilization and achievement, the Soviet Union extended an invitation to visit the USSR to Prime Minister Liaqat Ali Khan of Pakistan in 1950 and never contemplated such a courtesy to Nehru in the Stalin period.

It is not often remembered that in the period from 1947 to 1953, the USSR was neutral in the Kashmir debates in the Security Council. It was detached on the resolutions constituting the UNCIP, the proposals made by General McNaughton (Canada), the selection of Sir Owen Dixon of Australia as mediator (1950), and, of course, indifferent to Commonwealth mediation (1951). The USSR criticized Anglo-American interference (which the British delegate described as fantasies), but even so, the Soviet Union never obstructed Western diplomacy during the period. When direct Indo-Pakistan talks were taking place (1951-53), Nehru had warned that the great powers should keep out of the problem. However, the West did not anticipate that instead of the U.S.-Pakistan mutual security arrangements (1953-54) doubling the pressure on India, it would only provoke disenchantment and defiance and lead to the ending of discussions on the plebiscite modalities.

The endorsement of Kashmir's accession to India during the visit of Khrushchev and Bulganin only followed the Baghdad Pact and SEATO. The first Soviet veto was exercised in 1957, and by that time even Ambassador Gunnar Jarring of Sweden had reported that the "situation" had materially changed. In brief, it was the intrusion of the Cold War which polarized and militarized South Asia. In India the increase in the military budget gathered momentum only after the India-China War of 1962.

China's relations with the subcontinent also contradicted the Cold War syndrome of global bipolarity. The United States, USSR, Pakistan, and indeed, China and India as well, were taken aback when the Sino-

Indian crisis of confidence erupted in the wake of the 1959 revolt in Tibet. During the period from 1959 to 1962, the USSR oscillated between commitment to fraternal China and friendship for India. What is of interest to recall is that after the Sino-Indian conflict (and the Cuban missle crisis) was over in 1962, the Soviet Union was not even alarmed at the rise of U.S. influence.[2] There is no evidence that the Soviet Union did anything to frustrate the W. Averell Harriman-Duncan Sandys' shuttles between India and Pakistan. One might speculate that had Anglo-American diplomacy succeeded in bringing about pledges of peace and mutual respect and de facto acquiescence of existing lines of control, it would have been a sort of forerunner of Tashkent. The USSR might even have welcomed it.

Cemented only by their separate hostility to India and disregarding their communist-anti-communist professions, China and Pakistan developed their bilateral relations. However, the United States was not even seriously concerned when, at the height of the Vietnam War (1967-69), China and later the Soviet Union supplied military hardware to Pakistan, which was still a U.S. ally.

The next crisis in the subcontinent was the Indo-Pakistan war of 1965. Although the USSR quietly aquiesced in American attempts at Indo-Pakistan rapprochement in 1962, the United States actually encouraged the Soviet role as mediator after the 1965 India-Pakistan conflict and expressed satisfaction at the success of the Kosygin diplomacy at Tashkent in 1966. This was the symbolic obiter dicta of the 125-year-old British policy of containing Russia and preventing it from politically reaching the subcontinent and its limitrophic warm waters—not 1979-80 when alarms were raised after the Soviet invasion of Afghanistan.

While professing to defend and promote democracy, the United States chose to build its relations with nondemocratic governments in Pakistan. Similarly, the Soviet Union has maintained relations with India's communist parties, but whenever there was a conflict between support for the established central government of India and their ideological confrères, Moscow supported the former, after leaving the pro-Soviet parties in a state of dismay. The policies of both superpowers have been ideologically agnostic; their propaganda and rhetoric have only caused confusion.

Notwithstanding the leverage of arms supply and economic aid, both superpowers have found that the regional powers were never wholly politically pliant, even on non-subcontinental issues. The United States never really controlled Pakistan's foreign policy. Pakistan's position on Israel was always critical of the United States; SEATO all but died when China was most hostile and the United States was actively canvassing for political support on Vietnam. India was no doubt sensitive to the Soviet position on Hungary in 1956 and supported the USSR on some issues on the international agenda, but it remained detached and neutral on the Sino-Soviet rift, even when Sino-Indian relations were at their worst. Later, India was to refuse to endorse the Brezhnev doctrine for Asia and the notion of the nonaligned as the natural allies of the Socialist bloc.

What is common in all these cases is the deviation from the conventional wisdom that the bipolar Cold War syndrome dominated and determined the problems and politics of the subcontinent throughout these decades. It was the hypnosis created by East-West postures—taken too seriously, both by protagonists and opponents—which culminated in the tragedy of the 1965 conflict.

Most of these fallacies could have been foreseen. Whatever mutual assurances, public and confidential, were exchanged between the United States and Pakistan, Pakistan never had any heart in the fight against communist states, and it was naive to think the United States could ever be militarily involved against India. The latter might have been more diplomatically agile in forestalling the U.S.-Pakistan security arrangements before 1953 and might have preempted the development of the China-Pakistan connection in the early 1960s, which led to military supplies and a coordinated anti-Indian diplomacy. But, generally, various intellectual failures led to the exacerbation of regional problems by great power politics and allowed the illusions to persist as long as they did. The resultant frustrations of all the powers in the quadrilateral were largely avoidable.

1965-1980: The Region on Its Own

The 1965 conflict was a dramatic jolt to the Cold War paradigm, and Tashkent was a turning point. It was really the end of a decade of East-West competitive globalism in the subcontinent. Contrary to the spirit of their military agreements, American weapons were used by Pakistan against India. The United States then stopped military and economic aid to both India and Pakistan, causing dismay, especially to Pakistan. While the two superpowers made coordinated efforts to defuse the 1965 conflict and subsequently muted their competition in the subcontinent, China turned blatantly partisan, and through frivolous but calculated ultimata sought to influence the military outcome. But even China was not prepared to intervene directly in a conflict over Kashmir —which, after all, was only a Pakistani national purpose. Tashkent was a setback for China, but China persisted in cultivating Pakistan against what it perceived as India's double alliance with the United States and the USSR.

Some misperceptions that the East-West syndrome dominated regional politics in the seventies are also worth recapitulating.

After 1966, while nurturing its relations with India, the USSR sought to stymie China by developing parallel relations with Pakistan, and, as stated earlier, for a while sought to increase its leverage through arms supplies to Pakistan. The U.S. tilt in the 1971 conflict on the subcontinent was an aberration, primarily due to the U.S. pursuit of its globalist policies vis-à-vis the USSR. The Nixon-Kissinger policy reflected their enthusiasm at the prospect that Pakistan would act as an intermediary for the development of strategic relations with China against the Soviet Union.

During the early stages of the Bangladesh crisis, the attitude of both superpowers was similar. The Soviet Union did not encourage the dismemberment of Pakistan. But it was sagacious enough not to obstruct the inevitable, while the United States sought in vain to manage the conflict and put pressure on India. The Indo-Soviet Treaty was negotiated because of the fear, perhaps exaggerated, of the misconceived U.S. tilt and China's hostile attitude to Bangladesh's desire for independence. Anyway, the dispatch of the carrier *Enterprise* has become to the Indian mind a symbol of attempted American coercion, just as Pearl Harbor remains the image of perfidy, and Munich of appeasement.

However, after Bangladesh came into existence there was nothing left of the tilt and of the U.S. notion of a military or political parity between Pakistan and India. Even Dr. Kissinger (during his visit to Delhi in 1974) recognized the emergent preeminence of India in the subcontinent. President Carter went further and saw India as a regional power with a critical role in subcontinental security. (The other regional hegemons were to be Iran, Brazil, Nigeria, and Egypt.) This notion of India as the regional dominant power produced resistance and did not facilitate subcontinental diplomacy.

Earlier, India and Pakistan had found to their surprise that both superpowers were united and earnest in their endeavor to ensure the adoption of the NPT (1968). Both of the regional powers refused to sign it. After the passage of the U.S. Nonproliferation Act (1978), the United States again found that both India and Pakistan were unwilling to surrender their nuclear option. As a result, aid was cut off to Pakistan and, notwithstanding an existing bilateral agreement, fuel was delayed for the Tarapur reactor.

By the mid-seventies, and after nearly fourteen years of one-sided partiality for Pakistan, China also veered to a more evenhanded attitude toward India. In 1976, Sino-Indian relations were restored to the ambassadorial level, and, after the visit of the Indian foreign minister to Peking in 1979, the strident Chinese commitment to Pakistan's position on Kashmir was muted, although not abandoned. The Sino-Indian territorial settlement remains unresolved, but if we set aside worst-case scenarios, Sino-Indian relations are now more of a political than a security problem. Sino-Indian relations have since then again had their ups and downs, but this has related to Afghanistan and Kampuchea and not to India-Pakistan or India-China problems.

By 1976, what was significant in the attitudes of the United States, the USSR, and China was that, with differing rationales, all of them were moving away from the imposed either-or commitment and partisanship for India and Pakistan. Of course Washington, Moscow, and Beijing remained vigilant that the subcontinent as a whole did not slip into the orbit of a rival power, but the trend toward military nonalignment of the subcontinent caused no alarm in any of these capitals. The two levels of politics—the global and the regional—were being decoupled. There was quiet hope, if not positive encouragement, that the normalization of India-Pakistan relations would evolve through bilateral diplomacy. All three great powers happily acquiesced in (or positively welcomed) the agreements reached between the countries of the subcontinent during the years 1976-79.

This was a significant change, but it was slow and undramatic and went largely undetected by analysts and regional public opinion. The improvement in the political climate was not reversed in 1977 when the Janata government came to power in Delhi or when Bhutto was replaced by a military regime in Islamabad. It was not even deflected by important events such as the Saur Revolution in Afghanistan (April 1978) and the collapse of the Shah's regime and his exile (1979). The foreign policy approaches of the Democratic Socialist Republic of Afghanistan under Amin (on Iran, disarmament, and other East-West issues) were wholeheartedly pro-Soviet, but this did not bring about a precipitate improvement in U.S.-Pakistan relations. The United States continued to turn down Pakistan's requests for A-7 aircraft probably because India and Pakistan had maintained a dialogue and had more or less agreed that Afghanistan was an internal problem, and the United States did not want to complicate its relations with South Asia and fuel an arms race.

Suddenly, with the Soviet invasion of Afghanistan in late December 1979 (ignoring the lessons of three decades), the two Cold Wars—the global and the regional—were reenmeshed. What we have seen in the past five years is a telescoped reenactment of the tragic story of South Asia after 1954. Not that it was impossible to perceive that there was no new or imminent threat to the subcontinent; because of the hold of Cold War analysis and the fears and suspicions it embodied, instead of quarantining the conflict, the regional and nonregional powers allowed tensions to revive and to give a dramatic spurt to what had been a flagging arms race. Afghanistan provides another case study of the failure of contemporaneous judgments and false analysis, which led to tragic, self-fulfilling prophecies.

Afghanistan and Regional Stability

I have written elsewhere on Afghanistan and will no more than briefly summarize my own understanding.[3] The 1978 revolution succeeded because of accidents and not because of masterminded external direction from Moscow. The Khalq was probably surprised to find itself in power as a dominant partner in the new "Democratic Republic of Afghanistan." However, the regime started splintering within weeks, but that too was because of local dynamics. Overruling its coalition partner and disregarding its nationalist supporters, largely under Hafizullah Amin's leadership, it embarked on an overrapid transformation of a medieval religious tribal society into a socialist state. The Kremlin had naturally welcomed and throughout 1978 gave unreserved support to Amin. However, in due course, the Kremlin discovered that the forced advent of communism was alienating a country that had never been hostile to the USSR under the overthrown monarchy and the previous conservative oligarchy.

Having failed to moderate Amin—an obviously delicate task—the Kremlin planned and fortuitously failed the attempt to replace Amin politically or physically eliminate him in September 1979. Amin survived but was disillusioned at his discovery that his loyalty to Moscow was paradoxically forfeiting their support. He then turned nationalist and made concessional overtures; internally to the tribal leaders and Mullahs and externally to Pakistan on Pakhtunistan. Amin may have hoped he could wriggle free of his dependence on the USSR and even make overtures to the United States, but instead, in impetuous, defensive anxiety about the potential dangers from an alienated Afghanistan, the Soviet Union saw no alternative but to launch a massive invasion to remove their erstwhile friend, Amin, lest Afghanistan become a Soviet Nicaragua.

The enormity of its military and political miscalculation is almost certainly now recognized by the Soviet Union. The Soviet action overlooked Russia's historical experience in Afghanistan and other more recent examples of outraged nationalism, such as Vietnam's intervention in

Kampuchea. It proved, in any case, to be an unexpected setback to Soviet policy in the Third World. However, scholars as well as the Carter administration interpreted the invasion of Afghanistan as the first step in a sweep toward the warm-water ports and a threat to the oil flows of the Gulf, linked to the American hostages in Iran. Reflecting the entrenched hypotheses, the invasion was viewed as a menacing strategic maneuver against the West and proof of ideological expansion. A local situation was thus transposed into an East-West problem.

None of these scenarios has come to pass, and we are left with unconvincing post hoc explanations justifying hollow fears. The Soviet expansion is deemed to have been halted because of prompt military reactions (the Rapid Deployment Force) and the international boycott and alarm. In any case, it is argued that the Soviet capability for future military advances has been improved, as if the Soviet Union has not always enjoyed a decisive military advantage in the whole area. It had been obvious for more than a decade—including when Soviet-Iraq relations were very close—that the USSR recognized that any provocation or direct threat to the oil carried the same hazard as overrunning West Berlin.

On the other hand, the exaggerated alarm of the United States and the subsequent involvement of the CIA has been conveniently used by the USSR as confirmation that the Soviet action was a necessary preemptive measure to prevent Afghanistan from becoming a Western satellite.

As in 1953-1954, Pakistan was able to play upon Washington's alarm, restore warmth to the tepid relations with the United States, and obtain massive commitments of American arms and economic aid. American policymakers again failed to recognize that Pakistan's most serious concern was not the Soviet threat (against which Pakistan is indefensible), but India. The nature of the weapons obtained and the location of the deployment confirm that Pakistan's primary purpose is to bolster operational capabilities on its eastern rather than northern or western fronts. The Pakistani, however, have shown greater diplomatic skill than in the fifties. Having used the Afghanistan developments to consolidate relations with the Islamic world and having been assured of American assistance and strengthened further their friendship with China, the Pakistanis have been careful not to offend or provoke the USSR. Thus, it should have come as no surprise to anyone (but the Cold Warriors) that Pakistan rejected the Pentagon's plea for RDF bases on Pakistani soil and that it does not echo the hostile approach toward, and apprehension of, the Soviet Union. Pakistan's circumspection with respect to the Soviet Union notwithstanding, Pakistani leaders once again failed to anticipate the predictable Indian reactions.

India embarked on a massive program of defense modernization with purchases from both the USSR and the West. These purchases more than matched Pakistan's planned military aid from the United States. In turn, Indo-Soviet relations were strengthened. The initial attitude of the government of India (as, to some extent, that of the United States) was complicated by the coincidence of the domestic general election with the Soviet intervention in Afghanistan. In the 1977 Indian elections (and even though Pakistan was also having elections), no foreign policy issues were raised in the campaign. In 1979, international issues had figured prominently during the preelection debates. The initial reaction of the new Indian government to the Soviet intervention, as expressed in the speech of the Indian ambassador in the General Assembly debate on January 11, gave credence to the official Soviet explanation that its forces were invited into the country. This view reflected the election theme that relations with the Soviets had been allowed to deteriorate in the 1977-79 period. The Indian position changed soon after the new government was in power. Within weeks, the government of Indian publicly urged a Soviet withdrawal and a political solution. However, the consequences of the abstention on the crucial resolution before the U.N. could not be undone.

My own guess is that if Mrs. Gandhi had been in power after 1977 (or if the Janata government had remained in office until 1982), the initial Indian reaction would have been different. India might well have anticipated that the United States would react with alarm and how this would be used by Pakistan to obtain a resumption of military aid, in a way similar to that in 1954. It is worth recalling that Mrs. Gandhi had for years resisted the purchase of the Jaguar. It was the Janata government's decision to purchase squadrons of this subsonic deep-strike aircraft which provided the rationale for the supply of ultrasophisticated aircraft like the F-16 to Pakistan. The U.S. administration's commitment to contain the "evil of Communism" and to reestablish military superiority compounded the reenactment of the 1954 syndrome, but that came a whole year later. If the Indian approach to Pakistan in January 1980 had been similar to that of the foreign minister's speech in Karachi in June 1981, the subcontinental arms race might not have assumed its present dimensions. If India had anticipated the nonaligned vote on Afghanistan, India might have been better placed to play a more effective role in counseling Soviet withdrawal and rescuing Moscow from the Afghan quagmire. Afghanistan provided a unique opportunity to initiate steps toward an India-Pakistan settlement, an opportunity that was allowed to slip by. Paradoxically, the anti-American and anti-Pakistan hawks in India played into the hands of the Pentagon, and the anti-Indian and anti-Russian militants in Pakistan must have provided grist to the Soviet military mill rather than to the political strategists in the Politburo.

A Solution for Afghanistan

Many efforts to find a solution in Afghanistan were proposed in 1980-81, but they all failed and were abandoned. The only serious attempt still active is under the auspices of the U.N. Secretary-General through parallel, indirect talks—that, too, at six-month intervals—between his representative on the one hand and the governments of Afghanistan, Pakistan, the USSR and possibly Iran on the other. It is not surprising that the U.N.-sponsored initiative has not met with success. The U.N. is always paralyzed when facing violent conflicts, especially where a superpower perceives its interests to be involved. The USSR cannot be compelled to evacuate its forces from a neighboring country, especially as the United States makes no secret of its covert support to the *Mujahiddin*. Moreover, any timetable for a Soviet withdrawal could only be predicated on obtaining the agreement of the Mujahiddin within Afghanistan and in Pakistan to a cease-fire. The U.N. has no means even to reach Afghan insurgent groups, much less persuade them to lay down their arms while the Soviet Union remains engaged in operations against the consensus of the Afghan nation. It was to be expected that the U.N., by its very nature, would be stumped. Meanwhile, the tragic conflict continues in Afghanistan.

My own analysis, now more than five years old, was that the problem and its chronology had been subjectively interpreted, and therefore serious efforts to find a political solution were never launched.[4] Afghanistan became a part of the East-West Cold War. The crux of the problem now was the traditional and heightened security anxiety of the Soviet Union and the outraged nationalism of the Afghan people. My recommendations were based on the premises that the greatest danger was not of further Soviet advance and threats to Western interests, but of problems for Pakistan and in turn for the stability of relations in South Asia. The regional stakes demanded a harmonized regional initiative because that alone had some chance of persuading the Soviet Union to withdraw and restore Afghanistan to nonalignment.

Going by the approximate parallels of Soviet withdrawal from Austria and Finland, I urged as a precondition that the region and Afghanistan must (like Sweden) declare its neutrality and demonstrably become a buffer between the superpower strategies. The countries in South Asia and the Gulf could collectively reaffirm their nonalignment by reiterating their refusal to provide bases, storage dumps, or any secret contingency commitments to either superpower. Thereafter, the entire nonaligned movement (thus exerting the most telling possible moral pressure on the USSR) could select a nonaligned observer group from countries like Kuwait, Algeria, India, Tanzania, Syria, Indonesia, and Pakistan. All of these countries have urged Soviet withdrawal but are not implacably hostile to the USSR. Such a mission was not likely to be rejected by the Soviet Union. Once installed in Kabul, the nonaligned group, with their supporting corps of officers, could urge and observe the reduction and grouping of Soviet forces, to be followed by a cease-fire by the *Mujahiddin,* their return from exile, and their peaceful rehabilitation. The international community could provide the economic aid to meet the immediate needs of a shattered economy, and the mission could act as the funnel for its distribution. The next step could be to summon a traditional Loya jirga on the 1973 pattern. Such a purely Afghan body could either reaffirm the pre-1978 constitution or draft a new one. The mission could observe the elections under the constitution and the formation of a new government. At this stage, with the liaison of the nonaligned mission, the new government could negotiate a new Afghan-Soviet treaty patterned on the Soviet-Finnish treaty, that is, giving the USSR the right of consultation and intervention in case Afghanistan were to compromise its nonalignment, and at this time the residuary Soviet forces (and the nonalignment mission) could be withdrawn.

This is a brief summary of what was, in any case, a bare-bones outline. Unlike other proposals, it tries to ensure through preliminary steps and subsequent integrated measures that Soviet security will not be endangered. Although the U.S. covert support would have to end at the first stage (it is in any case militarily marginal), the proposal does not envisage that the insurgent groups would lay down their arms without some visible safeguards and a credible promise of regaining their national personality and Afghan nonalignment.

My own view is that *faute de mieux,* there is still time for the region to seize the initiative on Afghanistan. It is a lesser hazard than the present drift, in which Washington has no policy or solution, Moscow is in a no-win situation both politically and militarily, and South Asia cannot be reconciled to the loss of Afghanistan. In any case, Pakistan must be saved from the most serious situations. Even if the Soviets make no aggressive moves, the presence of the refugees could jeopardize Pakistan's integrity and even create semi-autonomous ministates on the frontier and in Baluchistan, thus changing the geopolitical complexion of the region.

The pervasive notion that the USSR has come to stay is a kind of moral reconciliation with the right of intervention by superpowers on the basis of their own assertions of *droit de limitrophe*. The security and political concerns of the United States, the USSR, and China in relation to the Afghanistan imbroglio are obvious. In their view, the security and economic futures of India and Pakistan are subordinate. The subcontinent must reckon with the mix of common and adversary interests of the nonregional powers. Even if the Soviet withdrawal does not come about, a harmonized regional nonaligned approach could be the catalyst to slowing the debilitating arms race and the threats to their economic futures and to regional stability. The real challenge is to statesmanship in the region, and this brings me back to the importance of Indo-Pak political normalization.

The India-Pakistan Conflict

Whether the problem and solution of Afghanistan is distinct from or linked with that of South Asia, we must recognize that its chief adverse fallout has been on India and Pakistan. The process of uncoupling South Asia from the Cold War that has been underway at least since 1971, if not 1966, has been reversed. Nonalignment, to which every country including Pakistan now pays homage, has reverted to a balancing dependence on competing superpowers rather than detachment from them. The future danger for both is becoming a convenient argument in East-West relations.

Fortunately, the repetition of the fifties scenario did not stop with the negative consequences of the subcontinental arms race and revived tensions. The old lessons—that becoming an adjunct to superpower politics and strategies brought lesser security at higher costs—soon began to tug at policymakers. After commitments to a program of massive militarization in the subcontinent, which may eventually run to $20 billion, it seems to have again been realized that ultimately relations with one's neighbor are critical to the respective security futures of both states. Presumably it was this logic that led Pakistan to reverse its earlier position and to offer an unconditional no-war declaration with India. India hesitated, but with unambiguous support of public opinion, responded with a counter offer of an Indo-Pakistan Treaty of Peace and Friendship. In the same spirit, both India and Pakistan responded positively to the Bangladesh initiative for a South Asia forum for regional cooperation. Since then, regular high-level visits have started between Delhi and Islamabad. These are unprecedented modalities which neither country can casually break off in the future.

The institutional innovations are of little more than potential importance if political attitudes remain inhibited. One cannot conceal that the old cancer of suspicions, the chicken-and-egg accusations, and the subcontinental variant of a quest for parity and military superiority as a precondition to meaningful arms restraint have again come into play. It is an open question now whether we are in the pre-1965 situation (heading for a conflict) or in the mid-seventies situation (with the prospect of step-by-step easing of Indo-Pakistan tensions).

The answer does not lie with the extraregional powers. For all their separate or collective power and leverage, Washington, Moscow, and Beijing cannot determine which way the region will turn—to war or to peace—or whether, when, and how the arms they sell or supply will or will not be used. The decision rests squarely in Islamabad and Delhi. No longer a government spokesman and officially uninformed, I can only speculate with the license of no responsibility. But I do know that the challenge to follow a constructive rather than a destructive path is not beyond the capability of Indian and Pakistani bilateral diplomacy.

The overriding impediment is the intellectual torpor of the Cold War. In the past, some national policy goals were misconceived, but that problem was compounded because the motives, power, and capacities of the other powers were misjudged. It is useful, before we think of security futures, to think of the fallacies that have been exposed in these decades.

The resilient old notion that India and Pakistan are not reconciled to each other's existence has all but died; it is realism to recognize that the Kashmir dispensation cannot be unscrambled without the hazard of a major conflict. (Although, as with German reunification, de jure confirmation of present reality may be a political problem, existing boundaries have to be accepted with a sense of finality.) Other fears or illusions are also almost gone: that India and Pakistan could be surrogates of different superpowers, and that one or the other could be manipulated for competing superpower strategies; that Pakistan is truly anti-Soviet and pro-American, or that India is necessarily interested in undermining Western interests to subserve Soviet strategic goals, even where its own were not involved; that the benevolent commitment of one power would support or rescue its alleged "client" in any regional conflict; that outside powers can prevent a regional conflict; and finally, that the superpowers would oppose (or even be able to obstruct) any regional settlement bilaterally reached if it was based on military neutrality.

The recognition of past mistakes in the international politics of South Asia is only one aspect of moving toward stabler security futures. To muster the confidence for positive purposefulness, it is useful to recall that the record of India and Pakistan in domestic achievement and in bilateral diplomacy is not quite as dismal as in sometimes supposed. It is well to recall how in many important aspects the prophets of doom were belied, and successes exceeded even nonprejudiced expectations.

Only a little more than a decade ago, both India and Pakistan were dismissed as international basket cases. Yet their success in food production can surely be compared with that of any developing country. Their separate achievements also should be recalled. India has indigenized democracy, domesticated ideologies, and, notwithstanding eruptions, secularized politics. It has diversified its economy, built up a technological infrastructure, and, overcoming the drag of its social system, modernized without a conservative backlash. Pakistan has belied fears that it would disintegrate. The consensus in India does not now question Pakistan's identity or longevity. (An incidental consequence of the change of central government in India from 1977 to 1980 is that Pakistani fears of Hindu chauvinism have all but disappeared.) After initial consolidation, Pakistan made unexpected progress in the fifties and sixties and confounded gloomy forecasts for its economic recovery after the loss of Bangladesh.

Even in their bilateral relations, in the miasma of suspicions and publicized differences, the record of working compromises and even unilateral gestures is generally overlooked, beginning with Mahatma Gandhi fasting to compel payment of the financial resources allocated to Pakistan. It is barely known that even after the Kashmir incursions, Jawaharlal Nehru nearly dismissed a cabinet colleague, who, after the Standstill Agreement expired in April 1948, stopped the flow of water for the West Punjab Canal System. The Nehru-Liaqat Pact on minorities was a rational compromise which worked satisfactorily. More recently, it was Mr. Bhutto's decision to withdraw the registered complaint with the International Civil Aviation Organization (1976) regarding the stoppage of overflights (after the destruction of an Indian Airlines plane in Pakistan in 1971). Bhutto's action made possible the restoration of diplomatic relations and road, rail, and civil air connections, both of which had been envisaged under the Simla agreement. Pakistan handled the second highjacking of an Indian aircraft in September 1976 with skill and zest, enabling the safe return of the passengers and the plane, even though the highjackers had Azad Kashmir affiliations and had expected support from Pakistan. For its part, India did not raise objections when Pakistan applied to join the nonalignment movement. India and Pakistan have cooperated sincerely and often provided joint leadership on North-South issues and in formulating the outlines of the New International Economic Order.

The Salal Dam agreement was a microcosm of Indo-Pak problems but became an example of successful bilateral diplomacy. For seven years, a purely economic hydroelectric project on the Chenab river in Kashmir was delayed because Pakistan suspected that it was primarily intended to facilitate military operations. Had this dispute been referred to international arbitration under the provisions of the Indus treaty (as it nearly was), it would have become a second "Kashmir." The last-minute bilateral negotiations revealed that the fears were unfounded and that the scenarios envisaged by Pakistan would have done more harm to India than any conceivable damage to Pakistan. The agreement was initialed in 1976 by Mrs. Gandhi and Mr. Bhutto, and it was confirmed in 1978 by their respective successor governments, making it a noteworthy example of binational bipartisanship. These and other examples are surely reasons to have confidence in the capacity of Indian and Pakistani diplomacy.

But diplomacy also has its own Gresham's Law. The present political climate does not reflect a confidence in bilateral diplomacy. It will require a major intellectual effort to muster the political will to prevent a slide into mutually reinforcing suspicion and actual conflict.

Both sides have to remind themselves of the lesson furnished by the downfall of the Shah of Iran: national security in the twentieth century is multidimensional, a mix of internal and external factors, and it requires a blend of political responsiveness, social justice, and economic growth, not just firepower. Political, governmental, and nonofficial opinion must focus more than ever on the long-term internal consequences of Indo-Pakistani paranoia.

Except in unlikely contingencies, India has been secure against external imposition. However, it has to appraise the needs and expectations of a population that will grow to one billion by the end of the century and to prevent internal disaffection from turning into violent disruption of its democracy. Pakistan has similar economic problems, but as a priority, it has to effect a transition to a representative form of government, to find the equation between Islamic ideology, the Shariat, and the imperatives of modernization. Both India and Pakistan have had a foretaste of the serious regional problems that (except for the case of Punjab in India) result from insufficiency and disparities in national economic growth. No outside power can cap these smoldering volcanoes.

An objective perspective also cannot deny that the long-term problems of the South Asian countries can be solved only through their cooperation. India, Pakistan, Bangladesh, Nepal, and Bhutan are all dependent on the common Himalayan watershed and ecology. By the denudation of its Himalayan forests, Nepal may, for example, have contributed (but compounded by India's own deforestation) to halving the useful life of

developmental irrigation projects in the Gangetic plains. Perhaps Nepal
had no alternative. Until it can develop its hydroelectric potential and sell
surplus power to India, it has few other sources with which to earn its ru-
pee requirements. As an upper riparian, India holds the same threat over
Pakistan. Surface and ground water flows and pollution defy sovereignty, however militarized the frontiers! The Indus Water Treaty was generally acclaimed, but it was predicated on the presumption of permanent
hostility, or at least the impossibility of cooperation between India and
Pakistan, even with respect to resources that neither can exploit unilaterally. A large share of the $6 billion (1960 prices) disbursed under the
Treaty was expended not to supplement but to substitute existing head-
works and canal links; the longer-term problem remains. Pakistan has 79
percent of the water flow of the Indus, but India has the mountain sites
that would enable both countries to harness the flow of the Indus for
many purposes. The fact that the two countries belong to an integrated
drainage basin is an irrevocable reality which history and suspicion cannot change. Pakistan's ties of religion with West Asia can be psychologically reassuring and even economically rewarding, but they cannot alter
the fate that links it to India.

Apart from water and ecology, there are more tangible gains to be realized from regional complementarities that can contribute to national
development strategies—if only the region's economic interdependence
were squarely recognized. SAARC promises only limited beginnings in
this exploration. After meetings between unofficial economists, The
Committee on the Study of Cooperation in South Asia has projected a
fuller picture of the benefits in important sectors like energy, industrialization, transport, population control, and technology sharing, which
can only follow rational coordination within the region without compromise to any sovereignty. Such regional economic cooperation will depend
on regional initiatives. Great powers could facilitate it with the promise
of an imaginative response (such as the U.S. response to Europe in the
form of the Marshall Plan), but it would be futile and indeed counterproductive to imagine that they had the power or leverage to knock South
Asian heads together.

Against these long-term problems and potential must be placed the opportunity costs of mutually reinforcing fears and mounting defense outlays, the more so if these trends are extrapolated for the next decade and
a half.[5] No one has ever projected what might have been the picture of
the Indian and Pakistani economies if only 50 percent of the total military outlays expended by the two countries on efforts directed against
each other had been available for developmental investment. I was assured by the most eminent economic official in India—admittedly with-

out detailed study—that both economies might have registered a minimum additional 3 percent growth rate. If compounded, both countries might have attained a per-capita income exceeding $1,000 and presented the same picture as the ASEAN countries.

Finally, harsh realism must also recognize that for all the weight of reason and international consensus, a New International Order is not imminent. Even if the global economic recovery continues, détente is revived, and East-West arms restraints are under way (an unlikely prospect in the present climate), international economic support for the Third World will range from meager to dismal. This brutal reality itself demands the end of psychological dependence on the East or West, either as a safeguard for security, as a source of economic rescue, or as a scapegoat for domestic problems.

This odyssey of intellectual reappraisal points to a reversion by India and Pakistan to the diplomacy of beneficial bilateralism. The military or political involvement of the great powers can only be defied jointly. Regional trust and peace, and external economic indifference, can only be ameliorated by greater cooperation and optimized self-reliance.

Toward a Regional Political Settlement

What could be the modalities for a political breakthrough in Indo-Pakistan relations? Most of the models—the Tlatelolco Treaty, the Sinai Accords, the MBFR—are either not applicable, or, for the moment, premature in the subcontinent. If we have to find a parallel—and no parallel is exact—it is in the steps envisaged in the Helsinki-Belgrade confidence-building scenarios between eastern and western Europe. The aim must be to cut through the vicious grip of mutual suspicions. Successful diplomacy must start with an appreciation of the national psychology and legitimate vital interests of the adversary: a sensitivity to the nationalism of others. This recipe for regional restraint and cooperation is not different from what the nonaligned have urged continuously on the superpowers: realistic limits to military vigilance and a vision of the economic costs in an interdependent world.

In relation to the six smaller neighbor states of the subcontinent, India has a special problem which bears comparison with the United States in relation to the world. Just as the United States (barring Soviet military capability) is disproportionately more powerful than all countries in the world, India is not only larger but industrially and technologically superior in South Asia. On different scales, both India and the United States face the expectation of generosity, understanding, and economic support by their "neighbors," but both are treated often unreasonably as a foil

rather than as a friend by smaller and weaker nations. Indian diplomacy
can no longer compartmentalize its relations with its neighbors. India's
inability to overcome the historic fears in Pakistan could be eased if simultaneously there were success in the improvement of relations with
Bangladesh, Nepal, Sri Lanka, and Bhutan. Contrariwise, tension with
any one country has tended to create apprehension in all the other states
of South Asia.

Although I do not minimize the role and responsibility of India to turn
the situation around, Pakistan also has to make a critical decision. It
cannot run with the hares of nonalignment and hunt in the superpower
game and still expect credibility with respect to its desire for more peaceful and cooperative relations with India. India has the obvious advantage
of defense in depth and is not likely to be blitzed into surrender. Even if
New Delhi does not receive in per-capita terms the kind of financial support that Pakistan is able to obtain, an arms race will not prove an effective method for the economic attrition of India.

Both India and Pakistan must also face the inherent dangers and uncertainties of nuclear weapons as a method of defense or coercion. Any
nuclear weapons capability, outside the full paraphernalia of mutually
assured destruction and fail-safe as well as verification technology will
only give an illusion of deterrent or compellent capability. In no scenario
can one be certain that a threat or an actual nuclear exchange will be limited to the regional level, or that radiation hazards will be confined to the
adversary's frontier. Furthermore, nuclear weapons cannot lead to the
reduction or substitution of conventional armed capability. Morally and
politically, the attempt to smother the nuclear option of either India or
Pakistan by the United States, the USSR, or both, was unrealistic and politically counterproductive. Whether Pakistan can even now refrain from
acquiring a weapons capability or whether it and India can be content
with the prestige parity of a bomb in the basement will also depend upon
their ability to achieve a climate of mutual trust between the two countries. If this goal proves elusive, the two countries will only flatter the superpowers by imitation—in an unrestrained and spiraling arms race.

Finally, the obvious truth must be stated: India has a vested interest in
Pakistan's integrity and prosperity. At the same time, Pakistan must accept that the ultimate guarantor of an optimal future for independent
Pakistan is a dynamic India, acting not as a regional hegemon but as a
power that is central to the viability of South Asia. Neither the United
States and the USSR nor China can be dependable allies or reliable patrons. Until the relations of the great powers undergo a sea change, none
of them can serve independently as an effective mediator. But all of them
—in varying measure—can be nonexclusive economic partners of South

Asian countries. The awe and the appeal of these great powers are exaggerated because of the failure to measure our own interests and capacities.

Looking back on the tragic story of the subcontinent, neither wisdom nor myopia has been the exclusive monopoly of the great powers or the regional ones. There was a naive nonlinkage between the two cold wars in the beginning, in 1947-53; it became vitiated by a perverse linkage in 1954-66, in 1971, and again after 1980; the present dangers can only be safeguarded with a deliberate delinkage. The only hope for Afghanistan —and South Asia as a whole—lies in regionalized nonalignment through regional diplomacy.

I remain persuaded that the countries of South Asia have the wisdom and the capacity to break out of the hypnosis of the past and to fashion a more stable security future. I would go on to add that a stable South Asia, which is the greatest open laboratory of the development and modernization process, could have a critical and unique role in narrowing the North-South chasm. Moreover, if South Asia could disengage from the East-West strategic game, it might actually be a relief and not a loss to both Washington and Moscow. The superpower strategies of deterrence are now essentially dependent on long-range missiles based in their homelands or at sea. A military presence or involvement outside their frontiers will evoke more and more political irritation, or even be a liability. They may also discover that the economic logic of arms control is undeniable. Stability in the regional subsystem may not jeopardize their interests or security. The real skill is to understand the role of nationalism in the region; the real challenge is economic: to be partners in the progress of a region involving one-fifth of the world's population. Similarly, if China envisages a revitalized role of leadership in the Third World, as is likely, it will prefer a parallel relationship with India and Pakistan which does not demand a partisan involvement on India-Pakistan issues. It might well be that this could initiate a process by which the Third World—the new world of the twentieth century—through its own variant of the Monroe Doctrine and the Canning Declaration could help rediscover the strength and so redress the balance and lost self-confidence of the affluent and powerful old world of Europe and America.

NOTES

1. See Sisir K. Gupta, *Kashmir: A Study in India-Pakistan Relations* (Bombay: Asia Publishing House, 1966).
2. John Kenneth Galbraith, *Ambassador's Journal* (New York: New American Library, 1970).

3. Jagat S. Mehta, "Afghanistan: A Neutral Solution," *Foreign Policy* (Summer 1982); "Solution in Afghanistan: From Swedenisation to Finlandisation," Kennan Institute for Advanced Russian Studies, Woodrow Wilson International Center for Scholars, Washington, D.C.
4. Ibid.
5. Editor's Note: Mr. Mehta has elaborated these views in his thematic essay, "Third World Militarization," in J. S. Mehta (ed.), *Third World Militarization: A Challenge to Third World Diplomacy* (Austin, Tex.: LBJ School of Public Affairs, 1985)

13

Prospects for Stability and Security in South Asia

K. Subrahmanyam

Image and Reality

There is a gap between image and reality with respect to the future security of South Asia. The image is one of a region engaged in an arms race. The reality happens to be somewhat different. With nearly 20 percent of the world's population, South Asia is responsible for about 1 percent of global military expenditure. Southwest and West Asia to its west, the Soviet Union and China to its north, and countries to its east and in Southeast Asia all spend much higher proportions of their GNPs and much higher amounts even in absolute terms on defense than the subcontinent does. In addition, there is a naval buildup in the Indian Ocean, and several hundred million dollars are being spent on bases at Diego Garcia, Masirah, and elsewhere.

The present period happens to be one of transition from an older generation of conventional weapons to a newer one. This is the third such cycle of weapon change after World War II. Because most of the developing countries derive their weapons from the developed world as it evolves from one generation of weapons to the next, the developing countries are compelled to follow suit. This is not a matter of choice, because it is not cost effective to maintain in operational condition obsolescent and obsolete weapons. If a country feels it needs an armed force, it makes sense to equip that force with the current generation of weapons. Therefore, there is today a compulsion imposed on South Asia to carry out a modernization program. Singapore, Thailand, Pakistan, the Gulf states, Saudi Arabia, and Egypt have all been cleared for receipt of one variant or another of the F-16. Consequently, India has to look at the MiG-29. At the same time it is worth noting that there is a certain stability in South Asian defense expenditures as percentages of gross national product over the last decade.

That part of Asia where India and Pakistan are situated has had its share of violent interstate and intrastate conflict. There are clashes on the Sino-Vietnamese and Thai-Kampuchean borders, insurgencies in Northern Burma and Afghanistan, a prolonged war between Iran and Iraq, occupation by Israel of parts of Lebanon and the West Bank, and civil war elsewhere in Lebanon. At the same time there are civil conflicts within India (Assam and Punjab), Sri Lanka, and Pakistan. Indeed, almost all states have violent conflicts of varying degrees of intensity owing to such factors as sectarianism within religions, differences between religions, multiple ethnicities and languages, and tribal groupings. This violence is often a result of rising political consciousness and is inevitable during the initial stages of nation-state formation. In the initial three centuries of nation-state evolution in the developed world, similar strife and violence took place in Europe and North America. The industrialized world has been at relative peace only after two terrible world wars; even today the IRA, Basque, and Croatian secessionist groups take their toll. These factors are mentioned not to justify violence in the developing world but to place it in an appropriate context. A realistic understanding of the situation in South Asia should eschew expectations of standards and norms of conduct for nations and societies that are unrealistic in the world as it is. South Asia cannot opt out of this world—particularly its developing portion—and therefore preachiness about rising defense expenditure in a world of grinding poverty and overpopulation is of little help. Whereas 20 percent of the global population in South Asia spends only around 1 percent of global military expenditure, the rest of the developing world (apart from China), with a similar percentage of the world's population, accounts for about 15 percent of global military expenditure. The same developed world that boasts of not having had a war since 1945 accounts for 80 percent of global military expenditure and is responsible for 97 percent of global military research and development and 97 percent of the world's arms trade.

Armaments by themselves do not produce insecurity (or for that matter, security). When Pakistan expanded its armed forces under Zulfiqar Ali Bhutto by about 70 percent and equipped them with $2 billion worth of equipment between 1972 and 1977, no one talked of an arms race in the subcontinent. Nor was there any such talk in 1978 when the government of India decided to make what was until then the largest single defense purchase for the country—the Jaguar deal—or when it initiated talks for an even larger arms deal with the Soviet Union in 1979. Those years are, for some inexplicable reason, often recalled nostalgically today in certain quarters. This is true not only of India and Pakistan. The period when the United States built the biggest arsenal ever conceived by man in history (in the sixties) and the Soviet Union followed that example (in the late sixties and early seventies) is now known as détente. It is evident that it is not so much the armaments but the politics underlying them that result in insecurity or tension. It is to these factors that one must pay attention in analyzing the prospects for stability and security in the subcontinent, or for that matter any other area of the world.

The equipment modernization programs of both India and Pakistan were initiated in the latter half of the seventies. Although the Reagan administration may have finalized the arms deal in June 1981, the Pakistani shopping list had been under discussion with the United States since the fall of Bhutto. It was discussed with the visiting U.S. Assistant Secretary of State Lucy Benson in late 1978. If the U.S. decision in April 1979 to invoke the Symington amendment in the wake of the assessment of Pakistan's nuclear efforts had not interrupted the process, the Carter administration might have entered into a similar arms deal even if the Soviets had not invaded Afghanistan.

Second, the relationship between India and Pakistan was on the mend during the Bhutto period. Diplomatic relations were restored, trade links were resumed, and large-scale travel between the two countries began. Trade declined from 1977 onward, and there are now ongoing discussions about a trade pact between the two countries. As already mentioned, both countries went in for major reequipment programs immediately after 1977. These facts have to be borne in mind for a realistic view of the developments that led to the present situation in the subcontinent and to see through certain synthetic myths.

Regional Security

The real problem in the subcontinent is the impact of the second Cold War (which began in 1978) on the political evolution of the area, exacerbating the tension and mutual suspicion among the constituent units. The perceptions of the nature of the relationship between the countries of the subcontinent and extra regional powers pursuing the Cold War create more of a sense of insecurity than the induction of military hardware on either side of the border. There are objectively valid reasons why this second Cold War creates such a sense of insecurity among the developing nations—especially the larger ones.

Although it is commonplace to refer to 140 instances of major interstate and intrastate violence in the developing world since 1945, it is not usually noted that in two-thirds of them there was direct or indirect intervention by the developed world with arms supplies to selected nations the preferred instrument of intervention. We are living in a world where the two superpowers have created for themselves exclusive instrumentalities which are proclaimed to give those nations a wide range of options between sending protest notes and landing the marines. When relations between the two superpowers worsen, Cold War considerations lead to intensified interventionism in the developing world. Because the industrialized world constitutes high stakes for the two superpowers and any war could escalate to the nuclear level, the two superpowers tend to maneuver for greater strategic advantage in the developing world, where their stakes are not high and where in a confrontation they can back down without much loss of face. The nonaligned nations pointed out as far back as the Algiers summit that limited deténte in Europe would not be viable and lasting.

During the first Cold War (from Churchill's 1946 Fulton, Missouri, speech to the 1973 Brezhnev declaration in Washington that the Cold War was over), the search was for military pacts to promote containment. After the failure of CENTO and SEATO and the erosion of the Rio Pact, during the second Cold War, the major effort appears to be to secure facilities for the use of military forces during various contingencies. In the developing world, very few of the nations have democratic governments with broad-based participation of elites in formulating foreign and security policies. It is feasible for a superpower to bring about a change in the external orientation of a nation by toppling its government in a military coup, by cajoling and buying off its leadership, by threat and coercion, or by supporting its parochial ambitions. This has happened in India's neighborhood in Bangladesh, Pakistan, Afghanistan, South Yemen, Somalia, and elsewhere. Security relationships of various kinds (involving the training of large numbers of senior military personnel and stationing large support teams in the recipient nations) become effective instrumentalities for intervention. The chain of events in Southwest Asia and the Horn of Africa from 1977 to 1980 illustrates how one intervention triggers a counter intervention. Afghanistan is the culminating point in one chain of such interventions. The establishment of the U.S. Central Command is an explicit expression of such a policy.

Concern for access to raw materials, especially oil, is very often advanced as the justification for such interventionism. Whatever the regimes, all developing countries are under compulsion to offer their products in the world market. Col. Qaddafi has never reneged on his contractual commitments. The Ayatollahs are pumping and selling as much oil as they can. The Marxist Angolan government uses Cuban troops to guard the U.S. oil company's installations. The Soviet Union sells titanium to Western Europe which goes into weapons targeted at the

Soviet Union. Most of these concerns are the result of security planning elites of various industrialized nations still being conditioned by outdated concepts and doctrines.

Such outdated concepts and doctrines are widely prevalent among the elites of industrialized nations, and a majority of the developing nations who borrow their threat perceptions from the former train their officers in the industrialized nations, thus generating various kinds of false ideas, fears, and complexes among the developing nations. Obviously, it is not possible for developing nations to fight prolonged wars without resupply support from industrialized nations, nor is it cost effective to keep under occupation large areas of foreign territory in an era when the political consciousness of the people has been aroused. If the war between Iran and Iraq has continued for four years, it is mostly because both sides continue to be resupplied on an intermittent basis. Without such external intervention and the interests of external powers in driving both sides to an exhausting stalemate, the war could not have continued for so long. When external powers do not get involved, wars in the developing world will come to an early end. Over a period of time, leaders in the developing nations will come to realize that in the present international milieu, war as an instrument of policy is not cost effective; this has been realized among the industrialized nations.

There is also too much loose talk and loose thinking on hegemonism. The two superpowers themselves find it very difficult to apply military power as an instrument of policy. The mighty United States had to withdraw from Beirut and is not able to have its way in Central America. The Soviets are not able to browbeat the Rumanians or easily counter the resistance in Afghanistan. The Chinese learned their lesson in Vietnam. In today's world the only possible hegemonism is technological hegemonism. Even economic hegemonism is becoming increasingly difficult and counterproductive. Unfortunately, far too many political-military establishments in the world have yet to realize the impact of these developments. Most of the security problems for the world as a whole and the developing world in particular result from this lag in understanding within the strategic establishments. The developing nations, even those who understand these factors clearly, are forced to arm themselves maximally in order to deter the intervention of the industrialized nations or the adventurism of neighboring developing nations whose leaders do not have a correct understanding of the current international strategic milieu.

Threats to Regional State Security

An often-repeated cliche is that the most difficult threat faced by the developing societies is poverty. As in all cliches, there is a large element of truth in this one. But removing poverty is a long-term endeavor. (Even in the affluent society of the United States, there are islands of malnutrition and poverty.) Therefore, talk of removing poverty as though it can be achieved overnight and attempts to sweep all other problems of nation building underneath the carpet of antipoverty verbiage contribute little to the actual removal of poverty. Unfortunately, this is what is happening in many parts of the developing world, especially in South Asia. Development and the removal of poverty require a sense of security. No government that is beset with problems of security will be able to attend to either need.

Today, the security of large developing nations like India and Pakistan is threatened by a multiplicity of factors. The process of decolonization was diverted into channels that threaten the newly emerged developing nations. At present there are thirty-two nation states with populations of less than two hundred thousand and another thirty nations with populations of less than one million. Another thirty-four nations have populations between one and five million. This global trend has spurred the ambitions of various small population groups to aspire to a sovereignty of their own. Whether it is the Nagas, Mizos, or Khalistanis in India, Tamils in Sri Lanka, or Baluch and Sindhis in Pakistan, they have all come under the spell of the disintegrated sovereignty phenomenon. Very often such secessionist tendencies based on such factors as religion (Pakistan itself, the Khalistanis, the Eelam Hindu Tamils), language, sectarianism, and tribalism become instruments of interventionism in the hands of industrialized nations. Developing nations too are not above taking advantage of such vulnerabilities. Thus, Nagas and Mizos have received arms and training from external sources. Although India has proclaimed officially that she considers it to be in her vital national interest to have a united, integrated, secure, and strong Pakistan, Sri Lanka, and other neighbors, such sentiments have not always been reciprocated.

Yet another vulnerability shared by many developing countries is fundamentalist religious revivalism. Today, most of the states of the developed world owe their stability to secularism. Nonetheless, where religion has become a factor in political life, as in Ireland, it has led to violent disruption. This is even more the case for developing states. Undue emphasis on religiosity in public affairs invariably leads to disintegrative sectarian divisions and violence. Iran's Shia Islam is considered to pose a threat to certain other states. In Pakistan there are demands for Shia representation in various public offices, institutions, and services, and for the enforcement of Fiqah Jafaria.[1] There are demands too for the distinction of the places of worship of the Qadiani sect, whose members number millions in Pakistan. Similarly, Buddhist fundamentalism has unleashed a sense of deprivation among Tamils in Sri Lanka. The Akali extremism unleashed other sectarian forces in certain parts of India in the wake of Mrs. Gandhi's assassination.

A nation, as John Stuart Mill concluded, consists of people who share the feeling of being a nation and a sense of common history. In this respect, in South Asia India has certain advantages. The idea of an India is many centuries old. Even when a trading company was registered in England at the beginning of the seventeenth century, it was called the East India Company, with factories in Surat and Bombay on the west coast, Madras on the southeast coast, and Calcutta in the east. At the beginning of the seventeenth century, when the nation state idea was new, India was recognized as an entity. If one starts questioning the unity of India, perhaps barring China and a few other very stable and established nation states, every other nation state's unity can be questioned. New nation states with no memory of a shared sense of history among its people can hardly indulge in the luxury of questioning Indian's integrity, since their own is more fragile and in greater peril under the assault of the widespread disintegrative tendencies referred to earlier. Sri Lankans would feel safer with a united India than with an independent Tamil Nadu. So should other neighbors. Hence former Foreign Minister P. V. Narasimha Rao declared in his address to the Kathmandu Council of World Affairs on November 29, 1981 that no neighbor of India is likely to benefit from the weakening of India. It is not certain that this has been clearly understood by all of India's neighbors.

Today, no nation state can be an island, totally isolated from developments in the neighboring states. The population explosion in Bangladesh and the steady infiltration of that population into Assam in the fifties and sixties has created a major problem of instability for India. The imposition of prohibition in 1976 in Pakistan has resulted in large-scale illicit distillation in Punjab and smuggling of several hundreds of crores worth of illicit liquor into Pakistan. In 1984, there were reports of narcotics from Afghanistan worth several hundred millions of dollars filtering from Pakistan into India to be exported to Europe and North America. Illicit traffic on this scale has inevitably led to illicit arms for protection, suborning of civil administration, the rise of organized crime, and its linkage to sectarian politics. The situation in the Indian Punjab is the result of the interaction of a number of such factors. Although I have no information on the state of affairs in Pakistan, Pakistanis also talk of the capture of illicit arms, large quantities of narcotics, and coup attempts. It should be recognized that those indulging in such activities have a vested interest in a turbulent state of affairs—the attention of the security forces is then diverted to the maintenance of law and order.

South Asia: Stability and Security

It is in light of such external and internal security problems in the subcontinent that issues of regional stability and security have to be analyzed. For the reasons already described concerning the second Cold War, which is a global phenomenon, it is difficult to separate and isolate South Asia's stability and security from major international security issues. For India, the security of its northern and eastern borders is tied up with Chinese policies toward South and Southeast Asia. Pakistan, on the other hand, claims to be part of Southwest Asia and the back door of the Persian Gulf. The very first issue in any discussion of the security concerns of India and Pakistan is defining the span of concerns of the two nations. Unfortunately, this issue has received inadequate attention, which complicates any useful dialogue because more than 40 percent of the Indian armed forces are meant for the security of the north and the east.

Second, this chapter has identified a number of external and internal threats that are commonly faced by all the nations of the subcontinent. A commonality of perception of and approach toward such threats is a prerequisite for regional stability and security. This, in turn, presupposes the evolution of a shared world view. The moment this factor is mentioned it is denounced as an attempt at Indian hegemonism.

Stability and security are value-loaded terms. In their imperial era the British used to boast of having ensured peace and stability in their Empire. To the anticolonialist freedom fighters, this was the peace and stability of the grave. It is not at all clear that all states in South Asia have shared interpretations of stability and security. The latter term presents greater complexity for definition. Security no doubt means the interests of the nation as defined by the ruling elite; however, in a democracy, there is broad-based participation by elites of different shades of opinion, which is not necessarily so in nondemocratic regimes, where such broad-based participation of elites in security policy is absent. This explains the continuity in policy between the Congress and Janata regimes in India or between the UNP and SLFP governments in Sri Lanka.

In making this point there is no intention of questioning the validity of the security interests pursued by the present administration in Pakistan. The difficulty arises because of an often-heard suggestion that there should be talks between Indian and Pakistani military commanders on force levels. Among knowledgeable people in India, this suggestion sounds somewhat strange. The mutual and balanced force reduction (MBFR) talks in Vienna are not conducted among military commanders but among teams of diplomats. Security perceptions and the steps necessary to counter them are part of the wider sphere of foreign policy and are not a matter for military commanders to settle. The MBFR talks are between two groups of nations who look upon each other as long-term potential adversaries with whom it is necessary to coexist peacefully because a nuclear war is unthinkable. Underlying the attempt at coexistence is the perception that systemic differences are irreconcilable and that therefore there must be an attempt to attenuate the risks of war. In India, no section of responsible public opinion wants Pakistan as a permanently hostile adversary with whom only peaceful coexistence (based on large military forces facing each other) is possible and with whom friendly relations are not. This is why it becomes necessary to consider how and by whom the security interests of Pakistan are determined. When we talk of stability and security in South Asia, are we talking about a framework of common security interests and shared perspectives of stability, or are we talking about the kind of permanent adversary context implied in the Vienna talks? Briefly, India offered Pakistan a friendship treaty because a no-war pact, like the MBFR, has the basic assumption of permanent irreconcilability and enduring hostility.

In fact, casual talk about discussions on force levels between military commanders (unthinkable at least in the Indian context, where civilian supremacy is an article of faith) that is targeted at uninformed visiting journalists, academicians, and political leaders evokes a comparison with the advertisements directed at ignorant Third World mothers by multinationals who manufacture baby food.[2]

Let us move from generalities to specifics. Between India and Pakistan there is only one contentious issue: Kashmir. Even concerning that issue, the Simla Pact has pledged both parties not to resort to force. There is a view in Pakistan that if Kashmiris have any grievances against India, it is for the Kashmiris to settle them. There is another view that the dispute on Kashmir could as well be left for future generations to resolve. There are other such issues elsewhere in the world which do not pose a threat to peace, and there is no reason why a Simla Pact that has preserved peace for twelve years should not continue to be effective indefinitely.

Pakistan does not appear to feel threatened by the Soviet presence in Afghanistan, although the refugees from across the border have imposed a very severe strain on Pakistan's economy and political and social fabric. Even though Soviet troops moved into Afghanistan in December 1979, there has been no meaningful attempt during the last six years to increase the number of Pakistani forces on the Afghan border. One may contrast this with the Indian action after the Chinese attack in 1962. A genuinely alarmed India raised nine divisions in two years and put them at high altitude, in snow, under canvas. Whatever may have been the original perception, an opinion is now gaining ground in Pakistan also that the Soviet move into Afghanistan falls somewhere between a defensive move and a costly mistaken attempt to maintain a particular type of regime in power.

Except for four divisions, the rest of the Pakistan army faces India. This may be because the chain of cantonments with living accommodations for the troops is along the Indian border and partly because the present internal situation in Pakistan under the martial law regime may have warranted the present pattern of troop deployment. In any case, as has been recently mentioned by General Zia ul-Haq, there are no accommodations for the troops on the western side. Thus, there is a certain permanency about the current pattern of troop deployment. Nor does one expect a reduction in armed forces at this stage, when the transfer of power to a civilian government has yet to take place. Sober recognition of these compulsions on the Pakistani administration creates problems of credibility with respect to glib references to troop reductions and redeployment. Such references, without any real underlying basis, reduce confidence instead of building it.

It is true that there is a great deal of distrust between the leaders of India and Pakistan. To some extent this is understandable because the wars of 1965 and 1971 occurred when the military was in power in Pakistan. Published Pakistani literature admits that both events occurred because of the Pakistani military leadership's inadequate appreciation of the realities of international politics. Although General Zia ul-Haq has displayed far greater sophistication and caution than his two military predecessors, there is in India a certain distrust of Pakistan's military leadership. Similarly, it is likely that the Pakistanis had a certain fear of Mrs. Gandhi in view of what happened in 1971. In India there is a genuine fear that the Pakistani leadership might miscalculate again, given the nature of its security relationship with the United States. These fears have been aggravated recently by the manner in which the Senate Foreign Relations Committee reversed its earlier conditionality on military aid to Pakistan. Pakistan is treated as a "front line" state although it has not shifted its troops to the Afghan border. Although the U.S. president cannot certify that Pakistan is not in the process of making nuclear weapons (as required by U.S. laws and against its own earlier commitments), the United States is to continue its arms aid. It is not my contention that Pakistan has no right to acquire nuclear weapons in a world where five nuclear weapon powers indulge in unlimited proliferation; nor is it my view that

United States has a right to intervene in Pakistani nuclear policy.[3] My point simply is that the United States is assigning greater priority to Pakistan as a "front line" state than to its loudly trumpeted stand on proliferation. Because President Reagan does not believe in free lunches, there are some very legitimate Indian suspicions about what the quid pro quo might be. In an Islamabad seminar, the American participants maintained that the present relationship is only a handshake and not the embrace of the fifties and sixties. But to India, U.S. actions do not look like a mere handshake.

India, being the bigger and more resourceful country, will attempt to keep an edge over Pakistan in military terms. India had been considerate in allowing Pakistan to reduce the gap in military disparity compared to that in 1965 and 1971. But it should be easily understandable that, given the ratio of size and resources between the two countries, India will maintain a certain superiority. That is a fact of life. However, that fact does not lead to the conclusion that India intends to threaten Pakistan or to exercise any hegemonism (whatever that term may mean).

One can understand Pakistan's sense of insecurity about intervention and threats to its unity and integrity because of the international factors enumerated earlier. If the Pakistanis would see it that way, then there is common ground between India and Pakistan on which to formulate policies that will ensure the stability and security of both, the strength of each augmenting the other. But that will essentially be a process of political interaction and harmonizing of the two world views. Hence, the Indian approach is political, and it took the shape of an offer of peace and friendship. The Pakistani approach so far has been a military and bureaucratic one—commanders' talks on force levels, mutual inspection, and a no-war pact. India fears that adoption of the military-bureaucratic approach may result in frozen hostility. Perhaps Pakistan will not be able to adopt a political approach until politics is restored to its proper place in that country. Since General Zia ul-Haq has assured us that this day is not far off, there is no harm in exercising some patience.

Looking to the Future

The South Asian nations are bound to be in a state of flux for many years to come. There are a large number of unresolved problems, mostly pertaining to the internal structure of each nation. A certain amount of internal violence is to be expected in some of these nations. If left to themselves, the constituent states will be able to handle domestic turbulence and will, one hopes, evolve toward modern statehood at a reasonable pace. But what is likely to destabilize the subcontinent in an aggravated manner and exacerbate tensions are interventions by external powers. For both superpowers, the subcontinent by itself is of lower priority than Southwest and Southeast Asia. This factor has attenuated interventionism, relatively speaking, but any attempt to involve a nation of the subcontinent in the tensions of Southwest Asia may trigger new interventions. Hence the Indians worry that parts of the subcontinent are included in the area of jurisdiction of the U.S. Central Command.

India is passing through a difficult phase, but India has enough strength and resilience to overcome its present difficulties. There have been some reports about external involvement in the troubles in Punjab. Part of this may be ascribed to the enormous illicit flow of narcotics into India and liquor into Pakistan and the accompanying organized violence and its linkage to sectarian politics. But any misjudgment or miscalculation (of the sort that occurred in 1965, when there were large scale anti-Hindi riots in Tamil Nadu, an acute food scarcity, and an inexperienced prime minister) regarding India's difficulties and any consequent attempt to take advantages of those difficulties will have grave consequences.

The coming years are crucial to both India and Pakistan. India has to find a solution to the Punjab issue. Pakistan has to prepare for the transfer of power to a civilian adminstration. It is difficult to foresee either stability in the region or freedom from a sense of insecurity among the nations of the area. That observation could as well apply to most of the developing world or, for that matter, to the whole world. But this does not necessarily imply interstate violence in the subcontinent.

The stability and security of India (which has within its borders one sixth of humanity) are vital to the stability and security of the entire region. In turn, the stability and security of the other constituent nations of the subcontinent are vital to India. Bangladesh and Pakistan are the eighth and ninth largest states in the world in terms of population. Nepal and Sri Lanka are medium sized states by international standards. Together, the area has nearly 20 percent of the world's population. These states have so many interacting linkages that the insecurity of any one cannot be without its impact on others.

There are two conflicting trends in the area. The first one seeks security by establishing linkages with extraregional powers. The Shah of Iran provides an example of this approach. Various parts of the world have drawn the lesson that such reliance on external sources for security is not viable in the long run. Sometimes undue reliance on external support complicates the solution of domestic security problems. A second trend is for the nations of South Asia, most of which are large and medium nations by international classification standards, to develop their own perceptions of security and to attempt to come to terms with local realities.

This is necessarily a slow and painful process, especially when one considers that politics—both internal and international—does not play its natural role in all South Asian countries. However, the realization is growing that external support cannot provide solutions to problems arising from internal factors; in that respect neighboring countries with whom one's own security has a symbiotic linkage may have a more constructive contribution to make. As the subcontinent completes the fourth decade of its political independence, myths of Indian dominance or hegemony are bound to lose most of their credibility. The South Asian Association for Regional Cooperation is a pointer in this direction. Just as security and stability cannot be assured for any part of the world, so they cannot be for South Asia. But in an insecure and unstable world, the chances of greater mutual understanding, greater economic and other interactions, and a more realistic assessment of national roles in the region and the world as a whole are steadily increasing among the states of South Asia.

NOTES

1. *Dawn,* April 15, 1984.
2. I owe this comparison to my colleague Col. R. G. Sawhney (Retd.).
3. Editor's note: Mr. Subrahmanyam's views on nuclear proliferation and Indo-Pakistani nuclear "options" are concisely presented in two *Times of India* articles, July 20, 1985 and July 30, 1985. For a longer statement, and other Indian views, see K. Subrahmanyam, ed., *Nuclear Proliferation and International Security* (New Delhi: Institute of Defence Studies and Analyses, 1985).

14

The Security of South Asia: Analysis and Speculation

Thomas Perry Thornton

Speculation about the future of South Asian security can be discouraging because the range of this future seems to lie between the undesirable and the unacceptable. There may be some bright spots though, and if we are to consider them in a realistic framework, we have to start out with some basics.

South Asia is a subsystem of the global or international system. I shall set forth some of its particular characteristics later in another context and only note here that despite its lack of formal institutions or even shared objectives, South Asia definitely constitutes a system. Nations are drawn into mutual relationships by geographic proximity, shared problems, and even mutual hostility, and South Asia has all of these in abundance. The South Asian subsystem is highly vulnerable to outside intrusion or intervention because of the splits within it; indeed, in some regards its internal situation is about as bad as it can be since the two major members are in especially dangerous imbalance. Pakistan is neither strong enough to assert itself effectively against India nor is it so weak that it can readily acquiesce in a subordinate position. The model is much more of France and Germany than the United States and Canada, or Malaysia and Indonesia. The imbalance is further aggravated because India is not as self-confident as the United States or even Indonesia; hence, it is loath to go the extra mile in its relations with Pakistan.

The result of this combination of regional tensions has been a remarkable demonstration of how the global (East-West) polarization can impose itself onto a regional polarization. The outcome has been the classic interaction between the two systems and has presented opportunities to the superpowers to intervene in their own interests. There have been ups and downs in this relationship that are familiar to all of us, but we must focus on the fact that (1) these vulnerabilities have led to very high levels of outside intervention in the past, and (2) the potential for renewed high levels of intervention persists. Finally, we should bear in mind that the intrusion of global issues upon the South Asian system and its individual members is not limited to the traditional menu of security and political tensions associated with the U.S.-Soviet rivalry, but also includes many of the "new" global issues such as nonproliferation, human rights, and ecology.[1]

Post-Afghanistan Possibilities

The dreary history of Indo-Pakistan relations can be largely skipped over. The early 1970s had provided some hope for a settlement of the regional problems that occurred after both the Simla Conference and the more realistic attitudes of both sides that had emerged around the middle of the decade, but this hopeful course of events fell prey to the general worsening of the international climate in the late 1970s. These changes affect heavily the entire southern rim of Asia; the Soviet invasion of Afghanistan, with its profound implications for South Asia, was a particular milestone in South Asian affairs. It was not necessarily a turning point since India and Pakistan might choose not to let it affect their postures vis-à-vis each other, but it was indisputably a milestone, for the invasion and the attendant shift in broader international relations contained the potential either for reversing and obliterating the progress that had been made earlier in the decade in Indo-Pakistani relations or for providing an impetus to higher levels of cooperation.

— A positive chain of events would build on the improved relations of the 1970s, react to the Afghan invasion by joining India and Pakistan in something resembling a joint security approach to the affairs of the subcontinent, and through that cooperation, give strength to the broader stirrings of regionalism that were manifested in the South Asian Regional Cooperation (SARC) meetings (more recently, South Asian Association for Regional Cooperation (SAARC)) themselves in part a reaction to the Afghan events.

— A negative chain of events would build upon a combination of the history of mistrust between India and Pakistan and the new assertion of global priorities symbolized by the Soviet invasion of Afghanistan and renewed American interest in the Persian Gulf region. The Soviet invasion would in this case trigger an extensive American involvement with Pakistan which would provide India with an excuse to step away from the reassessment of its ties to the Soviet Union that had begun in 1976.

The former chain of events would strengthen the autonomy of South Asia (i.e., its ability to settle its internal disputes without external involvement and to determine the terms on which the superpowers would relate to the region). The latter chain of events would reintroduce global polarization into the subcontinent in a virulent form and undermine the ability of the regional nations to deal with the outside world on their own terms. Neither of these tendencies has won out completely; there is no clear reading from the past or even from the present of how the future may look.

There are a number of realistic possibilities for the future of South Asia: either a regional security regime imposed from outside (and in South Asia that probably means imposed by the Soviet Union), or a repetition of the 1950s in which the regional polarity becomes subsumed in the global polarity, both of which would critically undermine the autonomy of South Asia and its constituent parts—not only India and Pakistan, but also the smaller nations that will be swept up in the tide. A third possibility, Indian regional hegemony, would probably enhance regional autonomy but at the cost of Pakistan and the other regional states. Finally, there could be regional cooperation structured around SAARC, the idea of joint defense or some other framework that would provide autonomy based on acceptance of a deftly exercised leading Indian role.

The Gloomy Probabilities

These are theoretical models of the future, however, and the safest predictions are almost always for projection of current trends—that is, "Things will be just like now only more so." There is much to be said for this kind of a prediction in South Asia. Consider, for instance, how little this system has changed since 1947 despite a series of wars, outside intrusions, and internal upsets. Pakistan is now split and recognizes the reality of Indian primacy, and Soviet domination of Afghanistan has moved from potential to real, but the system is fundamentally much the same as it was a generation ago. Alternate outcomes were possible, but the principal members of the system could not agree on anything that was less unacceptable to them than the status quo. The same situation persists now; even the nuclearization of both countries is more likely to reinforce the current trends than to alter them radically.

Afghanistan was a challenge to South Asian security that had the potential of reshaping the security management of the subcontinent and its relationship to the international system. Some striking change in the situation might still trigger such a basic reappraisal, such as a qualitative change in the level of Soviet threat to Pakistan, but the odds here, too, seem to be against any sharp changes. Although their tone became more menacing during 1984, the Soviets seem to have established a level of activity that meets their needs and does not exceed the bounds of others' tolerance. This is a situation that can and probably will persist for quite a long time. Should the Soviets succeed in the distant future in imposing their will in Afghanistan, significant problems of Pakistani security will arise, and these will have serious implications for India. Prospects for a just settlement of the Afghan situation are poor, mainly because Moscow cannot see any settlement that would give reasonable guarantees of protecting its interest; nor have the costs been high enough to induce Moscow to take some risks. Both sides of this equation are susceptible to change, but only with great difficulty, and the levers available are mostly either inside Afghanistan or at the global level. A united front of India and Pakistan could play an important role, but their present disarray makes it unlikely that they will do so.

The future of Indo-Pakistani relations, always a matter for conjecture, has been further beclouded by the changing political situations in the two countries. In India, the resounding mandate given to Rajiv Gandhi could provide the basis for statesmanlike moves toward reconciliation, but there is no guarantee that this will be Gandhi's near-term course. Pakistan is in a state of political transition that makes it a less-than-ideal negotiating partner for India, but it appears to have much to gain from a resolution of the two countries' differences. Separatist tendencies in both countries pose major problems; a major attempt by Sikhs to form an independent state in Punjab could bring disaster for all concerned. I do not, however, believe that the unity of either country is in jeopardy. War scares apparently have little to do with reality, and although there is always some danger that such forecasts will become self-fulfilling, neither India nor especially Pakistan would have anything to gain from a war. If that is the case, then, why should we worry much about the course of events in South Asia? This is, after all, a long-running saga with which we have all learned to live.

The answer to that question lies in the potential for markedly better and markedly worse outcomes for South Asia than muddling along. There is no a priori reason to assume that one or the other of the extreme outcomes is more likely, but certainly a good outcome is so much to be preferred to a bad one that it is worth devoting some effort to bringing it about. If the year or two around 1980 was a milestone—a window of opportunity perhaps—that opportunity is fast slipping away, because, as we noted earlier, the negative course of events may win out over the positive one; the momentum supplied by the Soviet invasion is dissipating. Although Pakistan has exerted itself to maintain its nonalignment and keep open its dialogue with India, it is tempted to revert to its practice of earlier years and seek outside patrons as a means of offsetting Indian strength. Since Pakistan cannot, however, opt out of South Asia, this is a course leading to regional disaster. Correspondingly, and in response,

India is tempted to draw ever closer to the Soviet Union as its external patron. The Indian act of taking Soviet support while giving little tangible in return is one of the more outstanding feats of the contemporary international scene; we cannot assume, however, that it can go on forever.

Islamabad and New Delhi have developed a dangerous new momentum in their arms-procurement policies. Pakistan has found a way to partial modernization of its forces, India is engaged on a procurement program well in excess of anything it needs to deal with Pakistan, and both sides are markedly upgrading the level of sophistication of their arsenals. Arms procurement does not necessarily cause war, but it increases the danger. Furthermore, neither nation needs nor should it afford this level of weaponry. Although cooperation in dealing with the nuclear issue could be a useful point of contact between India and Pakistan, it is not a sufficiently likely prospect to offset the negative effects and even dangers of competitive Indian and Pakistani nuclear weapons programs.

The psychological deterioration of the climate is also troublesome. The generational change that many had hoped would reduce bitterness between India and Pakistan may have had some positive effect, but it has had a number of drawbacks as well, and these have at least offset the benefits. Current news coverage and political posturing verges on the criminal as each country maligns the other.[2] In earlier years, perhaps, each side genuinely harbored the level of fear that it broadcasted. In the 1980s, exploitation of this kind of chauvinism can only be the result of extensive cynicism or of gross irrationality. Neither alternative is an encouraging prospect for peace in the mid to long range.

Possible Steps toward a Better Outcome

In seeking to reverse a trend that is sluggish at best and dangerous at worst, India and Pakistan have to address the dual problems of the internal weaknesses of their subsystem and its vulnerability to external exploitation. Although there are substantial problems involving Bangladesh, Sri Lanka, and Afghanistan, the key is for India and Pakistan to come to terms between themselves. The problem can be addressed conceptually in one of two ways: through focusing on small steps to build confidence (i.e., asking only the answerable questions at first), or through an attempt to grapple with the really tough issues in the hope of making a dramatic breakthrough that will sweep the lesser issues along in its wake. The problem is a common one, and we see it nowadays in such contentious relationships as those of India and China, China and the USSR, USSR and the United States, and the Arab nations and Israel. With the rarest of exceptions, history suggests that the best approach is one that avoids the most difficult questions at the beginning. It would probably be both foolhardy and naive to try now for a comprehensive Indo-Pakistani settlement that includes the Kashmir issue. On the other hand, history also suggests that unless a decision is made at the highest levels in both countries to press for broad improvement in relations, all of the progress made by the various subcommissions, committees, diplomats, and others working on Indo-Pakistani relations will be without a framework and will inevitably fail to bring about a genuine improvement in relations.

Since both India and Pakistan are associated with the small steps and dramatic breakthrough approaches, working in a middle ground which combines aspects of both approaches will also be useful as a demonstration of compromise between them. But the key is setting the priorities, enunciating them, and imposing them on government bureaucrats and spokesmen. For each side individually, the overriding requirement is difficult but essential: for Pakistan, that it learn to live within its geopolitical realities; for India, that it decide upon and pursue a responsible and generous role of leadership within South Asia, and that it make clear how it envisions this role. The gap between Indian regional realpolitik and the pseudo-Gandhian, nonaligned pieties that come from New Delhi is misleading and frustrating for those who in South Asia and elsewhere have to deal with India on these issues.

A menu of small steps can include a wide range of items, a number of which have been addressed already. Certainly improvements in trade, cultural sharing, motion picture exchange, study of joint economic ventures, and common economic development projects, can all do something to lower the level of mistrust and misunderstanding in Indo-Pakistani relations. As *The Statesman* has pointed out, however, these useful steps can be rendered futile if the overall tone of the relationship continues to be undermined by the unseemly complaints, accusations, and picking at old sores that emanate from semi-official and sometimes official organs of each country.[3] It is hard enough to make progress in the small steps without having them undermined by ill-advised rhetoric. Here, again, much depends on the willingness of the two governments to establish priorities and make them stick. It should go without saying that neither government should let their intelligence organizations play games with the other's domestic politics.

There are other steps that are not quite so small; namely, those relating to security matters, where sensitivities are particularly tender and understandably so, given the history of wars between the two countries. Obviously, much could be gained if the two were to consult with each other on their nuclear programs, thereby reducing mutual fears. (The results of such consultations might not be very pleasing to supporters of nonproliferation since both might agree that a small nuclear arsenal is a useful thing to have.) Quiet discussions about weapons procurement could not only reduce mistrust and tensions but might allow some savings in procurement budgets. Then there is the issue of confidence-building measures involving monitoring the other sides's troop movements and thinning out forces along border areas. Finally, defense ministries and the staffs of both countries' armed forces could profit from joint consultations on broader military topics—which, among other things, would permit some rethinking of the implications of the altered strategic situation that both face after the establishment of Soviet military power in Afghanistan.

Talks on military subjects are also no panacea, for military establishments at best reflect the fears and prejudices of their societies. (At worst, societies fan these fears and prejudices in order to enhance their own status, but that does not seem to be a major problem in either country.) Talks can, however, be useful if they focus on answerable questions and are directed toward finding agreement rather than posturing or providing a justification for the inability of political leaders to set priorities. Just what the most useful "answerable questions" might be is a matter to be decided by persons with a much fuller knowledge of military affairs than I possess. For what it is worth, I had occasion several years ago to put together a series of possible, answerable questions that might be addressed by India and Pakistan in preliminary security discussions.[4] It looked like this:

— To what extent and under what circumstances could India and Pakistan agree that outside involvement in the subcontinent is undesirable (rather than simply asking which superpower each side is seeking to exclude)?

— What, then, are the security requirements of the subcontinent as a whole (rather than the individual national requirements of Pakistan and India)?

— What are the strategic implications of the Soviet presence in Afghanistan for both India and Pakistan (rather than treating the matter as a purely Pakistani problem)?

—What is the *minimum* military force that each side needs on their shared border (rather than asking how much each needs in terms of the other's present deployments)?

— Working backward from that and adding the specific requirements for the Afghan and Chinese fronts, what are the total requirements of each side?

— How much procurement on each side represents bureaucratic considerations and a desire to have the most modern equipment for its own sake, rather than a response to requirements based on actual threat?

— Would calculations based on these questions represent a savings over present levels of equipment and expenditure? How much?

— What kinds and numbers of equipment does each side plan to procure in the short to mid term? What steps might each side take to reduce the perceived need for escalation in quality of equipment?

— Are there confidence-building measures that each side could offer and the other welcome, for example, notification and monitoring of major troop movements or changes in disposition of forces?

— What steps has each side *already* taken in the military and related political areas which merit the appreciation of the other sides (e.g., Indian restraint in exploiting the increased Soviet threat to Pakistan, and Pakistani determination to keep its external ties compatible with non-alignment)?

These questions indicate the other direction along which South Asia must make progress as they point to the wider transregional and global frameworks. For even if India and Pakistan do not have at each other in yet another bloody and senseless war, and even if they do succeed in getting their regional house in some semblance of order, there remains the equally important task of defining a more satisfactory relationship between the South Asian system and the global system. If India and Pakistan fail to do that, the negative scenario suggested earlier is likely to come into full control of the situation, and South Asia will remain a continuing problem on the international scene.

South Asia: Potential for Regional Autonomy

Among the various subsystems, South Asia is particularly well endowed with the qualities that protect autonomy from the intrusions of the global system, at least in political and strategic terms. The region contains vast human and material resources. Several regional countries possess impressive political skills and military establishments to back them up. The location of South Asia is favorable—it is well defined, defensible, and somewhat out of the line of fire of East-West hostilities. It also has, potentially at least, two of the most important structural elements stimulating autonomy—a significant but manageable external threat and a set of regional power dynamics that has been effectively clarified by the 1971 war (i.e., Pakistan can harbor no illusions of asserting regional primacy against India). Most important, perhaps, both India and Pakistan have developed considerable skill in dealing with the superpowers, and each has developed a healthy degree of skepticism about close relationships with a superpower patron.

While the United States and Soviet Union continue to produce genuine benefits for Pakistan and India, the costs of the relationships have become increasingly apparent. Pakistan has been very careful to avoid associating too closely with the United States; India continues to keep a substantial distance between itself and the Soviet Union. Where the subcontinental states have allowed themselves to be drawn closer to the superpower patron, the results have been cautionary (e.g., greater difficulty for Pakistan in dealing with India after the U.S. arms sales and the costs to India of recognition of the Heng Samrin regime). Despite the problems of the past five years, the overlay of East-West issues on the subcontinent is nowhere near as extensive as it was in the 1950s and 1960s; India has taken pains to maintain good economic and even political ties with the United States, and Pakistan has made clear its hopes for tolerable relations with the Soviet Union.

In an atmosphere of deteriorating (or at best, stagnant) relations between the two superpowers, a high degree of regional autonomy affords some degree of protection against being swept up into quarrels that have little relevance to the interests of the regional states. Both India and Pakistan are vital to the other's ability to play a larger international role and to each other's defense against threats and intrusions from abroad. They would be better positioned to deal with problems in the neighborhood of South Asia if they did so on a cooperative basis; the kind of Swedenization scenario that Jagat Mehta has suggested for the region as a means of resolving the Afghan problem is only possible through joint action; there may also be advantages to a joint approach in dealing with the oil-producing states of the Gulf region.[5] None of this, however, is possible if South Asia (and specifically India and Pakistan), remain at loggerheads and if they look to outside protectors to help them deal with their regional problems.

In developing regional autonomy, neither the system nor its individual members can expect much effective help from the superpowers themselves. Neither we nor the Soviets have much capability—and hardly more inclination—to isolate South Asia from broader international tensions. Short of truly extreme circumstances (perhaps imminent or actual nuclear war between India and Pakistan) we are not likely to work cooperatively in dealing with the region, and then it would hardly be on terms that would be welcome in Delhi or Islamabad. As a working hypothesis, most regional systems and their members should assume that the managers of the international system will be irresponsible in their dealings with regional powers and cannot be counted upon to take actions that will facilitate autonomy or even stability within the regional systems. Although as an American I believe that my country has generally acted responsibly, the effect of our interaction with the Soviet Union has more than cancelled out these positive measures; the problem lies in the working of the global system more than in its main actors.

I am equally unwilling however to subscribe to the idea that it is primarily the fault of the superpowers that the South Asian system is in such a poor state. That, in the sage words of Jagat Mehta, is "arrogance of conscience" (the belief that everything that goes wrong in the world is to be ascribed to the United States and the Soviet Union) and fails to come to terms with the fact that the problems of the regional systems are primarily internal.[6] Although our roles have not been all that creditable, neither we nor the Soviets should be used as scapegoats by regional leaders anxious to evade the responsibilities that are overwhelmingly theirs to bear.

As we have noted earlier, the ability of the South Asian system to assert autonomy is considerable, and the basis for an effective cooperative endeavor is present. Rather like the old Indian response to proposals for joint defense of the subcontinent, the question "against whom?" arises. The answer now is much easier—"against everybody." Given a choice among the United States, the Soviet Union, and China, few subcontinentals would have difficulty in finding somebody they want to keep out of their affairs. Should the countries of South Asia be able to get together and add up all of these outsiders rather than trying to play one off against another, they will have gone a long way toward assuming responsibility for their own fate rather than leaving it to those whose primary concerns lie elsewhere.

A regional subsystem can effectively assert its autonomy against the unwanted intrusions of the global system in two ways, most strikingly set forth in recent Southeast Asian discussions of the problem. The ASEAN countries see the alternatives as excluding the superpowers from the security management of their region through the establishment of a Zone of Peace, Freedom, and Neutrality (their objective in the hopeful 1970s) or else through a balancing of external involvement—the situation symbolized by American and Soviet military presence in Vietnam and the Philippines. (Neither of these options was of course available until the ASEAN states had found the means of dealing with their mutual disputes.)

For South Asia, the option of exclusion is a very difficult one. Moscow will continue to have vital interests in Afghanistan, and the United States will continue to assert its interests in the Persian Gulf and Indian Ocean almost irrespective of the wishes of India, Pakistan, and the other regional states. Unless India and Pakistan are able to guarantee (and to be credible, such a guarantee would have to be jointly given) that Afghanistan will be strictly neutral, that no outside power will come to dominate the Persian Gulf, and that the sea routes through the Indian Ocean will be protected, the superpowers will struggle against exclusion from the se-

curity management of the area around South Asia. Even under the best
of circumstances, it may be impossible for the Soviet Union to accept
such limitations on its access to South Asia. The USSR sees the region as
a natural sphere of influence and part of the containment ring around
China. The United States in contrast can be satisfied with an arrangement that guarantees equal denial of access to itself and the Soviet
Union; thus the struggle for autonomy in South Asia will have to deal
principally with Soviet intrusions and indeed it was the Soviet intrusion
into Afghanistan that triggered the recent wave of American activity. For
most of the 1970s we were happy enough with a situation of roughly
equal denial of security access.

For a variety of reasons, it does not seem likely that the South Asian
nations will be able to achieve sufficient unity of purpose in the foreseeable future, and superpower security involvement will remain a fact of
life. The issue then becomes one of balance. Historically, this balance
(such as it was) came about through alignment of superpowers with individual South Asian clients, at the cost of the latter becoming involved in
the former's causes. A more sensible kind of balance would be based upon a common assessment by the South Asian countries of the amount of
superpower involvement that they find useful and acceptable, and
sharing it about among themselves. Soviet port calls at Karachi and Indian purchases of American weaponry could be at least useful symbols of
such a situation; "genuine nonalignment" of both parties on international issues would be more substantial, as would a common position on
the Soviet role in Afghanistan and the American role in the Indian
Ocean. The level of superpower involvement would still be determined in
part by the amount of pressure that the superpowers were able to bring to
bear, but also by the desires of the regional states. In practice, this involvement should be high enough to provide reassurance to Pakistan but
not so great as to be incompatible with India's primary power role in
South Asia.

Even this relatively modest level of regional self-determination is well
beyond the reach of the South Asian states now. While they have been
able to moderate superpower involvement in quantitative terms, they
have not been able to take the qualitative step of regulating this involvement in terms of the interests of the system. From what we have seen earlier when considering the crucial variable of Indo-Pakistani relations, the
near-term prospects are bleak, and the extended forecast is hardly
brighter. Despite clear interests and strong capabilities, the security
future of South Asia may well be a projection of past and present
trends—fitful moves toward accommodation that never quite reach frui-
tion, bickering that leads to the edge of war and perhaps even into war,

and continuing openings for the superpowers to pursue their global interests at the cost of South Asian concerns. Indeed, on the latter point it is probable that the superpower role will become even more pervasive since it feeds upon the kind of chain reaction of fear and hostility that is growing between India and Pakistan. As an American, I am particularly saddened by the thought that the Soviet Union is much better positioned than America for such a contest in South Asia—perhaps to the point of uncontested regional supremacy, which would be a blow to Indian aspirations no less than Pakistan's.

Some Signs for Hope

I am loath to stop here, however, although both prudence and candor suggest that I do so. Perhaps I have paid my debt to candor thus far, and since prudence is not the sole guide in a speculative essay, I shall look for the promised bright spots. The situation between India and Pakistan may not be all that unpromising over time. On the Indian side, Mrs. Gandhi herself was part of the problem; Rajiv has hardly come to power with the image of being soft on Pakistan, but he and a new generation of leaders may review the costs and benefits of poor relations with Pakistan and conclude that the former have been outweighing the latter. Should the political process in Pakistan lead to greater democratization, prospects for dealing effectively with India could be enhanced. Even a military regime with a prospect of longevity could help by demonstrating to India that it has little to gain by waiting for change in Pakistan. The disappointing time in Indo-Pakistani relations that we saw during 1983 and 1984 could be only a trough from which the relationship could regain and exceed the modest high points of the early 1980s. Certainly the level of current institutional relationships provides a plateau for further progress that is much higher than in earlier years.

I am also encouraged by the implications of developments outside the region. First, individual nations and regions of the Third World are gaining considerably in military strength and capability, which results in an improvement of their position vis-à-vis the superpowers. Second, in a surprising number of parts of the Third World, regional groupings (with more or less formal organization) are coming into existence and realizing that they must take control of the fates of their own regions against intrusions from the superpowers or from strong regional neighbors such as Vietnam, Cuba, Israel, or South Africa. These are fragile trends but they are real and persistent. Do they apply to South Asia? Certainly the growth in relative power is striking in South Asia, the locus of one of the world's most impressive armaments races. Elements of regional consciousness and organization are also present. We have discussed some of these earlier, notably the tentative moves that both India and Pakistan have made toward cooperation. There has been much more exchange among the countries of South Asia in the past four years than at any time since partition, although the political will to capitalize on these beginnings is meager and the outlook is at best clouded. More striking is the emergence, out of SAARC, of the South Asian Association for Regional Cooperation which is struggling toward its chrysalis stage. SAARC does not stand alone in the world; its immediate neighbors are the Gulf Cooperation Council and the Association of Southeast Asian Nations, upon which it is modeled. Others, such as the Contadora Group, are further afield. At this early stage it would be foolish to expect much of SAARC, and in a large sense it does not make all that much difference what formal aspect the regional cooperation assumes. As an institution, SAARC may fade away as have many organizations in other regions, but it does offer an interesting model of how South Asian regional cooperation could develop.

At present, SAARC is not a security-oriented organization; that would put much too heavy a load upon the fledgling group, just as ASEAN long shied away from political and security matters. Further, SAARC is almost totally a hostage to the India-Pakistan relationship. If that collapses, SAARC will disappear overnight; India and Pakistan working cooperatively would either supersede SAARC or shape it to their desire. As long as the Indo-Pakistani relationship stays in the middle ground, SAARC can have a creative role. Its institutions can guarantee that communication between India and Pakistan will continue in almost all circumstances short of war, even if relations between the two deteriorate still further. SAARC can also provide a setting for each side to make concessions that it would be loath to make bilaterally, and it can soften the Indian insistence on bilateralism that so often sounds to neighbors like little more than a code word for hegemony. Conversely, it can provide India with a regional setting of some stability, out of which it can more effectively project its role on the larger stage. In a more highly developed form, SAARC could emulate ASEAN and act as a spokesman for the region in dealing with the outside world (e.g., the Gulf) on issues where individual members prefer to maintain some ambiguity.

This discussion has focused on India and Pakistan, but even though the other nations of South Asia are stars of a considerably lesser magnitude, they are not negligible quantities. They too are seeking a context within which to conduct their relations with India and project themselves internationally. Although New Delhi may prefer to deal with these other nations bilaterally, this is not a healthy situation, nor is it one that can be maintained indefinitely, especially with a nation as large as Bangladesh. Lacking a reasonable regional framework, Bangladesh and others will increasingly look to outside equalizers as Pakistan did in the 1950s. This is hardly in India's interest. The presence of these nations in the regional grouping can also serve to produce a more comfortable setting for the Indo-Pakistani relationship, helping to contain and shape it.

SAARC (or something like it) and the Indo-Pakistani relationship can thus be mutually supporting and beneficial to all of the regional states only if India and Pakistan want and are willing to work for it. It is not now clear that India and Pakistan are so disposed; the shock of the Soviet invasion of Afghanistan was apparently not enough to refocus their attention away from an agenda of disputes and fears that outsiders see as little more than a facade for indecisiveness and an excuse for pursuing quarrels that may have some domestic payoff. But things look different from the inside. The history of Indo-Pakistani conflict urges caution, and fears are understandably exaggerated when the stakes are high and are one's own. How many bilateral relationships in the world could not be characterized in the same way? But for India and Pakistan, these are excuses rather than justifications, as are the corresponding arguments for the United States and the Soviet Union.

Great effort and commitment is needed in both Islamabad and New Delhi. The challenge has been passed by before, and the costs have been high. This time, however, there is something new. India and Pakistan have it fully within their capability to shape the future of their part of the world. If they fail to do so, the blame rests squarely on them, regardless of how the superpowers behave, for the terms of superpower behavior in South Asia can now be determined by the South Asians working together; it is theirs to determine what the future will be.

The American Role

Obviously, this new situation does not absolve the superpowers of responsibilities in their behavior toward South Asia. In the last analysis, a global nuclear war would render vain just about anything India, Pakistan, and their neighbors had accomplished. It also is incumbent on the superpowers not to commit aggression against any or all of the South Asian states or to put irresistible political pressure on them. The injunction is most appropriately directed toward Moscow, based on past performance and future capability. But what should the United States be doing? Because this is not a subject of this conference but only a response to the proddings of my own conscience, I shall be exceedingly brief:

1. We need to better understand and respect the capabilities of the re-

gional states and their interest in autonomy. We are not dealing with client states nor "underdeveloped" countries.

2. Do no harm. There is not much we can do to encourage South Asian regional cooperation and conciliation, but our power to do damage is vast. We should not use it—least of all inadvertently as we have done at times in the past. We must, however, make it clear that we favor positive regional developments and do not desire a continued split between India and Pakistan. (This is not an idle admonition; it has been argued that continued Indo-Pakistani hostility is in our interest as a means of gaining extensive access to Pakistan in support of U.S. Persian Gulf interests.)

3. We must not overlay South Asia with the East-West confrontation or even give grounds for suspicion that we want to do so. That is not in our interest. Specifically, we should do whatever we can to minimize the East-West aspect of the Afghanistan issue (although our control over that is very small) and be seen to favor and actively support realistic moves toward a just settlement.

4. We will have to accept that Pakistan is first of all and ultimately tied into the South Asian subsystem. Pakistan has an important role to play further to the west, but attempts to treat it as somehow independent of its South Asian context are unrealistic.[7]

5. It behooves us to "deglobalize" the situation in South Asia insofar as it is possible, but still to maintain the kinds of global capabilities that make such a policy realistic. Specifically, this approach involves the maintenance of global economic and security structures within which regional capabilities can develop with some assurance. Neither nonalignment nor regional autonomy can flourish if the United States (or, if you will, the Soviet Union) relinquishes its superpower role. The global nuclear balance is the condition of all international relations at this stage of history. For the nations of the Third World, so is the maintenance of an American distant operations capability that at least matches the growing capabilities of the Soviet Union. Although this may be of less immediate importance in South Asia than elsewhere, it is not irrelevent, and in a changed security setting for the region, even the Indians might come to see Diego Garcia as a useful thing to have around—at comfortable distance.

NOTES

1.   See T. P. Thornton's "Between the Stools? U.S. Policy toward Pakistan during the Carter Administration," *Asian Survey,* 22, No. 10 (Oct. 1982), 959-77, for a discussion of the impact of the broad range of issues on U.S.-Pakistan relations.

2.   See for instance the array of articles on page 13 of the March 31, 1984, issue of *Statesman Weekly,* which carries a positive item on Indo-Pakistani relations but then submerges it in a welter of alarmist pieces, notably an inflammatory speech by former Indian defense minister R. Venkataraman. It would be only slightly harder to find corresponding examples in the Pakistani press.

3.   Editorial, January 28, 1984, commenting on the incongruity between sub-commission meetings designed to improve Indo-Pakistani relations and the simultaneous issuance of the sharply anti-Pakistani (or, at least, anti-Zia) brochure at a meeting of the All-India Congress Committee.

4.   In connection with a July 1981 meeting at the London International Institute for Strategic Studies. That meeting was the first step in the dialogue between Indian and Pakistani as well as third country strategic specialists, that was continued in the Urbana, Illinois, meeting of 1984.

5.   Jagat Mehta, "A Neutral Solution," in *Foreign Policy*, No. 47 (Summer 1982): 139-53.

6.   Jagat Mehta made this point in his presentation to the conference, "Third World Militarization: A Challenge to Third World Diplomacy," held at the LBJ School of Public Affairs, University of Texas, February 29-March 2, 1984.

7.   I have dealt with this problem in some detail in a paper prepared for the U.S.-Pakistan Bilateral Forum, held in December 1984 at the University of California, Berkeley. The proceedings of this conference are published in Leo E. Rose and Noor A. Husain, eds. *United States-Pakistan Relations* (Berkeley, Calif.: Institute of East Asian Studies, University of California 1985).

15

Conclusion

Stephen Philip Cohen

The prospects for South Asia are at once gloomy and hopeful—no simple statement can encompass the many factors that seem to push in one direction or pull to another. Further, there are new elements (such as nuclear proliferation) which will have complex and unpredictable consequences. The contradictions and disagreements among the authors of this book—as well as their points of agreement—fully illustrate the difficulty of the situation. It is both futile and inappropriate to sum up what others have written, but some significant themes do emerge which provide some indication of the prospects for stability and peace in South Asia. These can be themes grouped into five major categories: 1) the very different perceptions of Indians and Pakistanis about key issues; 2) the nature of the regional security structure that has evolved in South Asia; 3) the particular military balance between India and Pakistan; 4) their nuclear situation, and 5) the role the United States plays in the resolution of key regional disputes.

Perception and Image

One need not be a psychological reductionist to recognize that the images of each other held by Indians and Pakistanis contribute significantly to hostility between their states.[1] This hostility has two aspects: the conflicting identities of the two states and the problem of generational continuity. There are also important perceptual obstacles associated with America's involvement in South Asian affairs.

State Identity

The very identities of Pakistan (an avowedly Islamic state, the first such nation created in the modern world) and India (a predominantely Hindu but secular state with a large Muslim minority) stand as a challenge to each other. Pakistanis still find it hard to accept that millions of contented Muslims live reasonably Islamic lives in "Hindu" India, because much of the impetus for the creation of Pakistan was based upon the premise that South Asian Muslims—forever in a minority—could never achieve safety and freedom in a vast Hindu sea. Conversely, Indians find it difficult to accept that Pakistan is a functioning and reasonably successful state, and many Indians fear the attraction of Pakistan for "their" Muslims.[2]

Pakistan's Islamic orientation has also given rise to important strategic differences between the two states. Pakistanis tend to look to the Middle East and like to portray themselves as a Southwest Asian or even Middle Eastern power. Indians remain skeptical of this effort, even as they fear that it might succeed, and they prefer to emphasize Pakistan's subcontinental (and thus Hindu-influenced) roots. Thus, as K. Subrahmanyam and others have noted, even cultural artifacts such as films and cuisine are linked to the question of national identity.

Complicating matters, India and Pakistan have diverged signficantly from the British, parliamentary, democratic norm. Indians in particular are scornful of Pakistan's history of military rule, often using it as an excuse to avoid serious discussions with their Pakistani counterparts. Yet they have no such problem in dealing with totalitarian dictators and military rulers elsewhere in the world. Pakistanis, on the other hand, regard the Indians as having betrayed the assurances to minorities (such as Muslims) that the British provided; they see India as a thinly disguised Hindu state under continued Nehru family domination.

The Generational Dimension

Between partition and the mid-1950s a consensus developed in both India and Pakistan around the idea of hostility to the other. This situation has its parallels in the Arab-Israeli dispute, the dug-in fears of the U.S.-Soviet relationship, and, earlier, in Franco-German hostility. The "hostility consensus" is based upon real concerns and fears, but it also exists because some groups in each state find it useful to keep the threat of the other alive. Thus, Thomas Thornton argues in chapter 14 that among the new generation, Indians and Pakistanis are less able to get along with each other than their predecessors and that the regional psychological climate has deteriorated. This insight has not yet been tested by empirical study; indeed, there has been no serious cross-national research conducted among the nations of South Asia,[3] which suggests the need for a closer look at the problem.

I would argue that the process of generational change now underway is likely to have contradictory implications for the prospects of regional accord. It is true that the members of an older generation knew each other intimately; many grew up in what is now foreign territory and have powerful memories of life in pre-partition India. But these memories are mixed: some remember the horror of partition and its attendant communal riots, all can recall the everyday slights and insults that necessarily occur when two religious or ethnic groups find themselves in close proximity.

But members of the younger generation—those born after partition—will have their own advantages and disadvantages in coming to grips with the realities of regional politics. First, they naturally tend to question the dogmas and prejudices of their elders, and generational change will naturally lead to the diminution of some historic fears and stereotypes. But countering this change will be their own deformed understanding of "Pakistan" or "India." The results of an examination of the textbooks, novels, and scholarly studies written in each country about the other are not reassuring. Even more distressing are the systematic distortions taught in the universities and military academies of both states.

Without systematic research on the problem, it is difficult to predict whether the "new" generation of leaders coming to power in India and Pakistan will be better able to resolve their differences and dampen the corrosive effect of religious, racial, and regional stereotypes. (This would seem to be an ideal question for SAARC to examine.) What does seem likely is that such a reconciliation will have to take place under very different conditions from those that prevailed in 1947-49. Let us turn to some of these new circumstances, in particular the altered regional security structure and the greatly enhanced power at the command of leaders in both countries.

A Regional Security Structure: Dissensus

There is a critical difference between many Indians and Pakistanis about South Asia's "natural" or proper strategic structure. Indians like to believe that they inherited the strategic responsibilities once held by the British and that the defense of the subcontinent is indivisible. To most Indian strategists, Pakistan's effort to build a separate military machine not only threatens India but will be ineffective against a major external threat since Pakistan does not have the depth or the resources to stand alone.

Conversely, Pakistanis have tended to believe that the defense of the subcontinent is divisible and can be shared by India, with Pakistan holding responsibility for the Northwest and India for the Northeast.

All of this is purely theoretical since India and Pakistan remain each other's major threat. They have been unable to agree upon a structure in which the smaller South Asian states can coexist with a more powerful and developed India. Bangladesh, Nepal, and Sri Lanka have tried to accommodate Indian power in various ways, although they have each sought political protection via close relations with major outside powers and have been enthusiastic supporters of a regional association (SAARC) that might tame Indian power. Only Pakistan has tried to contain Indian power by seeking outside military ties.

The difference between Indian and Pakistani views on this critical question is exemplified in the language they use to describe India's regional position: Noor Husain and A. I. Akram of Pakistan call India's goal "hegemonist"—that is, India seeks to dominate completely its smaller neighbors and to turn Pakistan into a Bangladesh, rather than agree to a proper division of responsibility for subcontinental defense. That may be true of some Indians, but not of all of the contributors to this volume. Jagat Mehta and P. R. Chari (who uses the phrase "regional preponderance" to describe India's position) seem to be willing to accord Pakistan a regional role and adequate capacity for self-defense. Indeed, even K. Subrahmanyam has recently written of Pakistan's nuclear option, acknowledging that such an option is a legitimate objective for a state with an acute two-front security problem (a category that includes India).[4]

The first step in forging a regional security doctrine that can be accepted by all South Asian states (and ratified by major external powers) may be the abandonment—or rigorous clarification—of such vague and emotive terms as hegemony, dominance, preponderance, and superiority, all of which have been used to describe India's ambitions and position, and none of which actually correspond to a changing reality. Again, there has been little serious analysis of the minimum conditions under which the security of the smaller and weaker South Asian states can be assured, without heavy intervention and ties to major outside powers, that in turn threaten India's position. Indeed, can India come to tolerate the limited external connections by Pakistan or Sri Lanka or Nepal as the price for regional cooperation on other issues such as trade, regional defense, and sharing of water resources? Can the smaller states, especially Pakistan, resist the temptation to bring in such outside powers?

Since India accepts massive military assistance from outside states, it can hardly object in principle to such practices by Pakistan. What Pakistanis fear most is that Indian objections to American military sales are not based on principle, but on the desire to monopolize military power in the subcontinent. Although India can impose such a veto over Bangladesh, Nepal, or Sri Lanka, it will have a hard time doing so in the case of Pakistan.

While there is, as yet, no consensus on the regional strategic structure, there is room for cooperation on peripheral matters. All of the South Asian states belong to the nonaligned movement, and all have a shared view of the evils of colonialism, racism, and economic exploitation. They are all opposed to "foreign bases," and they all recognize (albeit not publicly) that the Soviet occupation of Afghanistan represents a real threat to regional integrity. They have all embraced the concept of a regional organization (SAARC), albeit with varying degrees of enthusiasm, and there remains the hope (expressed by some of the contributors to this volume) that SAARC will eventually serve as an instrument for the coordination of regional strategic policies.

In all of this commonality there is the making of a South Asian regional security doctrine. I have no doubt that this regionalism is an indirect response to the stark fact that the Soviet Union has occupied a major South Asian state since 1980. In these terms, regionalism is an inadequate response; SAARC will not be able to exert military or political pressure on the Soviets at this time. However, the process of regional consultation may make it easier for individual states (and especially India), both to pressure the Soviets and to provide tacit support for Pakistan's efforts to keep the Soviet Union from consolidating its power in Afghanistan. While Indian rhetoric has been unhelpful, there have been no known Indian actions that might indicate overt cooperation with the Soviet Union in squeezing Pakistan.

The Regional Military Balance: The Critical Unknown

There is no doubt that India has larger and more powerful military forces than Pakistan; it did achieve a major victory over Pakistan in 1971. Beyond that, there is uncertainty about 1) the degree of Indian superiority, 2) the trends in the military balance between the two states, and 3) the political implications of this balance. Appendix 1 presents some data on Indian and Pakistani air and naval ground forces and a discussion of some trends in the regional balance.[5] We shall consider the military balance as a factor in the overall regional strategic situation.

The chapters in this book demonstrate dissensus between and among leading Indian and Pakistani strategists on some fundamental military questions. K. Subrahmanyam and Jagat S. Mehta have quite different views about whether or not there is an arms race in South Asia and whether or not regional states are spending too much money on weapons; similarly, M. B. Naqvi differs sharply from the views of Noor Husain and A. I. Akram on the need for Pakistan to maintain a large military establishment to keep the Indians at bay; Naqvi proposes a strategy of unilateral disarmament. Actually, Subrahmanyam and Akram and Husain share a common perspective: that regional conflicts are not caused by the weapons per se, but by political tensions between India and Pakistan. (They differ, of course, about the origins of those tensions and the responsibility for perpetuating them.)

My view is that the weapons are important in their own right, in that both India and Pakistan are unusually vulnerable to threats from each other, and because both face a potential two-front war, neither can be sure that its present weapons inventory will be adequate to meet a worst-case situation.[6] The weapons themselves are not, of course, a cause of tension, but the inability of Indians and Pakistanis to talk about arms control, limitation, or restriction tends to give them a menacing symbolic quality out of proportion to their military importance.

A first step would be to confront the dual two-front problem. Can Indian defense needs be met by levels that do not allow India to overrun Pakistan? Will Indians tolerate a level of Pakistani armament that is adequate to insure that an Indian attack will not succeed, but that does not in itself threaten India? Realistically, it may be impossible for even unbiased military experts to work out a weapons mix that ensures the security of both states without threatening the other, although General Akram's suggestion that India could have forces 50 percent greater than Pakistan's is a starting point.

If there were to be discussions on overall levels of particular weapons types, they would have to account for qualitative differences among systems. This is not an insuperable problem, since India and Pakistan both lack the resources to equip their ground, air, and naval forces completely with the most modern weapon types. Finally, some systems might simply be banned or acquired in very small numbers. The interesting case under discussion is AWACS (Airborne Warning and Control Systems), which greatly enhance the effectiveness of interceptor and attack aircraft.

These are the areas where security and arms control concerns merge. Remarkably little thought has gone into this problem in South Asia because 1) it is difficult to apply the chief arms control criterion—stability—to a situation where both military powers have uncertain two-front security problems, and 2) India and Pakistan are psychologically predisposed to distrust each other. Nevertheless, there is a powerful strategic logic behind the argument that India and Pakistan might begin to cooperate with each other in certain arms limitation arrangements. Ultimately, they have a great deal to gain from such arrangements, and with adequate safeguards, would face little risk. History has shown that institutional and bureaucratic commitments to a worst-case threat analysis perpetuate some disputes long after the real threat has moderated or dissipated. But it also shows that change does occur—if slowly— as perceptions alter, as other and more real threats emerge, and as new concerns and interests replace old ones.

The Nuclear Factor

The most problematic regional military development is the slow crawl of both India and Pakistan toward a nuclear capability. Public evidence indicates that both states are within easy reach of a nuclear device. (India, of course, tested one in 1974.) Will they move to a new test, to the deployment? These are way stations along the nuclear road, although testing may, with some risk, be skipped. India and Pakistan could thus position themselves at the edge of weaponization without any public statement, test, or other indication of their plans. In this they would be following the Israeli example. They might even coordinate their nuclear cadence: both have an interest in keeping up with the other, but neither would find an outright nuclear arms race particularly useful.

Indeed, the present ambiguous situation seems to suit the interests and pocketbooks of both countries. A Pakistani bomb would mean the loss of American financial and military support and would be followed by a much larger Indian program. An Indian bomb might lead to greater prestige in the developing world, and even a Security Council seat, but it, too, would be followed by a Pakistani equalizer and might endanger India's access to Western high technology. Nuclear weapons are likely to remain attractive for both India and Pakistan for the foreseeable future, although not taking the final step has its attractions as well. Indeed, the present situation would seem to justify the position of Kenneth Waltz, Pierre Gallois, and, in India, K. Subrahmanyam, that proliferation can be stabilizing. There is already a de facto regional nuclear standoff, since both India and Pakistan have civilian nuclear facilities that are vulnerable to retaliatory attack by conventional forces. Nevertheless, maintaining the nuclear "option," let alone assembling, testing, or deploying nuclear weapons in South Asia, will create serious problems for regional states and others.[7]

First, there is little doubt that in the absence of agreement, regional nuclear proliferation would not decrease the need for conventional weapons and would be most likely to lead to a major overall increase in defense spending. Few South Asians are aware of it, but the ancillary costs of nuclear weapons—command and control systems, delivery systems, testing and development of new designs—far exceed the simple cost of fabricating fissile material into explosive devices. Of course, if agreement were possible on the limitation of conventional weapons, nuclear proliferation would be both less likely and less threatening.

Second, proliferation might not reduce the overall likelihood of war. It is argued by South Asian nuclear advocates that nuclear weapons will eliminate the possibility of conventional war between India and Pakistan as they have virtually eliminated the possibility of conventional war in Europe and elsewhere. However, the risk of nuclear war in South Asia might be judged somewhat higher. Not only are regional governments occasionally unstable, but they would be under great pressure to share nuclear technology with nearby states, and their systems would inevitably react with those of existing nuclear powers, especially the Soviet Union and the People's Republic of China.

Finally, regional proliferation will be regarded as a grave threat to the present nuclear regime. Even if it were to stabilize South Asia or bring advantage to India or Pakistan, proliferation would be regarded by the superpowers as a disastrous precedent for the Middle East, Latin America, and East Asia. It would certainly stimulate the development of SDI systems and might revive discussions of the preemption of fledgling offensive systems. It would be ironic if regional nuclear proliferation contributed to such responses, since nuclear advocates argue that it will tend to insulate South Asia from outside intervention.

To summarize, the nuclear dilemma is quite real. Going nuclear might immediately enhance the security of whichever state took the first step. Even if both India and Pakistan acquired military nuclear systems, it is possible to envision a stable, regional nuclear system. However, such a system could not be made leakproof and would be regarded as a threatening example by the present nuclear powers. They might respond with elaborate defensive technologies, but they are also likely to consider preemptive or counterforce strategies that would effectively cancel out whatever security gains were achieved by India or Pakistan. To my mind, the nuclear path is self-defeating, although one is compelled to acknowledge the hypocrisy of the major nuclear powers whose own arsenals are justly criticized by South Asians as wildly excessive. However, emulation of Western and Soviet error is not an effective strategy for correcting it.

The Role of Outsiders

One aspect of South Asia's regional security structure of interest to many contributors to this volume is the role that outsider powers might play in that structure. Noor Husain argues that China must be included in any regional agreements because it is a de facto regional power. A. I. Akram sees the Soviets and the Chinese as necessarily linked to

Pakistan and India, respectively, because of classical balance of power considerations. He does not count the United States as a major regional force. Jagat Mehta deplores the renewed extension of Cold War politics to South Asia after the Soviet invasion of Afghanistan, as does K. Subrahmanyam.

The American contributors also regard the external factor as important, but for different reasons. Selig Harrison suggests that the United States should have an expanded regional role, but one with a detached posture on the regional military rivalry, not one that tries to rectify artificially natural regional balances; William Barnds disagrees, citing the importance (and divergence) of American interests in Pakistan, and favors a balance between complex American regional interests and the level of American involvement. We could elaborate further, but there seems to be more disagreement among our contributors on this subject than on any other. I would not attempt to reconcile such divergent views, but we can offer some pertinent observations about the role of outsiders in South Asia.

First, no outside state has had a sustained regional involvement since 1947. American had no regional presence until the 1954 military alliance with Pakistan, and it then faded badly after the 1965 Indo-Pakistan war. The Soviets had a relationship with India from the early sixties, but this has been erratic and is now of real value only in its military dimension. What dominated both superpowers' policies was the perception that one (or more) South Asian states could be useful in countering another major power: the United States saw Pakistan and India in these terms vis-à-vis the USSR and China; and the Soviets view India in these terms, also vis-à-vis China. The Chinese also look at the region in terms of *realpolitik,* and find Pakistan a useful counter to both the Soviet Union and India (which they regarded as an American, and now a Soviet, tool). Thus, while ancillary motives are also involved (in the case of the United States, there are such issues as nonproliferation and human rights, whereas for the Soviets India has been useful as a window to the Third World—a role that is better played by more pliable states), these are not central to American, Chinese, and Soviet calculations. But South Asia's dilemma (and, ironically, hope) is that none of these external powers regards South Asia itself as central to the global strategic balance.

Second, with the exception of Pakistan's common border with Afghanistan and its proximity to the Gulf, South Asia does not contain strategic territory of any great value to outside powers. It does not contain vital mineral or other resources, nor is it a source of advanced technology. As Thomas Perry Thornton notes, this relatively out-of-the-way position can be regarded as a regional advantage, and the regional states themselves have the resources necessary to keep intruders away.

This position raises the question of policy guidance for those outside powers who, not having regional ambitions of their own, wish to ensure that the region remains free from domination by others. The policy imperative for such powers is that they must encourage discussions between India and Pakistan on critical security, military, and nuclear issues, bearing in mind their separate sensitivities. This, indeed, has been recent U.S. policy and shows signs of becoming Chinese policy.

The problems of such a policy (especially when conducted by the United States) are apparent, but are more of implementation than content. First, it raises Pakistani suspicions that the United States seeks a close relationship with India, abandoning Pakistan. This fear was one of the chief causes of the 1965 war. Conversely, Indians resent any American effort that appears to "equate" India and Pakistan. Any such policy must therefore provide special assurances to Pakistan that the U.S.-Pakistan partnership is valued, and to India, that its special status is acknowledged. As recent American administrations have discovered, this simple policy is difficult to implement, but all of the alternatives (siding completely with Pakistan, or with India, or withdrawing from the region entirely) suffer severe and obvious disadvantages.

Prospects

I envision four alternative security "futures" for South Asia. These are 1) the continuation of the status quo (that is, hostility between India and Pakistan just short of war, or perhaps leading to another inconclusive war); 2) Indian emergence as the regional dominant leader after the destruction of Pakistan's military capability; 3) increased Soviet influence to the point of managing the subcontinent; and 4) India acting as a regional leader in cooperation with Pakistan. The last alternative would involve real détente between India and Pakistan, the negotiation of a series of security and arms control agreements, and joint determination of relative force levels and disposition of major units in the context of an understanding that Pakistan could maintain a minimum deterrent.

The last future is not an impossible goal. The presence of the Russians in Afghanistan and the chaos in the Gulf may have encouraged regional states to move in this direction. What can be done to promote cooperation between these two states or at least to preserve their balanced imbalance?

First, it must be acknowledged that Pakistan's security will always rest upon India's restraint (or at least Indian calculations of gain and loss). Outside assistance to help Pakistan meet the threat from the Soviet Union has been necessary, but it will be futile without equally vigorous efforts to help Pakistan normalize its eastern border with India. President Zia (unlike most of his predecessors) recognizes the need for a political reconciliation with India rather than an effort to match Indian power militarily. Further, Indians are now coming to recognize that a weak Pakistan is no less a threat to them than an excessively strong one. There is an appropriate range of Pakistani military power above which Pakistan becomes a threat to India and below which it becomes a temptation. The determination of these levels is perhaps the most critical regional security issue, although it is difficult to deal with because both India and Pakistan have a legitimate two-front security problem.

Second, there still remains a great deal of uncertainty concerning regional nuclear proliferation. Does Pakistan intend to acquire a full-fledged nuclear system? Would even a lesser capability be tolerated by India, and if it were, would the United States be willing to continue a conventional military relationship with Pakistan? This seems to be the way in which the region is evolving, but there are enough uncertainties (including those surrounding India's own nuclear ambitions) to make the nuclear issue both urgent and critical for regional and nonregional states. Ideally, India and Pakistan can be encouraged to work out their own regional nuclear arrangement, which could be ratified by others, but this raises serious protests among Indians (who resent the equation with Pakistan) and among antinuclear advocates who would resist any agreement that did not meet Non-proliferation Treaty standards.

Third, there are areas where the major outside economic powers can make a useful contribution to regional stability by offering inducements to regional strategic cooperation. There are a number of joint river and water projects that could be pursued by India and one or more of its neighbors; there is a need for expanded regional, cultural, technical, and educational programs (which could be addressed through the SAARC forum) that would benefit from outside support.

There will some day also have to be movement on those territorial disputes that are also disputes over national identity and purpose. Kashmir is the most obvious problem, and its most recent manifestation— the struggle over the worthless and remote Siachin Glacier—is like a fight between two bald men over a comb. One hopes that India and Pakistan will address their differences across the negotiating table, where they can also seek out and pursue common interests, rather than have those differences assume the form of absurd military conflict.

I have never thought that the problems of South Asia were insuperable, nor that the role of outside powers, and especially that of the United States, is necessarily disruptive or divisive. Without accepting Indian claims to dominance (or a latter-day form of paramountcy) Indian ambitions could be accommodated in the framework of a regional system that both keeps the peace and allows a considerable degree of freedom for its smaller states—especially Pakistan—and that channels outsiders into useful regional roles.

Finally, although this may seem to contradict the entire thrust of this volume, the regional notion of "security" will have to be redefined and broadened. We must be willing to look beyond military calculations to address other dimensions of security. In the last analysis, security involves the preservation of deeply held, shared values; military power is merely a means to that end. India and Pakistan may have already compromised many such deeply held values (including some that they hold in common) by the very process of acquiring and deploying large armed forces to protect them. The United States, on the other hand, has so often pursued such a narrow definition of "security" when addressing the region—for all practical purposes, it has been one or another form of anti-communism—that it has neglected the threats to other important U.S. regional interests, especially the survival of democracy in large, pluralist, and relatively poor states.

The security problems that we have examined in this book—the India-Pakistan conflict, the Soviet presence in Afghanistan, and the logic of nuclear proliferation—deserve our full attention, but I believe that each, in its own way, is manageable. More important, compared with the common problems of poverty, injustice, and ignorance, these security problems assume less threatening proportions.

NOTES

1. For two statements of the problem of perception, see Robert Jervis, *Perception and Misperception in International Politics* (Princeton, N.J.: Princeton University Press, 1976), and Barry Buzan, *People, States and Fear: The National Security Problem in International Politics* (Chapel Hill: University of North Carolina Press, 1983); the latter book discusses the India-Pakistan relationship as a "security complex": a durable pattern of hostility and alignment.

2. The best systematic study of Indo-Pakistani conflict in the context of ethnic irridentist theory is in Sumit K. Ganguly, *The Origins of War in South Asia: Indo-Pakistani Conflicts since 1947* (Boulder, Colo.: Westview, 1986).

3. See Stephen Philip Cohen, "Image and Perception in India–Pakistan Relations," in Shivaji Ganguly and M. S. Rajan, eds., *Great Power Relations, World Order, and the Third World* (New Delhi: Vikas, 1981).

4. The contemporary discussion is reminiscent of those that raged around the British term, "paramountcy," that was used to describe the British claim to strategic dominance over, and the conduct of external relations of, the princely states not included in British India.

5. See Douglas C. Makeig, "The Simmering Subcontinent," *Journal of De-*

fense and Diplomacy, 3, No.7 (July 1985): 22-27, and Robert G. Wirsing, "The Arms Race in South Asia: Implications for the United States," *Asian Survey,* 25, No. 3 (March 1985): 265-91.

6.   Stephen Philip Cohen, *The Pakistan Army* (Los Angeles and Berkeley: University of California Press, 1984), pp. 14-29.

7.   I have examined the various policies that are included in the rubric of "nuclear option" in *Perception, Influence, and Weapons Proliferation in South Asia,* a report prepared from the Department of State, Bureau of Intelligence and Research, August 20, 1979, Contract #1722-920184, 58 pp. unclassified.

Appendix 1

The Regional Military Balance

Stephen Philip Cohen

Although South Asia is a distinct geomilitary entity, it is quite difficult to outline the contours of the regional military "balance" between India and Pakistan. Apart from the eternal problem of translating measurable military force into strategic and political influence (which is, after all, the purpose of such force), there are a number of region-specific complications:

—Both India and Pakistan have legitimate two-front security threats. A level of military power adequate to deal with one front may be totally inadequate to deal with threats coming from two directions. Consequently, there are important parallels between Indian and Pakistani strategic planning and that of several European powers during the heyday of the Eurocentric balance of power system.

—Virtually all of Pakistan's modern weapons and most of India's come from outside the region, which makes both states vulnerable to manipulation of spare parts, supplies, and replacements during a war that lasts more than a week or two.

—Outside powers also possess important intelligence and political resources which could significantly affect the conduct of a war, but neither India nor Pakistan can be assured that such assistance will be forthcoming in time of crisis.

—New military technologies, especially the advent of nuclear weapons, complicate the war plans of both states. The problem is just now being addressed by the armed forces of both countries, but they are unlikely to come up with better answers than Soviet, NATO, or Israeli strategists, who still grapple with the nuclear-vs.-conventional weapons issue.

—The regional military balance can be affected by unpredictable domestic political events. This was the case in Pakistan in 1971, when the army was bogged down in an unsuccessful attempt to quell an uprising in East Pakistan, and it may be the case in India in recent years because of the army's extensive involvement in "aid to the civil power" operations in the Punjab, Assam, and elsewhere.

—Finally, the reader is reminded that the performance of armed forces during wartime (or even during actions short of war) is wildly unpredictable, no matter what technical or numerical superiority exists. Preparation for war is a science; its conduct is an art. In relatively short wars (such as are likely to occur in South Asia) chance, and luck play a very great role—as do such intangibles as leadership and morale.

—The following table and figures are grouped by subject. Most data are drawn from the IISS Military Balance, a generally accurate source. Table 1 shows the current weapons inventories of India and Pakistan. Figures 1-4 trace the historic growth of air and armor systems in the region, manpower levels, and the ratio of major systems between India and Pakistan. Figures 5 and 6 trace the history of the total defense budgets of India and Pakistan and show the changes in defense expenditure as a percentage of government spending.

Table 1. Current Military Inventories: India and Pakistan

	India	Pakistan
Defense expenditure		
1984-84	$6.9 bn	$1.83 bn
Total armed forces	1,260,000	482,800
army	1,100,000	450,000
navy	47,000	15,200
air force	113,000	17,600
Paramilitary forces	260,000	164,000
Forces abroad	training units	30,000
Infantry div. equiv.	33	18
Armor div. equiv.	4	3
Mechanized divs.	1	—
Medium tanks (types)	700 Soviet T-54 and T-55 300 T-72 1,500 Indian Vijayanta	1,050 Chinese T-59, 405 U.S. M-47 and M-48 51 Soviet T-54 and T-55
TOTAL	2,500	1,506
AFV and APC	800	545
Modern combat aircraft (major types)	interceptors: 200 Sov. MiG-21 40 MiG 23MF 92 Indian Ajeet bombers 35 British Canberras 50 British Jaguars ground attack: 90 Soviet MiG-23Bn 40 Sukhoi 7-BM 50 Indian HF-24 7 French Mirage 2000	interceptors: 170 Chinese J-6 30 U.S. F-16 ground attack: 67 French Mirage—III/V, 41 Q-5 41 Q-5
TOTAL	846	375
Surface naval combatants (frigate & larger)	26	8
Carriers	1	—
Submarines	8	11 (incl. 5 midget)
Major orders	1,600 T-72 tanks 40 MiG-29 33 Mirage 2000 31 Jaguar, 165 MiG-27M; 6 submarines 1 carrier 2 destroyers 2 frigates	65 M-48 tanks; 10 F-16, 100 Q-5 aircraft; 3 frigates

Source: International Institute for Strategic Studies, *The Military Balance, 1985–86,* and various newspaper sources.

Figure 1. Aircraft Totals, India and Pakistan

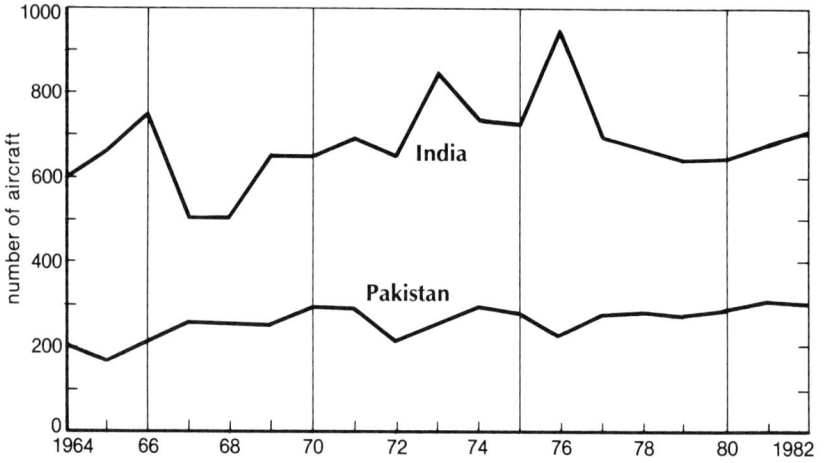

Source: International Institute for Strategic Studies, *The Military Balance*, various years.
Only combat aircraft are included.

Figure 2. Tank Totals, India and Pakistan

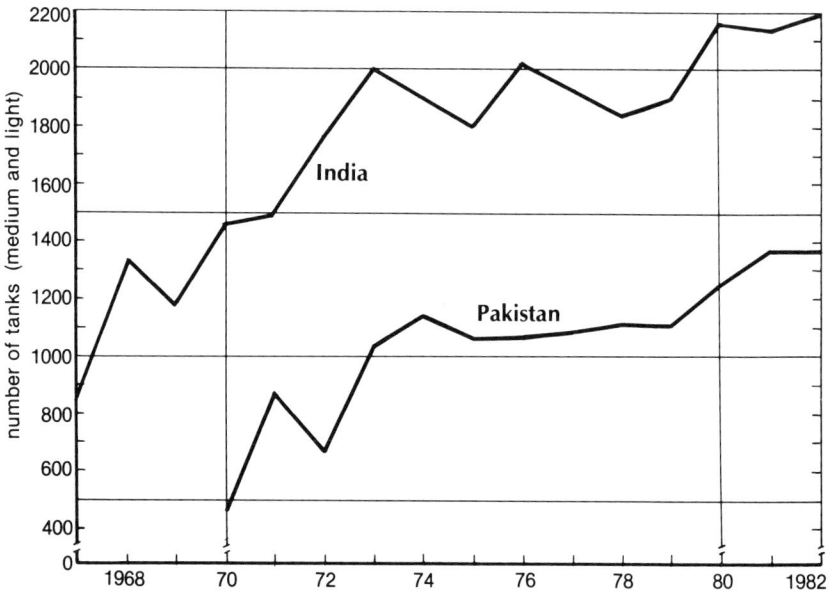

Source: International Institute for Strategic Studies, *The Military Balance*, various years.

Figure 3. Army Manpower

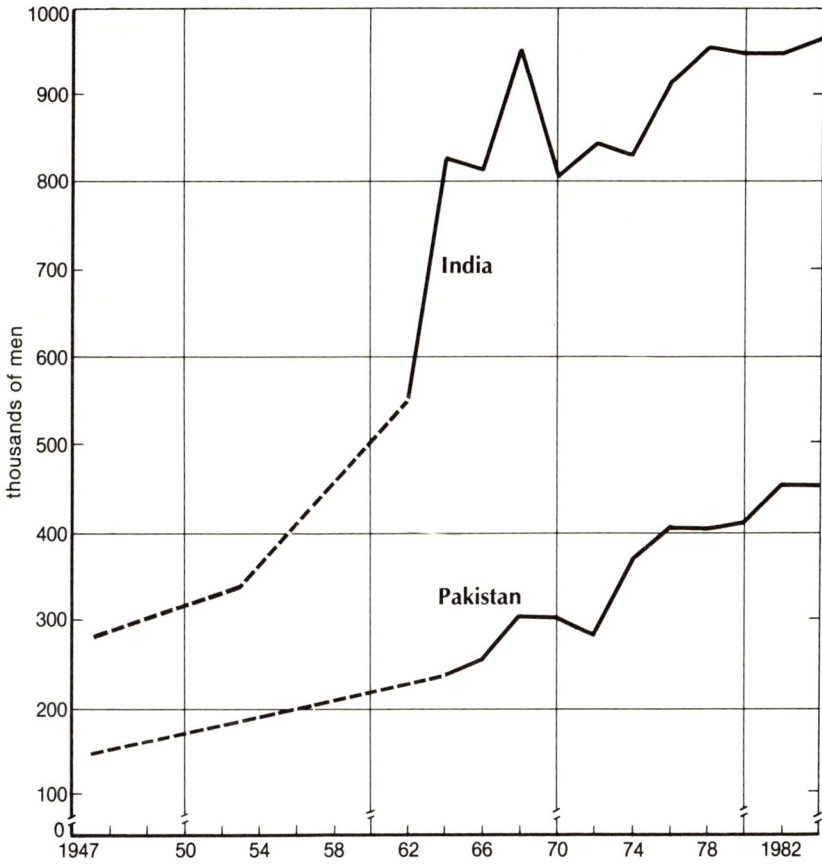

Sources for this chart include IISS *Military Balance*, and Lorne J. Kavic, *India's Quest for Security* (Berkeley and Los Angeles, Univ. of Cal. Press, 1967).

Note: Dotted lines represent estimations or approximations.

Figure 4. Ratio of Major Weapons Systems, India/Pakistan

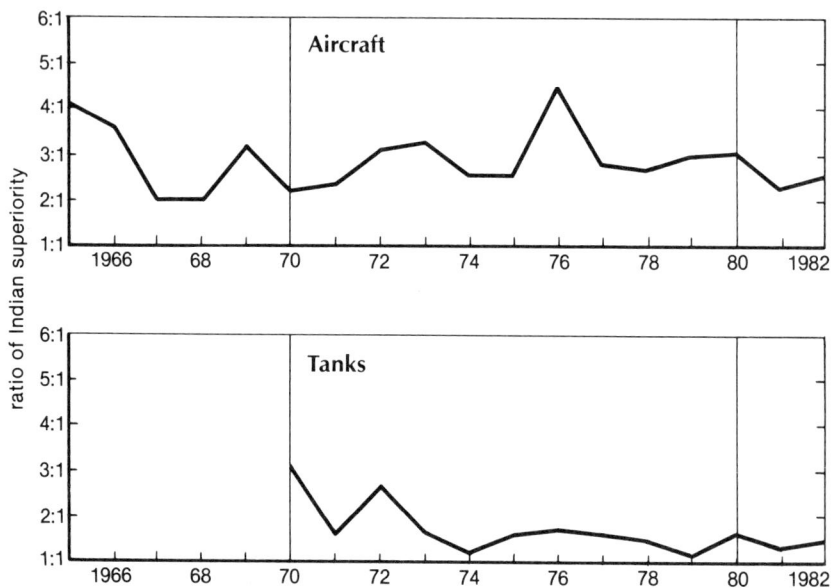

Source: International Institute for Strategic Studies, *The Military Balance*, various years.

Figure 5. Total Defense Budget

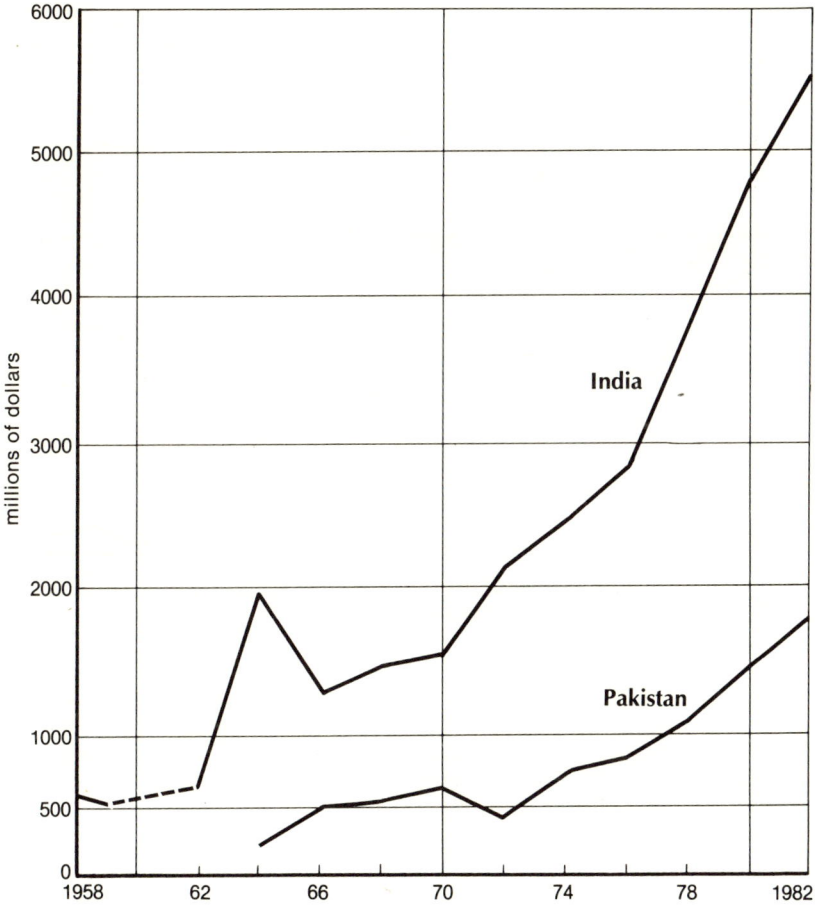

Note: Sources for this chart include IISS *Military Balance*, SIPRI publications, and various clippings. Dotted lines represent estimations or approximations. Due to shifting exchange rates, all the data in this chart is a rough approximation at best.

Figure 6. Defense Expenditure as a Percentage of Government
          Expenditure*

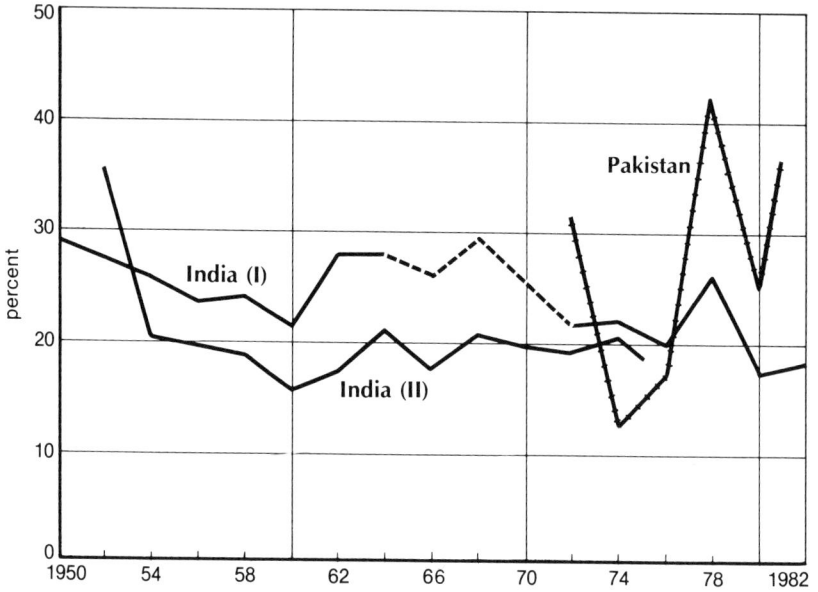

* India (I): Defense expenditure as a percentage of central government expenditure.

* India (II) and Pakistan: Defense expenditure as a percentage of government spending.

Note: The difference between India (I) and India (II) could be the scope of "government."
In addition, data for the India (II) graph were given such as "1952–53," and recorded in
the graph as "1952." Broken lines indicate estimations or approximations.

Sources for this chart include IISS *Military Balance*; Lorne J. Kavic, *India's Quest for Se-
curity* (Berkeley and Los Angeles, University of California Press, 1967); Raju G. C.
Thomas, *The Defence of India* (Delhi: Macmillan, 1978); D. D. Khanna (ed), *South-West
Asian Crisis* (Calcutta: Naya Prokash (dist.), 1981).

Appendix 2

Asia's Day After: Nuclear War Between India and Pakistan?

S. Rashid Naim

This study evaluates the likelihood of the use of nuclear weapons by India and Pakistan against each other, discusses the likely scenarios in such an exchange, and estimates the likely subsequent damage. It might seem a display of bloodthirstiness to examine such issues even before Pakistan has carried out a test explosion or before there is concrete evidence that India or Pakistan are actually building nuclear weapons. However, the fact remains that these developments could occur soon. In the absence of a study of the kind undertaken here no complete analysis of the consequences of regional nuclear proliferation can be made.

We do recognize that developing a workable bomb is not enough. Both countries, and especially Pakistan, have a long way to go toward developing effective delivery systems along with mechanisms to enable use and control of any weapons they develop. However, this study excludes discussion of such issues. We shall assume that both countries will succeed in either adapting the military hardware they possess for these purposes, or developing or acquiring the necessary delivery and C³I (command, control, communication, and intelligence) systems. The likelihood of a preemptive strike by India to prevent Pakistan from acquiring a nuclear weapon capability cannot be ruled out,[1] and again we will assume that this will not happen.

Since we are engaged in an exercise in scenario building, some general assumptions must be stated:

1. Pakistan carries out a successful nuclear test explosion.
2. Both India and Pakistan decide to manufacture nuclear weapons.
3. Both India and Pakistan succeed in acquiring or developing a bomb design.
4. Both India and Pakistan succeed in building a bomb.

5. Both India and Pakistan either adapt existing weapon systems or develop new ones capable of delivering nuclear warheads.

6. Both countries acquire or develop adequate C³I structures.

7. At any of the above stages India or Pakistan or both fail to launch a successful preemptive strike to prevent the other side from developing and building nuclear weapons.

All the above assumptions are likely to be met with reasonable certainty except 2 and 7, both of which essentially involve political decisions. These two assumptions are of course crucial, but in a worst-case scenario (from the point of view of the proliferation of nuclear weapons), both of these would be met.

The Effects of Nuclear Weapons

An atomic explosion releases energy in three forms: blast, nuclear radiation, and thermal radiation (heat). Blast is a high-powered "wind" that is forced away from the point of explosion and is caused by a sudden increase in pressure around the area of blast leading to overpressure. Although it lasts for only a short time after an explosion, overpressure is very destructive. Most of the material damage caused by a typical nuclear explosion on the surface, or at low or moderate altitudes in the air, is caused directly or indirectly by the shock (or blast) wave that accompanies the explosion. The magnitude of the blast effect depends on the yield of the weapon and the height of burst.

A second type of destructive energy released by a nuclear explosion is thermal radiation. Actually all the energy released by a nuclear explosion, including residual radiation from weapon debris, is thermal energy (heat), but what we define as thermal radiation is the part that can cause fire damage and personal injury.[2] Approximately 35 percent of the energy of a typical nuclear explosion at up to a height of 100,000 feet is in the form of thermal energy of this kind.[3]

Thermal radiation causes damage in two ways. First, it causes dangerous burns on human flesh. Second, depending upon the amount of combustible material in the area of the explosion, it can cause massive fires. A single megaton weapon can cause third degree burns up to five miles away, second degree burns up to distances of six miles, first degree burns similar to sunburn up to seven miles away.[4] The distances up to which burns are caused depend upon weather conditions; the behavior pattern of thermal energy is similar to that of sunlight. Thermal radiation also results in massive fires. According to some estimates, up to 10 percent of the buildings within the 5 psi ring may catch fire, whereas within the 2 psi ring, about 2 percent of the buildings may sustain fire damage.[5] The vertical updraft of heated air may cause a firestorm which can be made worse by existing winds.[6] Temperatures can exceed 1,000°C.

A nuclear explosion also releases radiation. Nuclear radiation is released in two forms: direct nuclear radiation and fallout. Direct nuclear radiation is a stream of atomic particles which may be injurious or fatal to a human being, depending upon the extent of exposure. Fallout is nuclear radiation caused by contaminated debris lifted by the explosion and carried by the wind to other areas. A dose of 600 rem within a short period of time (six to seven days) could result in fatal illness among 90 percent of the population exposed.[7] A dose of 450 rem within a short period of time could cause up to 50 percent fatalities. A dose of 300 rem would kill about 10 percent of those exposed.[8]

Prediction of Effects

This study will include two sizes of weapons: 20 kilotons and 1 megaton. These sizes have been chosen for several reasons. First, a 15 to 20 kiloton bomb is definitely within India's manufacturing capability. Second, if a fission-fusion-fission device (hydrogen bomb) is developed by either or both countries, the likely size will be 1 megaton, because weapons with larger yields would not be very useful. Large nuclear weapons are likely to be used against civilian targets as part of a countervalue strategy, and given the size of most urban centers in South Asia, a one megaton weapon would be of sufficient strength.

Because we only discuss the use of 15 to 20 KT or 1 MT weapons (and because some of the data on effects are available only for one of these sizes or for a different size altogether), a scaling formula is used to convert the area of a psi ring from an explosion of one size to the area of a psi ring of the same strength from an explosion of another size. This formula is:

$$\frac{D}{D'} = \frac{W^{(1/3)}}{W'}$$

Where W' is the KT yield from an explosion of known size, D' is the distance from the point of explosion of W' yield where a given overpressure occurs, W is the KT yield from another explosion, and D is the distance from the point of explosion of W yield where the same level of overpressure as in a W' yield explosion will occur.[9]

The psi ring is useful because some investigators calculate death and injuries by assuming that all people inside the 5 psi ring will die, and nobody outside it will die.[10] This same method is used in this study to predict deaths and injuries. The area (square miles) within the 5 psi ring is designated the lethal area, that is, the area within which all persons are killed. The lethal area is computed by means of the following formula: $A = \pi r^2$ where A is the area within the 5 psi ring, r is the radius of the 5 psi ring, and pi is 3.1416. The number of deaths caused by a weapon Td is determined by multiplying the given population density Pd by the lethal area A (Td = Pd x A).

A study of projected casualty tables in such works as *The Effects of Nuclear War*[11] and actual casualty figures in Japan given in *International Arms Control*[12] and *Effects of Nuclear Weapons*[13] shows that in nuclear explosions injuries generally do not exceed deaths, and when they do so it is only by a small fraction. In this study, just as we have used the 5 psi ring as the limit of the lethal area, we have also used the 2.2 psi ring as the outer limit of the injury zone; all persons outside the 5 psi ring but within the 2.2 psi ring are injured, and none outside the area of the 2.2 psi ring are injured. This formulation is based on the following reasoning: a study of the casualty figures, real and projected, in the above-named sources shows that the number of deaths declines sharply beyond the 3.25 psi ring and becomes relatively negligible beyond the 1.2 psi ring, whereas the number of injured survivors is the highest within the area between these two rings. Taking the median point between the 3.25 and 1.2 psi rings, we have therefore estimated that everyone between the 5 psi ring and the 2.2 psi ring will be injured, and no one beyond the 2.2 psi ring will suffer injuries. Like the use of the 5 psi ring to determine the lethal area, the use of the 2.2 psi ring to determine the zone of injury will make the task of calculating casualties easier without making too great a sacrifice in accuracy.

Property damage is defined in terms of square miles of built-up area destroyed. The 2 psi ring is used to determine property damage.[14] Using the calculation system in Glasstone and Dolan,[15] the area likely to be destroyed is shown in Table 1.

Variations in terrain and the possibility of a firestorm could affect

Table 1. Property Damage

Weapon Yield	Type of Burst	Radius of 2 psi Ring (miles)	Area Destroyed (sq mi.)*
15 KT	Air	2	12.5
15 KT	Surface	1.25	4.9
1 MT	Air	8	200.9
1 MT	Surface	5	78.5

*$A = \pi r^2$; r = col. 3.

these property damage figures by a factor of up to five.[16] As we shall see, certain features peculiar to South Asia would sharply increase the number of fatalities and injuries and amount of property damage implied by the method of calculation used in Table 1. I believe that casualty and damage figures projected by the above means are somewhat optimistic; actual figures are likely to be higher. Finally, it should be remembered that the figures generated by the above method are only approximations.

Factors Peculiar to South Asia

There are some additional factors that are likely to affect the extent of damage and casualties in South Asia in case of a nuclear war. First, the high population density would force casualty figures to levels much higher than those likely to be experienced in Europe, North America, or the USSR. However, these casualty figures will represent a smaller percent of the population of South Asia than the percentage of the population likely to be destroyed in Europe, North America, or the USSR because of the higher level of urbanization in the latter regions.

Second, the damage caused by thermal effects of nuclear explosions is likely to be more severe than in Europe, North America, or the USSR because of the very limited firefighting capabilities in the two South Asian countries.

Third, burn injuries would be a severe medical problem. The high probability that burn victims die if not promptly treated and the relatively sparse medical resources available could lead to very high mortality rates among the initial survivors of the attack. There are only 26 physicians and 75 hospital beds per 100,000 persons available in India and only 25 physicians and 50 hospital beds per 100,000 persons available in Pakistan.[17]

Fourth, although in more economically developed countries post-attack casualties could be limited by relying on the medical, shelter, and economic resources of the small- and medium-sized cities, this may not be true for nations that are less economically advanced. Except for a few large cities, neither India nor Pakistan (and especially the latter) has the necessary resources. In fact, it is very doubtful that post-attack recovery is possible for either country without massive outside assistance. Consequently one more point should be borne in mind: It is misleading to compare nuclear wars involving countervalue attacks (strikes against cities) with natural disasters. Nuclear attacks focus on the destruction of industrial, technological and administrative structures; those very institutions and assets that allow recovery from the effects of a disaster would themselves be totally destroyed.

Fifth, in economically less-developed countries a very high percentage of national value (administrative, technical, and industrial infrastructures) can be destroyed with relatively few warheads, since these are concentrated in small areas. Further destruction would require a large number of warheads. Figure 1 illustrates the point that only a few populated centers have to be hit to destroy what a nation values. The positive aspect, if there is any, is that this knowledge will keep civilian casualties confined to a few areas. This point should be kept in mind when discussing effects of a nuclear exchange between India and Pakistan and is especially applicable to the latter.

Weapon Systems and Their Impact on Strategy

Certain basic characteristics of any future Indo-Pakistani nuclear balance should be noted before we begin to create a scenario. India's greater resources and higher level of technological development would probably result in its having more nuclear weapons than Pakistan if the region were to be nuclearized. In the absence of a weapons manufacturing program in either country, it is not possible to project accurate figures about the number of warheads likely to be in the possession of the two countries by the 1990s; however, some rough estimates have been made. Richard Betts of the Brookings Institution has estimated that Pakistan could build up a modest nuclear force of between fifty and one hundred 50-KT weapons.[18] It is estimated that India is likely to be able to

Figure 1: Concave Vulnerability Function in Economically
            Less-Developed Countries

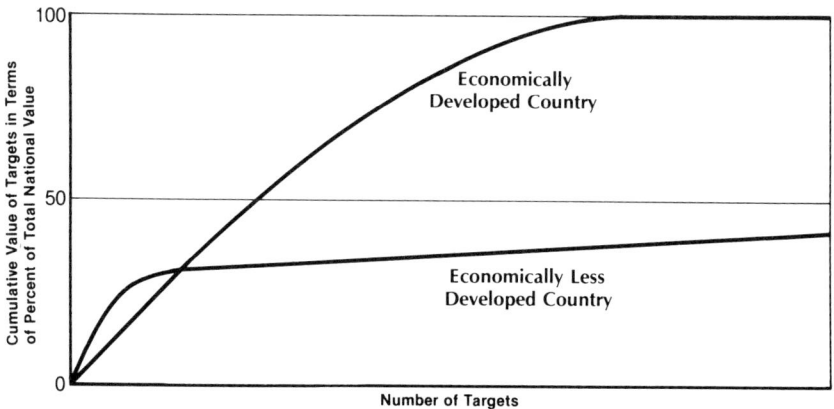

Source. P. Barker, "The Vulnerability of Pakistan to Nuclear Attack." Discussion paper. Hudson Institute. August 6, 1976.

build up and maintain a substantial lead in the number of warheads that each country possesses. A recent study of small nuclear forces estimates that in 1982, India had the potential to produce enough fissile material for a maximum of 53 warheads per year. This capacity would increase to 119 warheads a year by 1990 and 177 warheads a year by 2000. A maximum of 995 warheads may be accumulated by 1990 and 2,732 warheads by 2000. Similarly Pakistan's potential production capacity would be 21 warheads per year in 1990, increasing to 77 warheads per year by 2000. The accumulated total could stand at 300 warheads by 1990 and 1,070 warheads by 2000.[19] It must be noted that these figures are upper boundary estimates that assume efficient production and use of fissile material. The yield of these warheads would be the smallest possible needed to achieve an explosive chain reaction. Therefore these figures should be considered a loose general estimate rather than a precise measure of the equivalent megatonnage (EMT) or throw-weight capacity that the two nations are capable of producing.

The second chief feature of an Indo-Pakistani nuclear balance would be the relative vulnerability of the two countries. Pakistan's smaller size and greater accessibility to Indian attack aircraft make it more vulnerable than India in case of a nuclear exchange, since all of India is not within the range of Pakistani aircraft. Unless Pakistan acquires other delivery systems, it will not have the capability to threaten all of India in the near future.

This brings us to the question of delivery systems that the two countries have now or are likely to acquire in the near future. At this time both countries have modern aircraft capable of delivering nuclear weapons. India has the MiG-23, Jaguar, and the Mirage 2000, while Pakistan has the Mirage III and V and the F-16. Figures 2 and 3 show the areas in the two countries that are within range of these aircraft. As these two figures show, whereas all of Pakistan is within range of Indian aircraft, only the northwestern and western regions of India are within range of Pakistani aircraft. However, other delivery systems can also be utilized. According to one study, it is well within India's capability to develop IRBMs by the end of this decade. This study, based on India's recent advances in the area of space technology, states that India has developed the capability to put reconnaissance satellites into orbit, and the INSAT satellites, now being put into orbit, will substantially upgrade India's command and control capabilities. The study also points out that the SLV-3 boosters used by India to launch satellites can be converted into IRBM's with a range of about 930 miles (1,500 km). India is currently designing a powerful liquid-fuel rocket which could also serve as a delivery vehicle for nuclear warheads.[20] S. K. Ghosh, a senior official with the Indian Space Research Organization (ISRO) has observed that India

Figure 2. Range of Indian Delivery Systems

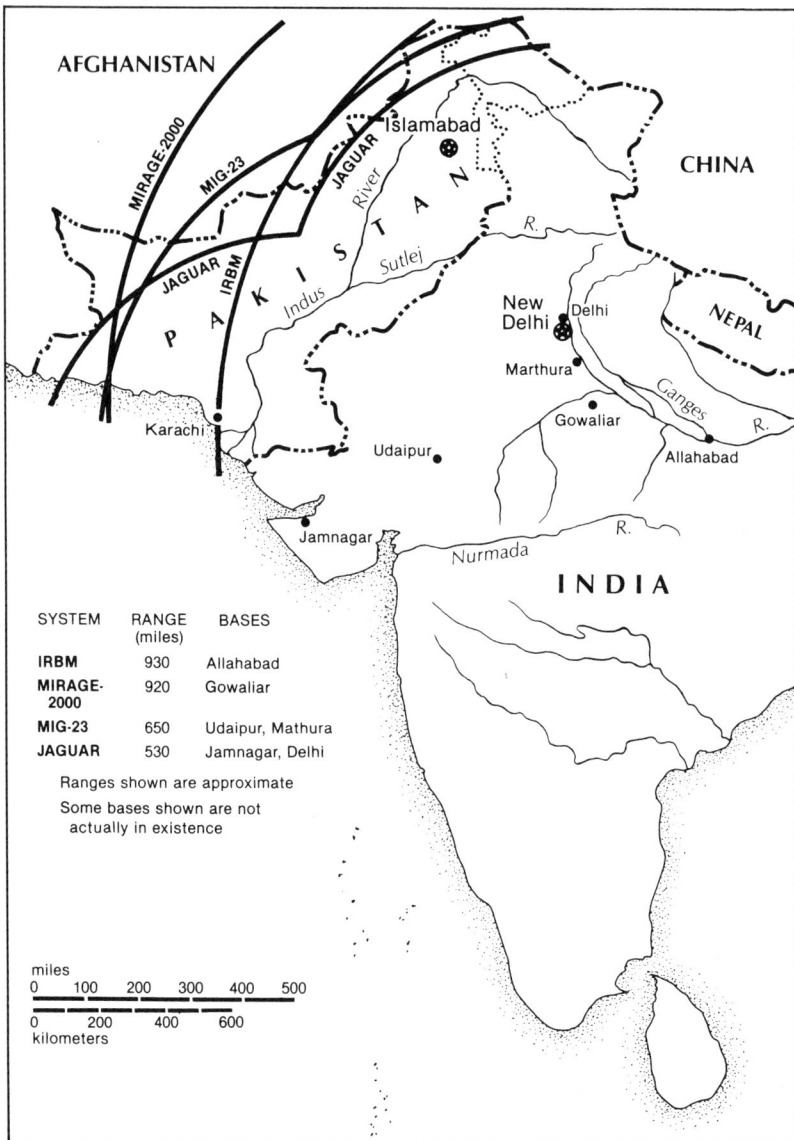

SYSTEM	RANGE (miles)	BASES
IRBM	930	Allahabad
MIRAGE-2000	920	Gowaliar
MIG-23	650	Udaipur, Mathura
JAGUAR	530	Jamnagar, Delhi

Ranges shown are approximate

Some bases shown are not actually in existence

miles
0   100   200   300   400   500

0   200   400   600
kilometers

Figure 3. Range of Pakastani Delivery Systems

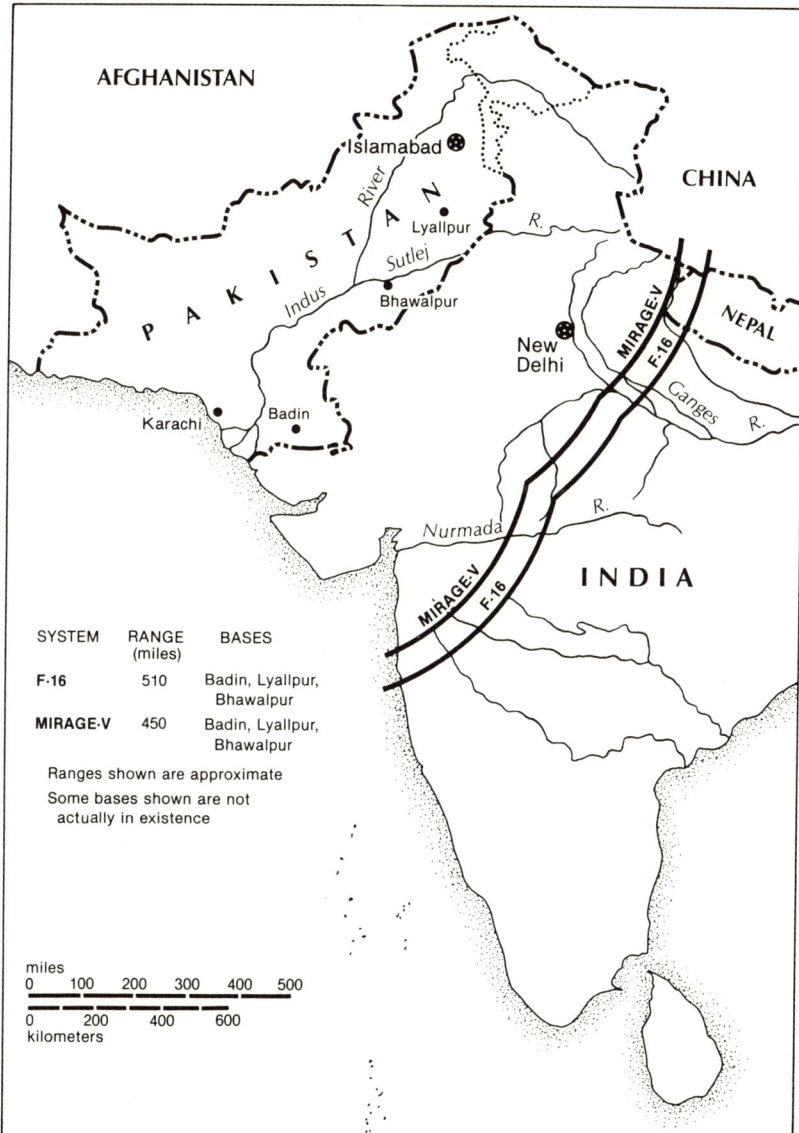

SYSTEM   RANGE   BASES
          (miles)

F-16   510   Badin, Lyallpur,
                     Bhawalpur

MIRAGE-V   450   Badin, Lyallpur,
                     Bhawalpur

Ranges shown are approximate

Some bases shown are not
actually in existence

could develop an IRBM prototype within two years.[21] If India were to develop IRBMs with a range of about 930 miles, it could maintain a nuclear strike force out of the range of Pakistani aircraft, yet capable of hitting almost all of Pakistan. Thus if and when the two countries acquire nuclear weapons, they will also have delivery systems; there need not be a time lag between the acquisition of the two.

All these factors would have an impact on strategy and should be kept in mind when discussing the uses of nuclear weapons by the two countries and likely scenarios in an Indo-Pakistani nuclear exchange.

Usability of Nuclear Weapons in South Asia - Constraints and Incentives

The crucial issue remains: What are the chances that nuclear weapons would actually be used by India and Pakistan against each other? Any examination of the constraints and incentives involved leads us to the conclusion that such use is very unlikely for a series of pragmatic reasons—some domestic, some regional, some international, and some geographic. We do assume that rationality and perspective are retained by regional decisionmakers during a period of crisis.

Use for Deterrence

A study of the Pakistani military strategic debate over the development of a nuclear doctrine seems to follow the predictable lines of nuclear strategy that have evolved elsewhere; that is, to adopt the general principles of deterrence, the main adversary being India. Advocates of nuclear weapons in India also justify their demands on the basis of the deterrence value of nuclear weapons against both China and Pakistan.

For Pakistan, the threats to strategic and military security are permanent and lethal. Most of these threats are associated with Pakistan's security dilemma vis-à-vis India, and more recently, the Russian occupation of Afghanistan. These external threats are compounded by internal instability and inadequate security-related resources.[22] Given the overall superiority of the powers that exert external pressure on Pakistan through their conventional strength alone, the possession and use of nuclear weapons for deterrence is very attractive and the idea could become even more acceptable as the imbalance in conventional military strength between Pakistan and India increases in favor of the latter. Indeed, it is possible to stand the proliferation chain argument on its head in the case of the Indo-Pakistan dyad. The argument has been that if China acquired nuclear weapons, India would acquire them and this in turn would lead to a Pakistani bomb. We can instead argue that Pakistan needs nuclear weapons to offset India's conventional military superiority. In order to prevent Pakistan from using these nuclear weapons for compellence (for example, in Kashmir) rather than deterrence, India needs nuclear weapons. As K. Subrahmanyam puts it (although in a different context), "nuclear weapons can be deterred only by nuclear weapons."[23] The proliferation of nuclear weapons into South Asia may indeed follow this pattern.

If the two nations develop striking power to the extent that their respective nuclear forces serve only to cancel each other out—that is, to deter use of nuclear weapons—diplomatic, political, and perhaps even conventional military interactions may proceed in much the same manner as before. There would be, however, one important difference. Direct external threats from India to the very existence of Pakistan as a state could no longer exist. On one hand, this could lead to fewer restraints on adventurist tendencies among Pakistani leaders; on the other hand, it would remove what is felt by many to be the root cause of the continuing conflict between the two countries, the widespread feeling among the Pakistanis that India is bent on dismembering and perhaps absorbing their country. The possession of nuclear weapons would enable the Pakistanis to inflict unacceptable punishment on India should the latter threaten the very existence of Pakistan. The positive effects of an increased sense of security among the Pakistani elite would far outweigh any negative impact caused by increased adventurism in its leadership. Although both nations have committed acts of brinkmanship in the past, policy formation and crisis behavior have on the whole been pragmatic and sober. Indeed, the acquisition of nuclear weapons by both sides may prevent even conventional wars between the two countries as leaders exercise extra caution for fear of starting a nuclear war.

The successful maintainance of a credible deterrence posture by the two countries against each other would, however, not be a simple matter. First of all it would require superior Pakistani technical ability to offset India's larger nuclear arsenal (which is inevitable given India's greater resources and the threat it faces from a nuclear China), and the fact that, whereas all of Pakistan is within strike range of Indian planes and missiles, all of India, including missile launching areas are not within range of Pakistan (see Figures 2 and 3). Thus Pakistan would need superior technology to prevent India from carrying out a decapitating first strike against Pakistani nuclear weapons. Given India's current technical superiority, it is hard to envisage Pakistan acquiring the needed technical ability. In the absence of such security for a Pakistani force, acquisition of nuclear weapons would be more destabilizing than stabilizing, because the temptation to use the weapons before they are destroyed would be great.

Another related problem that could lead to similar premature use is that of Pakistan's possible inability to deliver a nuclear weapon under certain battle conditions. It has been pointed out that if Pakistan were in such dire military straits that it actually decided to use nuclear weapons against an attacking enemy, it might have already lost the military ability to deliver the warheads.[24] This situation could mean that the decision about to when exactly to use nuclear weapons would be left to the military, because it alone would best be able to determine when the armed forces were about to lose the capability to deliver the warheads. This would indeed be a very destabilizing factor!

A third problem with nuclear deterrence in the Indo-Pakistani dyad is that of command and control. Unless both countries developed strong C^3I, Pakistan, and to a more limited extent, India, would face a trade-off between viability and stability. Pakistan might encourage the adoption of Launch on Warning (LoW) postures. Needless to say, LoW is not conducive to confidence in robust mutual deterrence.

These three major problems would destabilize nuclear deterrence. If the two countries were to acquire nuclear weapons, it would be imperative that various steps be taken to overcome these problems so that credible deterrence might be established. We have already pointed out the conditions necessary for establishing credible deterrence by Pakistan and the problems that it is likely to encounter in establishing them. It must be asserted here that unless these problems are overcome, the introduction of nuclear weapons into the region would be extremely destabilizing. If Pakistan were to acquire nuclear weapons but not the necessary technology to make them invulnerable to a decapitating first strike by India, the incentive to launch a preemptive strike during a crisis or adopt a Launch-on-Warning strategy would be great. Such vulnerability of Pakistani weapons could also provide India with incentives to use nuclear weapons. First, the option of neutralizing Pakistani nuclear weapons with little or no loss would be available to Indian decision makers. Second, the fact that, being aware of the vulnerability of their weapons, the Pakistanis might launch a preemptive strike would in turn serve as an incentive to India to preempt them.

Protection is not enough. The Pakistanis must develop a capability to deliver such weapons during a crisis situation, even after its armed forces have been severely mauled in a conflict with India. Lack of an ability to do so would have the same impact on the deterrence strategy and decision-making calculus of both India and Pakistan as the vulnerability of actual warheads.

Adequate C^3I would also be needed. Here again it is Pakistan that would face greater problems because of its lower level of technological achievement. Adequate C³I would be needed not only to deter adoption of such strategies as Launch on Warning, but would also have to be geared to ensure that unauthorized use cannot occur. Both sides would have to know enough about each other's C³I to promote confidence in the unlikelihood of preemptive and unauthorized use. It would therefore be necessary to establish communication links between the two that are specifically geared to such communication and coordination of information. It should be noted that besides solving the problems discussed above, other measures would also be needed to establish a credible deterrence posture. These measures would include successful communication by one side to the other of an ability and will to use nuclear weapons if the security of the state is threatened beyond a certain point. It would also be necessary to elaborate a clear deterrence doctrine that would inform the other side about the conditions under which a non-nuclear conflict situation would escalate into nuclear conflict.

Use for Compellence

Compellence would only work if one side were to have a monopoly of nuclear weapons or a military superiority that would make it impossible for the "compellee" to retaliate against the "compellor." At the very least, the demands made by the "compellor" should not be viewed as so outrageous or so destructive to the nationhood of the "compellee" as to make these demands unacceptable even under threat of nuclear attack. If the "compellee" had a nuclear force of its own, chances of successful compellence would be very low indeed. One of our assumptions has been that both sides acquire nuclear weapons and the means to deliver them. Under such conditions, use of nuclear weapons for compellence would be impractical.

Let us take the example of Kashmir. It is hard to imagine either India or Pakistan giving up the areas of Kashmir under their control to the other side because of nuclear threats, especially if both had nuclear weapons. Both countries consider control over their part of Kashmir vital to their national character, albeit for different reasons. Neither would give up control in the face of nuclear threats that could be countered by nuclear weapons in its own possession.

The successful use of nuclear weapons for compellence by one side would lead to a rapid escalation of such use, a situation equally unacceptable to both sides because of the destabilizing effects it would have and the risk of a subsequent nuclear exchange. Thus constraints on use of nuclear weapons for compellence are strong, and it is doubtful if attempts at such use would succeed.

The use of nuclear weapons for compellence by a small group of fanatics on either side—"blackmail"—will be discussed below in Scenario F. Here it is sufficient to conclude that it is impractical and unlikely to be used by a state to achieve national goals.

Use as Tactical Weapons

Nuclear weapons may also be used to attack field formations during battle. It is our contention that differentiating between the tactical and strategic uses of nuclear weapons in the South Asian context is fallacious, if for no other reason than that of the number of civilian casualties that would occur on both sides. The situation here is different from that in Europe, where use of "tactical" nuclear weapons would not kill Russian and American civilians. (European civilians would of course die, and it is for this reason that the Europeans don't see much difference between strategic and tactical weapons.) The damage and loss of life that would occur in South Asia not only makes such a distinction a cruel joke but also a dangerous one. Escalation of "tactical" use into counter-city strikes (Scenario D) is almost inevitable, given the extent of the damage that would be caused by "tactical" use. Any quick, decisive result in a war is likely to come out of a battle in Punjab or Kashmir. Therefore it is this sector of the Indo-Pakistan border that has the highest level of troop deployment, and it is in this area that tactical nuclear weapons are most likely to be used. Given the high population density along both sides of the border in the Punjab-Kashmir sector, collateral civilian casualties and damage are likely to be very high. Once use of nuclear weapons, even tactical ones, has caused extensive damage and casualties in such border urban centers as Amritsar, Gujranwala, Ferozpur, Gurdaspur, Pathankot, Srinagar, Fazilka, Baramula, Lahore, Sialkot, Kasur, Gujrat, and Jhelum, the chances of escalation into counter-city strikes are very great. Thus use of tactical nuclear weapons against field formations in the Punjab-Kashmir sector would be tantamount to a large scale exchange between the two parties.

Use of tactical nuclear weapons further south along the Rajasthan and Gujrat border would not cause widespread collateral civilian casualties because of the relatively sparse population along both sides of the border in that sector. Therefore tactical use of weapons in this sector would not necessarily escalate into counter-city strikes. The danger remains, however, that once the nuclear threshold is crossed, such escalation would occur.

This discussion on use of tactical weapons has assumed that such use would be made against military formations of the other side before they cross the border. Once forces of one side have crossed the border and have occupied populated areas of the other side, the latter would be placed in a situation wherein use of tactical nuclear weapons against the enemy would mean causing the deaths of large numbers of its own population. Under such circumstances a country might choose to use nuclear weapons as envisaged in Scenario E below (Warning or Symbolic Attack) in order to force the enemy to stop his advance, vacate occupied territory, or both. The dangers of escalation from such use to counter-city strikes have already been discussed. On the other hand if a country decides to use tactical nuclear weapons against enemy forces on its own territory and incurs substantial civilian casualties in the process, it is likely to launch attacks on some of the enemy's population centers as compensation. The chance of an escalation to large-scale attacks on civilian targets in such a situation is self-evident.

Beside the danger pointed out above, two additional factors add to the risks of actual use of nuclear weapons if "tactical" weapons are developed and deployed. First, it would provide policymakers with what could be perceived as an intermediate option between no-use and annihilation, which would undermine deterrence. Secondly, and because of the first, it would be easier to make the decision to use nuclear weapons in the hope that "tactical" use against military targets would limit retaliation by the other side to similar levels. As we have seen, however, once nuclear weapons have been used in any form, all bets are off about rationality and restraint, creating a dangerous situation that could lead to counter-city strikes. Such escalation might result from miscalculation about the enemy's real intentions, even though only "tactical" use was made of nuclear weapons, or a steady escalation of use of smaller yield weapons into use of larger yield weapons.

However, the development of nuclear weapons for tactical use is not unlikely and is the main danger that would arise from acquisition of such weapons by India and Pakistan.

Other Constraints

The ultimate constraint on using nuclear weapons in a situation where both sides have them is of course Mutual Assured Destruction (MAD). However, other international, regional, domestic, and geographic constraints, some fairly strong, also exist in South Asia.

Use of nuclear weapons in any but the most dire of straits is unlikely because of several international and regional factors. For India the main regional constraint is the China factor. Any use of nuclear weapons against Pakistan would have to take into consideration the impact on Sino-Indian relations. Even if China were to stand by and do nothing, such an attack would be likely to lead to a nuclear arms race with China. It is also doubtful that the Soviet Union and the United States would stand aside during such a conflict.

Then, of course, devastation from a nuclear war would open the door for the penetration of outside powers—China, the Soviet Union, and the United States— into the subcontinent, which would further reduce the maneuverability in international and regional affairs that India, and to a lesser extent Pakistan, have so painstakingly acquired over the past decades.

There is also the problem of setting a precedent. Small- and medium-sized powers do not want to legitimize the use of nuclear weapons or set precedents because they would then be open to similar attacks or threats from the big powers, with whose huge arsenals of nuclear weapons they cannot hope to compete.

Yet another constraint on the use of nuclear weapons by India and Pakistan against each other which is often overlooked or underestimated relates to the composition of the population of India. Any strikes on major urban centers in India would cause many casualties among Indian Muslims who are intermixed with the non-Muslim population. Table 2 shows the percentage of Muslims in the populations of towns likely to be hit in a counter-city strike of the sort outlined in Scenario D.

It is not my contention here that the Indian Muslim factor would prevent an attack on Indian cities; rather, I argue that it would be a major constraint on Pakistani behavior in all but the most severe of crises, where the very existence of Pakistan was at stake. The impact on Indian Muslims of a nuclear attack on India would be a factor that Pakistani decision makers would have to take into consideration for several reasons. The more important of these reasons are: the ideology behind the creation of Pakistan, the maintaining of which is essential for the continued existence of the state; the role that Pakistan has sought to play in the Muslim world; the support and concern, at least rhetorical, for the Muslims of India expressed by all sections of the Pakistani elite; the likely rise in influence of Hindu communal organizations in India which would take advantage of heightened anti-Muslim sentiments and the collapse of law and order to indulge in large-scale killings of Muslims; and, last but not least, close familial ties between Indian Muslims and Pakistanis of Indian origin (*Muhajirs*). The latter are an important force in Pakistani politics and hold key political and bureaucratic positions. Here it is important to note that, contrary to the arguments made by some Indian analysts,[25] the more conservative, religious, and "Jihad"-oriented a Pakistani government is, the less likely it is to use nuclear weapons against India because of the impact, both direct and indirect, such an attack would

Table 2. Percentage of Muslims in Projected Population of Indian Towns Likely to Be Targets in a Pakistani Counter-City Strike.

City	Population* (1990)	Percentages Muslim†	Muslim Population (Col. 1 × Col. 2)
Bombay	11,914,900	14.12	1,682,400
Delhi	9,118,600	7.40	674,800
Ahmedabad	3,164,100	14.58	461,300
Agra	1,041,800	16.34	170,200
Gwalior	944,300	15.00	141,600
Jaipur	904,600	18.71	169,300
Baroda	821,400	12.00	98,600
Amritsar	813,500	0.42	3,400
Indore	798,900	12.41	99,100
Ludhiana	775,800	0.10	800
Surat	693,500	24.00	166,500
Jallandhar	590,900	0.08	500
Meerut	528,400	39.00	206,100
Jodhpur	467,000	20.00	93,400
Ghaziabad	174,700	24.00	41,900
TOTAL	32,752,400		4,009,900

* Based on 1971 or 1981 censuses. The prevailing growth rate in each city has been used to project the 1990 population.
Source. Statistical Pocket-Book of India 1980 (New Delhi: Ministry of Planning, Government of India, 1981), pp. 5, 10-12.
†*Source.* N. A. Siddiqui, *Population Geography of Muslims of India* (New Delhi: S. Chand & Co., 1976), pp. 66-98.

have on Indian Muslims, and on Pakistan's own position within the Muslim world.

On the other hand, Indian Muslims would also be a factor in the Indian government calculations if that government ever planned to launch a nuclear strike against Pakistan. I would like to make it very clear here that although the loyalty of Indian Muslims to India is not in question, at the same time the fact that Indian Muslims have close familial ties with 80 percent of the population of Pakistan's largest urban center, Karachi, cannot be ignored.[26] Again, such considerations might restrain rather than prevent Indian decision makers from using nuclear weapons. In this regard it is worth noting that in past conflicts between the two countries, some of them very bitter, neither side has resorted to indiscriminate attacks on population centers. In the case of the 1971 civil war in Pakistan, atrocities were committed against fellow Muslim South Asians by the Pakistani army. The likelihood that this will occur again is not very high, given the consequences.

The third set of constraints relate to the geographical proximity of the two states and various meteorological factors. The close physical proximity of the two states makes it inevitable that fallout from nuclear explosions in one would affect the territory of the other. The heartland of Pakistan—the Indus Valley region of Pakistani Punjab—runs parallel to the strategic, rich, and now restless state of Punjab in India. Any attack on Pakistani cities in the "heartland" of Pakistan (five out of eight cities in Table 7 fall within this region) would mean that deaths and damage from fallout would affect Indian Punjab. Similarly, attacks on Indian Punjab cities, indeed even on Delhi, would result in some fallout deaths and damage in Pakistani Punjab. The extent of damage would depend on wind direction and force, which varies at different times in the year (see Figure 4).

We see that during the period of the Northeast Monsoon (December to March), fallout would be carried back to India. Similarly, during the Southwest Monsoon (June to September),[27] fallout would be carried back to Pakistan. Therefore, to prevent damage to itself from fallout from its own weapons, India would have to attack during the months of April through October, whereas Pakistan would have to attack during the months of October through May. Even without strong winds, damage to the border regions of the two countries would be substantial. Fallout damage to the two Punjabs would be of great economic and political

Figure 4. Wind Direction during the North-East and South-West
Monsoon Seasons in South Asia[32]

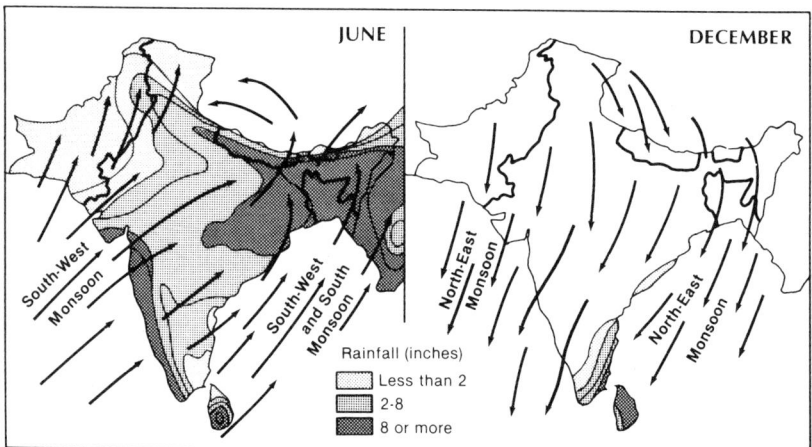

Source. J. Bartholomew, *Oxford School Atlas of India, Burma, and Ceylon* (London: Oxford University Press, 1968), p. 15.

significance if the two countries were to survive as states after a nuclear war. This would be yet another constraint on the use of nuclear weapons for any purpose other than deterrence.

It is therefore clear that besides Mutual Assured Destruction, other constraints exist on use of nuclear weapons in general and on its use for any other purpose than deterrence in particular. These constraints would play an important restraining role. At the same time the importance of these constraints should not be overestimated. The best and most effective constraint would still be MAD.

As already noted, the chances of a strategic nuclear exchange between India and Pakistan (provided the conditions necessary to achieve nuclear stability outlined above are met) are very low. The probability of such an exchange is about the same as that of a strategic exchange between the United States and the USSR. The ability of both sides to inflict unacceptable damage on the other, indeed, to threaten each other's survival as states or even civil societies, is deterrence enough against such use. It would compel both sides to limit their ambitions at the expense of the other, and force both elites to end exaggerations of external threats to security.

The development and deployment of tactical nuclear weapons, however, would sharply increase the chances of use of nuclear weapons. Even if such use is initially of a limited nature, it is, for reasons already discussed, very likely to escalate into major nuclear strikes. Thus if nuclear weapons are ever used by India and Pakistan against each other on a large scale, such use is likely to escalate from "tactical use."

Scenarios

One can create scores of different scenarios likely to occur in a nuclear exchange between India and Pakistan. In the next section I discuss six of the most likely ones. All these scenarios assume that a political decision to use nuclear weapons has already been made. The dynamics and likelihood of such a decision are discussed later.

Scenario A: Attacks on military targets and formations
Scenario B: Attacks on military targets and limited strikes on economic targets
Scenario C: General attack on military and economic targets
Scenario D: Counter-city strikes
Scenario E: Symbolic/warning strike
Scenario F: "Blackmail"

I shall take up each of these scenarios, briefly identify the goals and targets, and calculate the estimated damage likely to result from each. Before we proceed, a note about the projected casualty figures is in order. *These projections are only general estimates*; precise calculation of casualties would be very difficult if not impossible.

Scenario A

This scenario envisages an attack by India or Pakistan on the other's military targets and formations. Such an attack would hit major cantonments within striking range and would be a part of a strategy of compellence or would be designed to fulfill tactical military purposes. The goal would be the destruction of the enemy's major military formations in order to prevent a conventional attack, or would be a prelude to military action by the attacking side.

Since the aim would be to destroy concentrated military personnel and equipment, 20 KT weapons are likely to be used. These would fulfill the purpose of the attack and minimize collateral damage. For the same reason surface bursts are likely to be used which would result in 5 psi rings of a radius of .8 miles, 2.2 psi rings of a radius of 1.3 miles, and 2 psi rings with a radius of 1.4 miles.[28]

Table 3 through 8 identify targets and summarize casualties likely to be caused by such an exchange.

These figures are of initial casualties; they do not include casualties that would occur from the delayed effects of such an attack.

The targets listed above are mainly army cantonments. A nuclear attack by either country would also seek to destroy both nuclear weapons and delivery systems and would involve attacks on air fields and on missile sites. These attacks might also consist of 15-20 KT weapons set for surface burst. The number of airfields targeted would depend upon the deployment policy adopted by Pakistan. Two broad options are available. Given the accessibility of almost all of Pakistan to Indian aircraft, Pakistan might choose to concentrate its nuclear weapons and aircraft committed to a nuclear attack mission on a few air bases, concentrating its defenses on protecting these bases from a surprise attack. On the other hand they might adopt a strategy of dispersal, making it more difficult for India to carry out a decapitating air strike because of the problems of coordinating and successfully carrying out several air strikes simultaneously. Whatever deployment policy is adopted, the location of nuclear weapon air bases is likely to optimize distance from the frontier (the farther away the better, giving more warning time in case of an attack) with penetrability of Pakistan's own air strikes (the shorter the distance from the frontier, the better). Given the above, the airfields likely to be used as bases for nuclear weapons and attack aircraft include Badin, Bhawalpur, Peshawar, and Lyallpur. These would be targets of an Indian attack.

Table 3. Casualty and Damage Projections: Limited Attack on Military
Centers of Pakistan

Target Cantonments	Population of City (1990)*	Estimated Deaths†	Estimated Injuries**	Property Destroyed (sq mi)‡
Karachi	8,337,100	128,900	211,541	6.16
Lahore	4,599,900	66,100	10,800	6.16
Rawalpindi	1,427,100	68,300	11,200	4.12
Hyderabad	1,088,000	44,600	73,200	4.12
Peshawar	383,100	27,500	45,100	3.08
Sialkot	283,200	20,400	33,400	6.16
Quetta	282,600	35,500	58,300	6.16
Bhawalpur	261,900	18,800	30,900	6.16
Wah Cantt.	222,100	148,000	74,000	6.16
Gujrat	212,500	15,300	25,100	6.16
Sahiwal	51,600	3,700	6,100	6.16
TOTAL	17,149,100	577,100	579,641	61.60

* The populations for these cities have been calculated by projecting the growth rate for
each city between 1962-72 to 1990. The only exception is Wah Cantonment, the population
of which grew by 194% between 1962 and 1972, because of the development of the cantonment into a major arms production center during this period. The growth rate between 1972
and 1990 for Wah has therefore been calculated as 5.92%, which is the average growth rate
of Pakistani cities between 1962-72. The 1962 and 1972 population figures are from *The
Statistical Abstract of Pakistan 1980* (Government of Pakistan: Islamabad 1981), pp. 5-7.
Figures have been rounded off.

†The method used to calculate deaths is outlined in the text. Ground Zero is located at
the center of each cantonment. Population density and city area figures are from Kureshy,
pp. 86-96. The population density throughout the area of each city is considered to be
uniform. The figures have been rounded off.

** The method used to calculate injuries is outlined in the text. Ground Zero is located at
the center of each cantonment. Population density and city area figures are from Kureshy,
pp. 86-96. Population density throughout the area of each city is taken as being uniform.
The figures have been rounded off.

‡Built-up area destroyed is calculated according to the method described in the text. The
size of built-up area destroyed varies because of the location of each cantonment.

*** 100% of the population of Wah cantonment will be affected because of the large
military contingent in the population which is located in the cantonment area, and the fact
that the few civilians live in areas adjacent to the cantonment.

The greater range of Indian nuclear capable aircraft along with the
fact that all of India cannot be reached by Pakistani aircraft (at least the
new modern sophisticated aircraft—Canberra bombers which have
greater range are slow and vulnerable) makes the Indian task of deployment less complicated. Likely air bases include Delhi, Mathura, Gwalior,
Udaipur, and Jamnagar. Air bases located close to the frontier would

not be used because they would be more vulnerable without any payoff in terms of increased penetrability of aircraft based there. (See Figure 2.)

If India were to acquire or develop IRBMs, it could deploy them as far east as Allahabad and still cover the core areas of Pakistan. These missile sites could only be reached by Pakistani aircraft if they were to carry out one way attack missions.

Both countries might locate their nuclear attack forces at new air bases. Such bases may be built away from population centers to reduce casualties in case they are attacked. On the other hand, they might be built close to civilian centers and thus signal to the opposing side that an attack on these bases would cause so many civilian casualties that any chance of limiting the war and preventing Scenarios B, C, and D would be an illusion.

The discussion here has concerned itself with attacks on military targets in cantonments and on some air bases; it has not discussed attacks

Table 4. Casualty and Damage Projections: Limited Attack on Military Centers of India

Target Cantonments	Population of City (1990)	Estimated Deaths*	Estimated Injuries	Property Destroyed (sq mi)†
Bombay	11,914,900	136,900	224,600	6.16
Delhi	9,118,600	40,700	66,900	4.62
Ahmedabad	3,164,100	153,500	251,900	3.08
Agra	1,041,800	91,100	149,400	6.16
Gowaliar	944,300	18,000	25,400	6.16
Baroda	821,400	4,200	6,900	6.16
Amritsar	813,500	15,500	21,900	6.16
Ludhiana	775,800	14,800	20,900	6.16
Jullandhar	590,900	11,300	15,900	6.16
Rajkot	529,100	10,100	14,200	6.16
Meerut	528,400	10,100	14,200	6.16
Jamnagar	408,400	79,300	13,000	6.16
Jhansi	337,300	6,400	9,100	6.16
Ajmer	334,300	6,400	9,000	6.16
Jammu	273,400	5,200	7,400	6.16
TOTAL	31,596,200	603,500	850,700	84.70

Source. J. Bartholomew, *Oxford School Atlas of India, Burma, and Ceylon* (London: Oxford University Press, 1968), p. 15.
Based on 1971 or 1981 census, the prevailing growth rate in each city has been used to project the size of the 1990 population. The figures are from *The Statistical Pocket Book of India 1980* (New Delhi: Ministry of Planning, Government of India, 1981), pp. 5, 10-12.
*The system used to calculate deaths is described in the text. Ground Zero is located at the center of each city. Population density and city area figures are from various sources, including Statistical Pocket Book. Numbers have been rounded off.
†Calculated as described in the text. The size of the built-up area varies because of the location of each cantonment.

on units deployed on the frontier. Use of nuclear weapons against the latter would constitute tactical use. The probability of such use has already been discussed. Because of the mobility of these targets and changing deployment postures, it is difficult to project targets and casualties if field formations are attacked with nuclear weapons. No such attempt is made here.

It is clear from the above discussion that even an attack limiting itself to military targets in cantonments and airfields using relatively small weapons (20 KT), and trying to minimize collateral damage (surface bursts), would cause substantial death, injury, and destruction of property. Some of the reasons for high casualty figures have already been discussed above. An additional factor is that the major cantonments which would be targeted are located within or adjacent to cities.

Scenario B

This scenario envisages attacks by India or Pakistan on not only military targets but also on major economic targets. Such an attack would again aim at fulfilling compellence goals. The attacks on economic targets would be more harmful to Pakistan for several reasons. First, whereas India can attack almost any economic target within Pakistan, large parts of India's industrial heartland—central Uttar Pradesh, most of Maharashtra, and West Bengal—will be out of range of Pakistani aircraft (unless one-way suicide missions are undertaken). Second, attacks on economic targets would mean a decision to fight a prolonged war, which would enable India to mobilize its superior resources and wear down Pakistan's ability to resist.

The military targets in this scenario would be the same as in Scenario A. Tables 5 and 6 list likely economic targets in an exchange aimed at major economic centers.

Table 5. Major Economic Targets in Pakistan*

A. Energy	1) Hydroelectric power stations
	a) Mangla
	b) Warsak
	2) Thermal power stations
	a) Multan
	b) Sukkur
	3) Nuclear power station
	a) Karachi
	4) Gas
	a) Sui gas fields
	5) Oil refineries
	a) Multan
	b) Attock

Table 5. Major Economic Targets in Pakistan* (cont.)

B. Nuclear Facilities	1) Heavy water
	  a) Multan
	  b) Karachi
	2) Enrichment
	  a) Kahuta
	  b) Sihala
	3) Fuel fabrication
	  a) Chashma
	4) Reprocessing
	  a) Chashma
	  b) Rawalpindi
	5) Research reactor
	  a) Rawalpindi

C. Irrigation and Water Resources	1) Mangla Dam 2) Tarbela Dam 3) Sidhnai Barrage 4) Sulemanki Barrage 5) Panjnad Barrage 6) Sukkur Barrage 7) Kotri Barrage

D. Industries	1) Iron and steel
	  a) Karachi
	2) Ordnance
	  a) Wah
	  b) Kamra
	  c) Taxila
	3) Chemicals and Fertilizers
	  a) Karachi
	  b) Lyallpur
	  c) Shiekhupura
	  d) Lahore
	4) Cement
	  a) Dera Ghazi Khan
	  b) Thatta

E. Transportation	1) Jhang Railway Junction 2) Hyderabad Railway Junction 3) Miamwali Railway Junction 4) Karachi Railway Junction 5) Karachi Port

* Choice of target is based upon economic value and size.

Table 6. Major Economic Targets in India*

A. Energy	1) Hydroelectric power stations
	a) Trombay
	b) Bhakra
	c) Kotla
	2) Thermal power stations
	a) Bhavnagar
	b) Agra
	c) Ahmedabad
	3) Nuclear power stations
	a) Narora
	b) Tarapur
	c) Kota
	d) Kakrapar
	4) Petroleum
	a) Bombay
	b) Baroda
	c) Mathura
B. Nuclear Facilities	1) Heavy Water
	a) Nangal
	b) Baroda
	c) Kota
	d) Thal
	2) Reprocessing
	a) Trombay
	b) Tarapur
	3) Research Reactor
	a) Trombay
C. Irrigation and Water Resources	1) Nanaksagar Dam
	2) Sardasagar Dam
	3) Nangal Dam
	4) Gangapur Dam
	5) Pong Dam
	6) Baira-Siul Dam
D. Industries	1) Bombay
	2) Faridabad
	3) Bhatinda
	4) Ghaziabad
	5) Mathura
	6) Agra
	7) Amritsar

Table 6. Major Economic Targets in India* (cont.)

	8) Ludhiana
	9) Ambala
	10) Baroda
	11) Jamnagar
E. Transportation	1) Railways
	a) Agra Junction
	b) Delhi Junction
	c) Amritsar
	d) Ambala Cantt
	e) Bombay Central and V.T.
	f) Baroda
	2) Ports
	a) Bombay
	b) Kandla
	c) Jamnagar

* These targets are within range of Pakistani Mirage III and Mirage V and F-16 aircraft.

Successful attacks on the targets listed in Table 4 would result in severe damage to Pakistan's economic infrastructure. For example, the destruction of the four hydroelectric and thermal power stations listed above would reduce Pakistani thermal and hydroelectric power production from 1,583 to 715 million watts. The destruction of the Mangla and Tarbela dams would reduce water storage capacity by 16.6 million acrefeet. The destruction of barrages listed in Table 4 would lead to the total disruption of control over irrigation in the Indus valley system. The destruction of the railway centers would paralyze rail transport in Pakistan. Destruction of Karachi's port would lead to total disruption of sea communications. Although all economic targets in India will not be within range of Pakistani weapon systems, the damage there would still be grave. Besides the deaths and injuries that would result immediately, the long-term impact of attacks on economic targets could include widespread famine, rampant epidemics, and the destruction of the two countries as viable economic systems.

The weapons used to achieve these results could have small yields. The civilian casualty figures in both countries would, of course, be much lower if attacks were limited to military targets only. These projections have not been calculated because data are unavailable on the size and density of population in some of the areas listed in the tables.

Scenario C

A more widespread attack on military and economic targets could occur, but this would be a case of overkill because damage done by destroying targets listed in Tables 5 and 6 would be enough to cause total economic disruption in both countries. Scenario C could evolve, however, as a result of steady escalation during a war in which retaliatory strikes would gradually lead to attacks on relatively minor economic or military targets. Such a development is unlikely, if only because the number of nuclear warheads that will be available to the two countries in the near future is limited. Given the concave vulnerability function discussed above, the limited number of warheads available would make a scenario like this impossible. In case of a really savage war, Scenario D is more likely to occur.

Scenario D

A more deadly use of nuclear weapons would involve strikes aimed primarily at the other's civilian population centers in case a policy of deterrence fails.

Unlike the other scenarios, Scenario D would involve the destruction of urban centers and the infliction of the maximum possible civilian casualties. Therefore, weapons with higher yields and air, rather than surface, bursts are likely to be used. Either a 1 MT weapon or several weapons with smaller yield could be used against each target. The 5 psi ring from a 1-MT air burst would have a radius of 4.4 miles, the 2.2 psi ring radius of 7.6 miles, and the 2 psi ring a radius of 8.1 miles.[29] Given the congested nature and small area of most South Asian cities, very high casualties would result. For example, the entire area of the city of Lahore would fall within the "Lethal Zone." Tables 7 and 8 give likely targets in a counter-city strike scenario.

As has already been pointed out, casualties are likely to be very high because of the congested nature of South Asian cities, the limited firefighting capabilities in most cities, limited medical facilities, and the total disruption of the administrative infrastructure on a national scale. Unlike the more developed countries, India and Pakistan would not be able to rely on the medical, administrative, and economic resources of the small- and medium-sized towns not hit in a nuclear war for relief operations. One of the results would be more deaths caused by nontreatment of the injured and by uncontrolled epidemics.

Assuming that a 15 mph wind is blowing over each city, fallout of 3,000 rem would cover a downwind area of 140 sq mi. (Exposure to more than 300 rem per week is likely to be fatal.) Thus eight such patterns cov-

Table 7. Targets in a Counter-City Strike against Pakistan

City	Projected population (1990)*	Estimated deaths†
Karachi	8,337,100	6,252,000
Lahore	4,599,900	4,500,000
Lyallpur	2,064,300	2,000,000
Rawalpindi	1,427,l00	1,400,000
Hyderabad	1,088,000	1,088,000
Multan	1,007,200	1,000,000
Gujranwala	885,300	885,000
Peshawar	383,100	383,000

* The populations for these cities have been calculated by projecting the growth rate for each city between 1962-72 to 1990. the 1962 and 1972 population figures are from *The Statistical Abstract of Pakistan 1980* (Islamabad: Government of Pakistan, 1981), pp. 5-7. Figures have been rounded off.

† The system used to calculate deaths is described in the text. Ground Zero is located at the center of each city. Population density and city area figures are from Kureshy, pp. 86-96. Figures have been rounded off.

Table 8. Targets in a Counter-City Strike against India

City	Projected Population (1990)*	Estimated deaths†
Bombay	11,914,900	8,936,000
Delhi	9,118,600	9,100,000
Ahmedabad	3,164,100	3,100,000
Agra	1,041,800	1,020,000
Gwalior	944,300	940,000
Jaipur	904,600	900,000
Baroda	821,400	800,000
Amritsar	813,500	810,000
Indore	798,900	790,000
Ludhiana	775,800	770,000
Surat	693,500	690,000
Julandhar	590,900	500,000
Meerut	528,400	500,000
Jodhpur	467,000	390,000
Ghaziabad	174,700	168,000

* Based on 1971 or 1981 census, the prevailing growth rate in each city has been used to project the size of the 1990 population. The figures are from *The Statistical Pocket Book of India 1980* (New Delhi: Ministry of Planning, Government of India, 1981), pp. 5, 10-12.

† The system used to calculate deaths is described in the text. Ground Zero is located at the center of each city. Population density and city area figures are from various sources, including Statistical Pocket Book. Numbers have been rounded off.

ering an area of 1,120 sq. mi. would hover over Pakistan. Similar fallout patterns would cover an area of 2,100 sq mi in India, which would cause additional deaths from exposure to radiation. These deaths are not included in the estimates in Tables 7 and 8. Given the population density of some of the areas surrounding the major cities targeted in this scenario, the number of such deaths would be very high.

Scenario E

Another possible scenario would involve a warning or symbolic attack by one country against the other. Such an attack could be used to deter, compel, or punish the other side.

India or Pakistan may detonate a single, relatively low yield weapon on the other's territory as a warning to the other side of its serious intentions in case of an attack on itself, namely, as deterrence. Such an attack could be carried out over a relatively sparsely populated part of the enemy's territory in order to minimize the chances of escalation. Targets could include western Rajasthan in India and the Baluchistan desert in Pakistan.

If the purpose of such an attack were compellence rather than deterrence, the target chosen would be of significant economic or psychological value to the other side. Possible targets in Pakistan would be a port like Pasni, the oil refineries at Attock, the electric power station at Warsak, or the Sukkur or Kotri Barrage. Possible targets in India could include ports like Dwarka or Jamnagar, the hydroelectric complex at Kota, oil refineries at Mathura, or the Nangal dam. These targets would be chosen to signal the serious intention of the attacker without causing so much damage as to force the other side to retaliate.

A third use of a nuclear device in a limited role could be to punish the enemy or "avenge national honor" by attacking a single target of some economic or symbolic value to the other side.

The major problem with this kind of use is that once the nuclear threshold is crossed, it is very unlikely that restraint could be exercised by either side, even if the political leadership wished to do so. Moreover, the slightest miscalculation about the real intention of the user could plunge the two countries into a full-scale nuclear confrontation.

Scenario F

Finally, a government or an extremist group in either country could use nuclear weapons to blackmail the other side. One such scenario could involve a plane carrying nuclear weapons that circles a major city of the other side while demands are being made of the rival government.

It is very unlikely that a government would engage in such an enterprise, at least overtly. A government that did so would either have to maintain the blackmail threat indefinitely or face inevitable retaliation if and when it ends the threat. Use of nuclear weapons for compellence is, therefore, more likely to take the forms described in Scenarios A, B, D, or E. A small group of extremists could get away with blackmail, but the demands they can make are limited in nature and scope. These demands would have to be for money or some other movable, concealable, tangible thing that they could prevent the other side from recovering once the blackmail threat is removed. The use of nuclear weapons by a group of criminals is likely to take such a form. This is a danger that is not specific to South Asia. At the same time it is imperative that new nuclear powers take steps to ensure the security of their nuclear weapons and develop procedures to prevent a gang of criminals or dissidents from stealing a nuclear device.

Conclusions

In concluding I would like to restate the parameters within which the arguments in this study have been presented and the assumptions that have been made. This study does not estimate the probability or possibility of a nuclear weapons program in the two countries; it does not seek to evaluate the technical ability of the two states to develop and maintain a nuclear force; it has not discussed in detail the role of other powers in an Indo-Pakistani nuclear equation; it has not considered the possibility of the export of a Pakistani "Islamic" bomb (which is at best an unpersuasive and unsubstantiated argument). All these issues have been discussed in some detail by others. However, after assuming that both countries have acquired nuclear weapons and the ability to deliver them, we have estimated the damage likely to be caused by several types of nuclear exchanges between India and Pakistan. We have also examined the likelihood of a nuclear war between the two countries.

In view of the above we reach the following conclusions about the usability of nuclear weapons in South Asia:

1. The introduction of nuclear weapons into South Asia would not necessarily be destabilizing, provided that it was not too rapid and asymmetrical in nature.

2. Nuclear weapons would probably be used to maintain a deterrence posture by both countries. However, four potential problems exist with regard to Pakistan's ability to maintain a stable and credible deterrence posture: its technical backwardness compared to India; the danger that Pakistan might lose the ability to deliver nuclear weapons because of losses suffered during conventional warfare; the relatively greater vulner-

ability of Pakistan to Indian attack than of India to Pakistani attack; and the need for the two sides to develop C^3I. These problems will have to be overcome to establish credible deterrence.

3. The use of nuclear weapons for compellence would be impractical unless only one side had nuclear weapons. If both have nuclear weapons, their use to compel compromise on vital issues of national interest would not be possible.

4. The use of nuclear weapons for compellence by small extremist dissident or nongovernmental groups cannot be ruled out. However, such groups could only achieve parochial, not national strategic goals.

5. The major destabilizing effect of nuclear weapons would be caused by any policy to use them as "tactical weapons." The adoption of such policies and the development of "tactical nuclear weapons" must therefore be prevented, if and when the two states acquire nuclear weapons.

6. Any use of nuclear weapons in the region, even on a small and limited scale, would cause very high civilian casualties and collateral damage and would be likely to cause escalation from a limited nuclear exchange into a major counter-city strike.

7. Besides MAD, other international, regional, domestic, and geographic constraints exist on use of nuclear weapons for any purpose besides deterrence. These constraints are significant.

Thus the acquisition of nuclear weapons by India and Pakistan will not necessarily lead to instability in the region. If both sides acquire nuclear weapons, a policy of using them for deterrence would be established and, if rationality and perspective were retained by decision makers in times of crisis, acquisition of nuclear weapons might actually lead to more stable relations between the two states. But if nuclear weapons are introduced into the region, it is imperative that this introduction be gradual and symmetrical and that the conditions necessary for a credible and robust deterrence be established.

NOTES

1. An interesting scenario leading to such a strike and its consequences is found in Ravi Rikhye, *The Fourth Round: Indo-Pak War 1984. A Future History* (New Delhi: ABC Publishers, 1982), chap. 3 and 4.

2. S. Glasstone and P. J. Dolan (eds.), *The Effects of Nuclear Weapons* 3rd ed. (Washington, D.C.: Department of Defense and Department of Energy, 1977), p. 276.

3. Office of Technological Assessment (OTA), Congress of the United States, *The Effects of Nuclear War* (Washington, D.C.: O.T.A. Congress of the U.S., 1979), p. 20, and Glasstone and Dolan, *The Effects of Nuclear Weapons*, p. 277.

4. OTA, *Effects of Nuclear War*, p. 21.

5. Ibid.

6. K. M. Lewis, "The Prompt and Delayed Effects of Nuclear War," *Scientific American* (July 1979): 40.

7. Roentgen Equivalent Man.

8. OTA, *Effects of Nuclear War*, pp. 19-20.

9. Glasstone and Dolan, *Effects of Nuclear Weapons*, p. 101.

10. OTA, *Effects of Nuclear War*, p. 19.

11. Ibid., p. 37.

12. J. H. Barton & L. D. Weiler, *International Arms Control* (Stanford, Calif.: Stanford University Press, 1976), p. 47.

13. Glasstone and Dolan, *Effects of Nuclear Weapons,* p. 544.

14. OTA, *Effects of Nuclear War*, p. 35.

15. These calculations were made on the "Nuclear Bomb Effects Computer" in Glasstone and Dolan, *Effects of Nuclear Weapons.*

16. Lewis, *Prompt and Delayed Effects*, p. 38.

17. Ruth Sivard, *World Military and Social Expenditures 1980* (Leesburg, Va.: World Priorities, 1980).

18. Richard Betts, "Regional Nuclearization and Political Tensions: South Asia," in J. K. King (ed.) *International Political Effects of the Spread of Nuclear Weapons* (Washington, D.C.: Department of Defense, 1979), p. 48.

19. From Rodney W. Jones, "Small Nuclear Forces," *Washington Papers* 103 (1984): 17.

20. J. F. Elkin and B. Fredricks, "Military Implications of India's Space Program," Air University Review 34, No. 4 (May-June, 1983): 56-63.

21. S. K. Ghosh, "India's Space Programme and its Military Implications," *Asian Defence Journal* (September 1981): 36.

22. See Stephen Philip Cohen, "Nuclear Issues and Security Policy in Pakistan," Paper delivered at the Annual Meeting of the Association of Asian Studies, Washington, March 1980, pp. 3-13.

23. K. Subrahmanyam, "Implications of Nuclear Assymetry" in Subrahmanyam (ed.) *Nuclear Myths and Realities* (New Delhi, 1981).

24. Cohen, "Nuclear Issues and Security Policy in Pakistan," p. 13.

25. See for example Maj.-Gen. D. K. Palit and P. K. S. Namboodri, *Pakistan's Islamic Bomb* (New Delhi: Vikas Publications, 1979), pp. 114-15.

26. Almost all *Mhajirs* have close familial ties with Indian Muslims that have not decreased over the years.

27. K. U. Kureshy, *A Geography of Pakistan* (Karachi: Oxford University Press, 1979), pp. 29-31.

28. These have been calculated on the "Nuclear Bomb Effects Computer": in Glasstone and Dolan.

29. These have been calculated using estimating methods in OTA, chap. 2.

About the Contributors

Lt. Gen. A. I. Akram (ret.) is President, Institute of Regional Studies, Islamabad, Pakistan.

William J. Barnds was Staff Director of the Subcommittee on Asian and Pacific Affairs and is now Director of the Japan Economic Institute, Washington, D.C.

P. R. Chari, I. A. S., is former director of the Institute of Defence Studies and Analyses, New Delhi, and is now Joint Secretary, Ministry of Defense, Government of India.

Pervaiz Iqbal Cheema is Chairman of the Department of International Relations, Quaid-E-Azam University, Islamabad, Pakistan.

Stephen Philip Cohen, Professor of Political Science at the University of Illinois, was on leave as member of the Policy Planning Staff, U.S. Department of State, 1985-87.

Selig A. Harrison is Senior Associate at the Carnegie Endowment for International Peace, Washington, D.C.

Brig. Noor A. Husain (ret.) was Director General, Institute of Strategic Studies, Islamabad, Pakistan.

Jagat S. Mehta is former Foreign Secretary of the Government of India

M. B. Naqvi is former editor of *Dawn*; he resides in Karachi, Pakistan.

S. Rashid Naim is a Ph.D. candidate in Political Science at the University of Illinois.

Leo Rose is in the Department of Political Science, University of California (Berkeley), the coeditor of Asian Survey, and served on the Policy Planning Staff, U.S. Department of State, 1984-85.

K. Subrahmanyam, I. A. S., was Staff Director of the Institute of Defence Studies and Analyses, New Delhi, India.

R. R. Subramaniam is a physicist with a special interest in arms control, and is a member of the Institute of Defence Studies and Analyses, New Delhi, India.

Thomas Perry Thornton, formerly of the NSC staff and the Policy Planning Staff of the U.S. Dept. of State, is Professor, School of Advanced International Studies, Johns Hopkins University, Washington, D.C.

Lt.-Gen. Eric Vas (ret.) is now a private defense writer residing in Pune, India.

W. Howard Wriggins is Professor of Political Science, Columbia University, New York, and has served as the U.S. Ambassador to Sri Lanka.

Index